D1594909

NASSAU
Suburbia, U.S.A.

NASSAU

SUBURBIA, U.S.A.

———◆———

The First Seventy-five Years
of Nassau County, New York

1899 to 1974

————

EDWARD J. SMITS

FRIENDS OF THE NASSAU COUNTY MUSEUM

SYOSSET, NEW YORK 11791

Distributed by Doubleday & Company, Inc.

GARDEN CITY, NEW YORK

1974

Library of Congress Cataloging in Publication Data

Smits, Edward J
  Nassau: Suburbia, U.S.A.

  Bibliography: p. 291
  Includes index.
  1. Nassau Co., N.Y.—History.   I. Title.
F127.N2S62   974.7'245'04
ISBN 0-385-08902-3
Library of Congress Catalog Card Number 74–16383

FOREWORD

RALPH G. CASO

Nassau County Executive

Anniversaries are times for looking back with nostalgia and looking ahead with confidence, for reviewing yesterday's hopes and renewing tomorrow's.

That is why it is so fitting that publication of the first scholarly history of Nassau County, written by a man who has made it a lifetime study, should coincide with our celebration of the county's seventy-fifth anniversary. The Nassau County of 1974 is far different from the Nassau County of 1899 and far different, too, from the Nassau County of 1999. In a very real sense, the year of our seventy-fifth anniversary is a unique milestone in the history that is traced in this volume. It is a year that marks an end and a beginning.

Nassau County in 1974 is at the end of two decades of unparalleled growth. It is the nation's premier suburban county—its most populous, its most advanced, its most diverse, one of its most prosperous. The first to feel the impact of the postwar suburban population explosion, it is a model for other suburban counties across the nation. Its institutions, its governmental machinery, its sophisticated programs are analyzed, studied and adapted by the new suburbs that are only now starting down the road that we have traveled.

Nassau County in 1974 is at the beginning of an era of settling in and settling down, of consolidating and absorbing past gains and preparing to meet new challenges. Newer, still semi-rural suburbs will outstrip us in population before this century ends. All of them can profit—as we can profit—from reading Nassau County's story.

Yet, there is a continuity in history. The Nassau County of today grew out of our rural past just as surely as the Nassau County of tomorrow will grow out of our suburban present. And the lessons that we should learn in studying our history are lessons in how to preserve the best of today's Nassau while being flexible enough to meet tomorrow's needs.

Nassau is a county of uniquely individual people and individually unique communities. Together they make a mosaic of past achievements in which we can take pride and future goals toward which we can work. This book should help us do both.

CONTENTS

PREFACE

The development of suburbia has been one of the major thrusts of American civilization in the twentieth century. Adjacent to New York City, Nassau County, with almost 1.5 million citizens, is a key suburban area. As both a participant in and an observer of Nassau's suburbanization, I have tried to provide in this work an over-all view of the major aspects of the changes the county experienced as it moved from a rural farming community into a highly intensified suburb.

The basic research for this history has taken place over a period of ten years and initially was intended to explore only the early years of Nassau's suburban development. However, the occasion of the seventy-fifth anniversary of the county in 1974 emphasized the great lack of printed material on the county's development. It seemed that this was a critical need for such a mature county, and therefore additional material was prepared to bring the Nassau story up to date to provide a basic history of the county. The years after World War II are exceedingly complex and filled with so much change and action that the chapters dealing with them provide merely a framework for what has happened. It will be up to future historians and writers to provide the detailed research and analysis to fill out this framework.

The reader will readily realize that this work is not meant to be the comprehensive final history of Nassau, but it is an attempt to explore and consider the great diversity of the county's history and development in the twentieth century. To the general reader perhaps this will provide a better understanding of his own community and its relationship to the county as a whole. Hopefully, scholars and researchers will become more aware of the extraordinary scope of subject matter that must be explored if we are really to understand the pattern of suburban development. This is a rich area to be mined and a great many more sociologists, economists, political scientists and historians should exploit the great potential suburban areas represent in adding to our understanding of American life.

It is quite deplorable that so little definitive scholarly work has been performed about a community the size of Nassau County with such a large and significant population. Perhaps the major reason is the great difficulty of performing local history research. Resources are scattered in many communities, there are only a limited number of secondary sources, and researchers must arduously mine newspapers, a variety of ephemeral paper material, and interviews with participants to provide the required information for meaningful interpretation. All of these techniques have been used in the preparation of this work.

Reviewing these scattered sources and collecting such a range of data would not have been possible if a great many individuals had not generously assisted me with both their time and knowledge. For many years my research efforts and analysis of Nassau County life have been assisted by Richard A. Winsche, historian of the Nassau County Museum, whose help has been invaluable; Dorothy V. Reinhard, my administrative assistant and organizer par excellence; Dr. Myron H. Luke, my undergraduate history adviser, who as a colleague has encouraged meaningful research into Nassau life; former County Executive A. Holly Patterson and his long-time assistant Forrest Corson, both of whom generously gave of their time and information providing the firsthand story and insight into Nassau's most explosive growth years.

I particularly want to indicate appreciation to James Gray, William Kaiser, Hank McCann, James Nagourney, Robert Ryan and Dr. Bayrd Still for textual review and assistance. The illustrations are a major accompaniment to the text and would not have been possible without the special help of Gloria Campbell, Elaine King and Marylouise Matera. Assistance was also provided by representatives of many organizations and my colleagues in the Nassau County Museum and county agencies.

My special acknowledgment also to the faithful services of my secretary Marjorie McMullan and to Rochelle Goodstein, who has efficiently prepared the major part of this manuscript. And finally, I hope in some way the value of this volume will be some compensation to my wife Ruth and sons John, Ted and Robert for their understanding and patience during my almost total absence from home for months during its final preparations.

Although the Frenchman Alexis de Tocqueville viewed American life over 125 years ago, he still provides a meaningful insight into our American character. De Tocqueville commented about democracy that it "does not give the people the most skillful government, but it produces what the ablest governments are frequently unable to create; namely, an all-pervading and restless activity, a superabundant force and an energy which may, however unfavorable circumstances, produce wonders." Although some observers decry the sameness of suburbia, I believe this volume indicates its enormous diversity and the extent of community and individual spirit that can produce such wonders!

E.J.S.

NASSAU
Suburbia, U.S.A.

The new Garden City Hotel in early 1900s.

CHAPTER I
RURAL QUEENS COUNTY

Resorts and Railroads

During the winter of 1900 as a new century dawned, a majestic brick hotel was rising on the Hempstead Plains that was a harbinger of the new era Nassau County was entering. Only a year earlier, on January 1, 1899, Nassau had become the sixty-first county of New York State, its 274 square miles including the towns of Hempstead, Oyster Bay, and North Hempstead, the three eastern towns of old Queens County.

Emerging from the ashes of a disastrous fire on September 7, 1899, the new Garden City Hotel was designed by the noted architectural firm of McKim, Mead and White to be a larger, modern replica of an earlier structure. This proud Georgian structure of brick and marble could be seen for many miles over the flat unused plains land surrounding it. It was to become the area's major landmark to thousands of weekend bicyclists and to the region's potato farmers as they tilled their distant fields. Such an elegant building really was an anachronism in the midst of this rural county, but it was a fitting symbol of the incoming tide of change which was to sweep over Nassau.

The late 1800s had seen the final hardening of political differences within Queens County which led to the creation of this new county. But they were also years when significant influences began to change the population and economic bases of the area. Already the beginnings could be discerned of a population growth which was drastically changing segments of the towns making up the new county—one of the nation's greatest surburban areas in its infancy.

In 1880 Hempstead, North Hempstead and Oyster Bay had a combined population of 37,647, which increased to 45,760 in 1890. During the 1890s the growth continued to pick up momentum, and the population reached 55,448 in 1900. Geographically this population was distributed rather unevenly throughout the area comprising Nassau County. The heaviest concentration of population had developed along the south shore, where a series of attractive communities was growing along the railroad line paralleling the bay front. Bordering the Queens County line were Valley Stream and Lynbrook, both essentially farming communities although the latter's name had been changed in 1894 from Pearsall's Corner because of the influx of new residents from Brooklyn. To the south of them stretching out onto the Rockaway Peninsula was the area known as the Branch. There such villages as Lawrence, which was incorporated in 1897, Woodmere and Hewlett were residential developments. Continuing eastward, there was a heavier population concentration in Rockville Centre and East Rockaway, which were incorporated into villages in 1893 and 1900 respectively. From the latter, a row of small maritime communities stretched eastward along the Great South Bay. Freeport, incorporated in 1892, was the second largest village in the county, with 2,612 residents. East to the county line, sparsely populated villages dotted the south shore.

Hempstead, long the center of population and retail business, was in the middle of the

Garden City in late 1800s, indicating sparse development of plains land. The cathedral is under construction, center of photograph.

John Duryea's country store at the corner of Front and Main streets, Farmingdale, 1890.

county. Incorporated in 1853, it had a population of 3,582 in 1900 and was the area's acknowledged commercial leader. Clustered to the north of it were Garden City and the new county seat Mineola on the border line between the towns of Hempstead and North Hempstead. From Hempstead eastward across the center of the county for sixteen miles lay the famous Hempstead Plains, a noted geographic feature of Long Island since colonial times, when they were used as common grazing lands. Little development had occurred on the plains except at their extreme ends. On the west, Elmont and Franklin Square were small farming villages. On the eastern end two larger, prosperous farming communities, Farmingdale and Hicksville, were growing villages, each with over one thousand residents.

Along the picturesque north shore, a series of villages was on the various necks of land projecting into the Sound and at the head of the harbors. Great Neck was closest to New York City and, with its neighbor Manhasset, was rapidly losing its agricultural character. Port Washington and Roslyn were rural business centers while farther eastward Glen Cove was an important industrial and business village. South of Glen Cove was Sea Cliff, which since its incorporation in 1883 had rapidly grown to a population of 1,558 as a result of its charm as a summer resort. Across six miles of rough north shore woodland from Glen Cove was the third-ranking community in the county, Oyster Bay, rural seat of the township of that name.

The essential factor which led to the

Mineola train junction, late 1800s.

growth of these communities was the Long Island Rail Road. By 1875 the multitude of small local railroad lines on Long Island had been consolidated into three main systems— the North Side, South Side and Long Island Central. In the period from 1880 to 1896 under financier Austin Corbin, the Long Island continued to grow. Corbin obtained control of the various systems and united them under one management. However, he still attempted to gain business other than local traffic and promoted a deep-sea port at Fort Pond at the tip of the island. From this port the railroad then would supply transport to New York City. In 1897 when William Baldwin took over as president, the line abandoned this promotion and settled down to its role as strictly a local railroad. With the construction of an extension from Great Neck to Port Washington in 1898, the system was practically complete except for some minor changes. Its three parallel roads through the northern, central and southern parts of the island, with occasional north-south connections, provided a comprehensive rail system.

Two problems hindered the railroad's development. At the Brooklyn end ferries had to be used to carry passengers to New York, creating a tight bottleneck; and despite the increasing growth of the island's communities, the railroad was never able to get out of financial straits. Finally in 1900, the Pennsylvania Railroad acquired majority control of the Long Island for $6 million and announced plans to build a grand depot in New York City which would be connected with Long Island by a tunnel. This move was enthusiastically welcomed in Nassau. According to the *Nassau County Review* of May 11, 1900, "the cool fields, ample beaches and picturesque hills of the island afford room for tens of thousands of cottages and if only the people could be assured of rapid transit and through trains such dwellings would be built."

Throughout the 1880s and 1890s the railroad had attempted to stimulate such commutation use and constantly promoted the advantages of living on Long Island, particularly in the area that became Nassau County. It proclaimed that since the rail-

Turn-of-century commuters awaiting the train at Sea Cliff station.

road had been built, "towns and villages have sprung up, the highways graded and a wonderful growth of seaside resorts developed. There are no more fortunate people than those who have established permanent residence on Long Island."

In a steady stream of publications, including books on Long Island, boardinghouse and hotel guides, and cyclists' booklets, the company reached thousands of homes, clubs and businesses with its message—the desirability of life in the country on Long Island. The new management of the line reaffirmed this policy in 1900, indicating that it hoped to foster the development of beach resorts and "supply swift express trains for commuters, enabling them to live out on Long Island all the year round."

Commuter use of rail service became noticeable from 1890 to 1900. During these years daily commuter trains on the Montauk (south shore) Division rose from twelve to nineteen and on the Main Line (center of island) from fifteen to twenty-three; and the Glen Cove and north shore branches also showed corresponding 50 per cent increases. Such sizable increases indicate the expansion of commuter traffic and the railroad's ready response to it. Carrying people back and forth to work and play, the wooden railroad coaches, pulled by belching steam

locomotives, were an essential part of Nassau life.

Although rail was the principal means to travel from the city out to the island, a great number of people became familiar with Nassau through bicycling. The new "safety bicycle" became the craze of the 1890s. Bicycle clubs existed all over the island, each village having "official" hotels of the League of American Wheelmen. On weekends hundreds of bicyclists would travel out to Nassau communities in special railroad cars. From central points such as Garden City, they would spread out, leaving few corners of the island unexplored. The craze reached one of its heights on July 7, 1899, when Charles M. Murphy raced behind a railroad train down a specially constructed runway between the tracks near Farmingdale. This fastest mile ever ridden earned him the title "Mile a Minute" Murphy.

The promotion of the recreational opportunities on Long Island was the strongest initial stimulus to the growth of its shorefront communities. The towns of eastern Queens County became known as a "great place for sports. The rich and the poor find amusement here." Throughout the county there were vacation communities where ball fields, boating, fishing, bathing, golf courses, race tracks, gun clubs, bicycling, hunting and polo

Bicyclists along the old Merrick Road.

Sportsmen at Port Washington Trap Shooting Club, early 1900s.

offered every imaginable recreational pastime.

All along the south shore the resort business was an important aspect of village life. The Great South Bay was a fabulous natural attraction swarming with fish and having excellent bathing and boating facilities both in surf and in still water. The convenience and charm of "sailing with careful boatmen who make their living as oystermen or fishermen" was proclaimed. All the communities had numerous small hotels, boardinghouses and summer cottages. In just one day in July of 1899, the railroad delivered 1,500 passengers to Freeport.

Strong attempts were made to develop a giant resort at Long Beach, one of the barrier beaches to which a rail line was extended in 1882. In 1880 a promotion syndicate obtained a fifty-year lease on the land from the Town of Hempstead and built a large hotel and cottages. Even though the resort was given heavy promotion it never achieved great profitability. The project passed through a succession of companies in an effort to refinance its operation, and in 1900 new plans were formed to create a fashionable winter as well as summer resort.

Along the north shore similar developments had led to its emergence as a resort area. These cool inviting hills and broad harbors were ideal for vacation pleasures, and each community had small boardinghouses and summer cottages. An additional stimulus was the accessibility to Long Island Sound. During the 1890s numerous yacht clubs were formed, including the famed Seawanhaka Corinthian Yacht Club at Oyster Bay. Sailing boats dotted the waters with gay vacationers enjoying fishing parties or clambakes. Seasonal wildfowl hunting was also a prime attraction.

City residents were particularly aware of this region's attraction since for many years steamboats had regularly made stops at the various shorefront communities and in summers made many special excursions to rural picnic grounds. In the 1890s Theodore Roosevelt established his home at Sagamore Hill

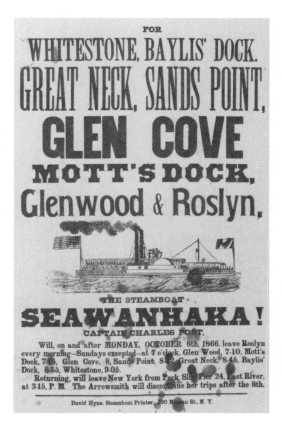

in Oyster Bay. Noting the charm of life there, he wrote in his autobiography, "the Sound is always lovely. In the summer night we watch it from the piazza, and see the lights of the tall Fall River boats as they steam steadily by." The steamer *Idlewild* made regular daily commuter trips from Nassau's north shore to New York in the 1890s.

Sea Cliff was the central summer resort on the Sound. It originally had been founded as a Methodist camp meeting ground, but by the 1890s it was an established community which tripled its population in the summer. The Sea Cliff House held three hundred guests, and another twenty smaller hotels such as the Sound View, Plaza Park and Bittershall Inn provided accommodations. The excellent shorefront with bathing pavilions made it an attractive summer home. Its residents were greatly interested in promoting this development. In the Sea Cliff village election of 1900, one candidate pro-

6   RURAL QUEENS COUNTY

Sea Cliff landing from the Illustrated Christian Weekly, *September 4 ,1875.*

View of the Metropolitan Tabernacle, Sea Cliff.

SEA CLIFF
SUMMER HOME,
FOR AGED AND INFIRM MEMBERS OF THE
Methodist Episcopal Church,
Of New York City.

posed "a large beer garden on the shore, with a large dancing pavilion" to attract the excursion steamboats from the city.

In that same election the local newspaper noted the significant fact that many voters who resided in New York for the winter months came out to vote. This trend was also evident elsewhere. Having become acquainted with the pleasant life on the island, many city people were establishing permanent residence there. As early as the 1870s, prominent men such as Charles Dana, and William Cullen Bryant before him, had liked the pleasures of country life so much that they established permanent homes on the north shore and commuted by steamship to the city. A major factor in this appeal was the good effect of a country atmosphere on children. As Theodore Roosevelt indicated, "There could be no healthier or pleasanter place in which to bring children up than in that nook of old-time America around Sagamore Hill." The area was promoted as ideal for gentlemen engaged in business in New York, and even Mayor W. R. Grace had a home in Great Neck. Roslyn and Great Neck

William Cullen Bryant in the study of his home, Cedarmere, at Roslyn.

doubled their populations in the growth engendered by this interest during the 1890s.

A significant part of this growth was the beginning of the trend which was to create one of the most fabulous areas in America—the north shore's Gold Coast. In 1899 Clarence Mackay established a tremendous estate on Harbor Hill overlooking Roslyn. This estate encompassed 650 acres and although it was called a summer residence, it was estimated that it cost $5 million to develop the elaborate gardens, roads and buildings.

A little farther inland in Old Westbury and Wheatley such millionaires as Edwin D. Morgan, Thomas Hitchcock and F. Ambrose Clark were buying large farms and establishing estates. These were the very rich of New York City, who now began the custom of having a Long Island place. It was usually a large farm with fields, meadows, wide green pastures, large and fine houses and stables. Estates were erected with extensive roads and mansion buildings—Wil-

liam C. Whitney's even included a moss-covered tile roof. There they could entertain in early summer and fall in "as fine style as anybody at any of the ducal houses of England." By 1900 these large, almost baronial holdings were becoming part of Nassau County life and rivaled in beauty and elegance the English showplaces which they emulated.

Of great influence in this growth was the importance of the country club, and two in Nassau County, the Meadow Brook and the Rockaway Hunting, were the most prominent in the New York area. The Meadow Brook in Westbury was rather unpretentious but its exclusive membership was not equaled "in horsemanship, wealth or social prominence." During the fall of the year its pink-coated hunt riders, following the baying hounds, participated in one of the most chic of the wealthy's leisure pastimes. In Cedarhurst the Rockaway Hunting was more prominent for its polo activities at this time.

Theodore Roosevelt enjoyed life at Sagamore Hill to its fullest and loved "a great many things—birds and trees and books and all things beautiful and horses and rifles and children and hard work and the joy of life." The family enjoying the bucolic pleasures of Oyster Bay, hiking or playing at the barn. The interior view of Sagamore Hill is after its restoration as a national historic site.

Sheet music of the 1880s.

Although these estates and clubs promoted the expenditure of a great deal of money in Nassau County, their owners played a relatively inactive role in county affairs. Most of these residents focused their interests on New York City or their social set rather than the local communities.

On the south shore the vacationists began to put down roots and build homes in the vicinity of the various railroad stations. This area grew as the most populous part of the county with the greatest amount of real estate activity. Because of the availability of large, level tracts of land, the real estate speculator and developer played a considerable part in this growth. Whole communities and a host of large subdivisions were planned by developers such as the Royal Land Company in Valley Stream, Hewlett's Land and Improvement Company, Freeport Land Company, Bellmore Land Improvement Company.

Promoters on the south and north shores chose attractive names for their projects such as Beechwood, Lakewood Settlement, North Country Colony, Roslyn Highlands and Sunnycroft as part of an effort to provide a comprehensive plan of a delightful suburban existence. None of these accomplished their grandiose plans but they did establish a pattern that was to be consistently followed in the future. Aiming at the average middle-class family, they developed homes and sites which encouraged the growth of population along the shore. Village residents generally welcomed this growth, particularly local businessmen.

The Rockaway Hunting Club in the southwest section of the county led to the development of more exclusive residential sections there. Garden City was also developing into a community for wealthy businessmen. Founded in the 1870s by A. T. Stewart, the great merchant, its growth had been stagnant until the 1890s. In 1893 Stewart's lands were acquired by several land companies including the Garden City Company, which began vigorous development of the village. With its hotel, casino, golf and gun clubs, the village became a center for fashionable New Yorkers coming to the area for sport and recreation. The hotel was a focal point of county social life, and in its ballroom and hallways decorated with Charles Dana Gibson drawings, visitors, including members of the Harriman, Morgan, Astor and Belmont families, were entertained.

Thus, by 1900 a definite change in Nassau's population was evident. Stimulated by railroad promotion of the area as both a resort and year-round home, its growth was increasing steadily. Along both shores attractive communities were developing for middle-class businessmen from the city, where their families could live in a healthy semi-rural environment. Less important in terms of numbers was the influx of the very wealthy, who established large estate communities in the northern portions of the county.

An Agricultural Economy

As this population development occurred, consequent changes were caused in the area's agricultural life. In the early 1800s, mills dotted every stream and inlet to handle flour milling. Grain production began to decline after the Midwest granaries opened, and farms converted to dairy use and sheep raising. As the large estates and small subdivisions were created, farm acreage dropped accordingly. From 1875 to 1900, farm acreage in the towns comprising Nassau County dropped from 90,738 to 69,357.

Not only was there a change in the number of farms but significant changes were taking place in the manner of farming. As early as the late 1880s, market gardening was becoming the prominent interest of the farmers. This shift in farmers' interest was evident at the Queens County fair, where the display of cattle, sheep and swine was now outnumbered by that of other departments. These fairs, run by the Agricultural Society of Queens-Nassau Counties at the permanent fairgrounds near Mineola, were an annual highlight for local residents. In 1899 over $13,000 in premiums was awarded.

Agriculture was a major ingredient of the county's economic base at this time. Of its 1,658 farms, 68.7 per cent were owned by independent operators. The size of the average farm in the county was 53 acres but many were more extensive. P. C. Barnum's farm in East Meadow was the largest with 1,200 acres, including a palatial residence and

Powell farm lane, Old Bethpage in the late 1800s.

Scenes at the Mineola fair around the turn of the century.

beautiful gardens. He operated one of the largest dairies in the metropolitan area and sold six hundred quarts of milk a day.

Milk production was still an important phase of agriculture in the county, and there were many dairy farms around Westbury, Hicksville and Syosset. These dairies shipped their milk by special railroad trains to New York City. However, by 1900 better refrigeration and increasing competition by upstate dairies had caused a serious decline in local dairies. From 1,430,011 gallons of milk sold in 1875, sales decreased to 996,855 gallons in 1900. More than one half of the milk and five sixths of the butter produced were consumed on the farms so that to a considerable extent this kind of farming was more for subsistence purposes than for income. There was little emphasis on livestock and the once significant sheep-raising activities had declined to only 550 fleeces in 1900.

The increasing demand and market for vegetables in New York City caused many farmers to concentrate on this type of production. Since they were close to the market, local farmers were able to raise perishable crops without danger of loss in transportation. Farmers in North Hempstead and Oyster Bay sometimes sent their loaded market wagons to the local train depot. Special cars were then used to carry the wagon, horses and all, to the city—America's first piggyback railroad system. The more usual method of shipment was to cart the produce by wagon and team, arriving at night. Generally the farmers themselves drove in and the largest part of the production was sold at wholesale to dealers in the Washington Market or in the market area near West Twelfth Street and Tenth Avenue. Some farmers remained in until daylight and sold their produce in the retail trade. Produce sent by the railroad or by sloop was generally consigned to commission dealers.

The farmers concentrated on vegetable production, particularly potatoes, rye, corn,

Loading market wagons on flatbed railroad cars for shipment to New York City.

A market wagon of the Velsor family ready for its journey to the city from Old Westbury.

cabbage, peas and cucumbers. Since they did not practice crop rotation, large quantities of fertilizer were used. Due to large production of certain crops, special processing facilities were built in some villages. Hicksville became the center of a considerable pickle industry. In 1898 a large pickle works was erected by the H. J. Heinz Company to process pickles, ketchup, vinegar and sauerkraut. The products were brought in from the surrounding countryside, processed and shipped in barrels to Pittsburgh for final packing. Many other independent kraut and pickle works were established there and in other communities. One of the pickling factories in Wantagh, Kaufmann Brothers, shipped twenty-four carloads of kraut to the city in the 1899 season.

Cultivation of potatoes was well suited to the soil of the flat farm lands. In 1875 some 214,672 bushels of potatoes were produced by local farmers and by 1900, a total of 873,859 bushels went to market from Nassau. Enormous fields of potatoes stretched across the center of the county, and natives were already promoting them as "the finest potatoes of the world." The one quarter of total farm acreage in the county which was used for market gardening and potatoes provided an income in excess of $1,200,000 in 1900. Only eleven counties in New York State led Nassau in potato production, and its per-acre yield was among the best in the state.

In the production of miscellaneous vegetables Nassau ranked second in the state after Queens County. At this time Queens still had considerable farm land, particularly a tremendous amount in greenhouse production. This gardening was so profitable and suited to the area that proposals were made to convert the salt marshes in the north shore harbors to market gardening use. So desirable were the vegetables from these lush fields that the best New York City hotels proudly proclaimed on their menus "Fresh Long Island Vegetables."

Conversely, as market gardening increased the production of grain declined. In 1875

over 4,000 acres were planted in wheat, but the acreage in this crop had declined to less than 1,588 in 1900. There was only a fraction over 2,000 acres left in oats and rye combined. Corn production still took up 9,753 acres, but the greater part of this was used for livestock feed. The virtual end of grain production was particularly evident in the decline of the milling industry. By the turn of the century only a few gristmills were still operating and even these were not grinding to capacity.

One unique development in local agriculture was a considerable garden seed, nursery and flower business. The seed production center around Floral Park was described by a contemporary as surrounded by "flowers of every description as far as the eye can reach. The railroad tracks for a mile is lined and bordered with fields of flowers, acres of exquisite gladioli, brilliant flaming cannas— all in luxuriant growth." The largest seed business was owned by John Lewis Childs, a native of Maine who had determined to be a florist. He settled in the little Long Island community of Hinsdale, which was a growing seed and nursery area. Gradually he built a massive operation including hotels, over twenty buildings, lumber and planing mills and his own printing plant. This plant, the Mayflower Press, annually produced hundreds of thousands of seed catalogues which were sent around the world, one year's run costing $85,000. The community was renamed Floral Park, received a first-class post office and set an example for smaller ventures of this type in other communities in the county.

Throughout the county there were also a number of nurseries and other establishments devoted to raising flowers and ornamental plants for the local and city markets. Among the leading nurseries was that of Isaac Hicks and Sons in Westbury, an old-established business which was devoted to propagation of hardy trees, shrubs, vines and fruits. They developed special hybrids and supplied much of the plant material for the extensive landscaping of the many great estates. Gar-

Saddle Rock Grist Mill, restored and still operating as a historic site by Nassau County Museum.

An active building in the center of historic Roslyn, the gristmill still exists as a tea shop.

The Plandome Mill continued to grind into the early 1900s, and was later converted to a residence.

Davison's Mill in East Rockaway became a lumber storage building and has been restored by the Old Grist Mill Historical Society of East Rockaway.

dens on these estates, such as the Pratts in Glen Cove, Coe in Brookville and Phipps in Old Westbury, would rank among the greatest in America. The combined florist and nursery business in the county accounted for over $275,000 in sales from locally raised plant materials in 1900.

Despite these changes in the quantity and nature of agriculture, the area still retained many rural customs and activities little changed since the 1700s. One significant custom involved the vast islands of marshland along the shores which contained a variety of salt hay. Each September, under regulations strictly enforced by the towns which owned these common lands, farmers would harvest this hay for use as winter forage. They would take up scythes and spend a week on the marshes, sleeping out and cooking over an open fire. While serving a utilitarian purpose, the time was also looked forward to as an occasion to celebrate the end of a long summer of work. This week and the annual county fair provided relaxation for the hard-working farmers. Farming dominated the county's economy but definite

Hicks's nursery crew moving an enormous tree destined for a Gold Coast estate.

Cutting salt hay on the marshes at Hempstead Harbor.

changes were under way which would soon diminish its status. The character of farming was changing from subsistence and dairying to market gardening while the growth of estates and commuter housing was seriously decreasing the land available for farming.

Along the south shore and, to a lesser extent, the north shore, the sea provided a livelihood for numerous baymen, clam diggers, fishermen and oystermen. This was essentially a very individualistic industry with few business organizations on a large scale. The inlets of East Rockaway, Oceanside, Baldwin, Freeport and Seaford were lined with boat and oyster houses. This rugged, independent group continued because of a love for the sea despite the hard manual labor involved. The folklore surrounding these unique men is replete with stories not only of successful catches but of the mystical attraction of the sea. Because this business was so individualistic with widely scattered producers and dispersed local and distant markets, there is little comprehensive data available concerning the scope of its operation.

One form of fishing which did require cooperative action and groups of fishermen was the catching of menhaden or "bunkers." These fish contained an oil which was extracted for use in paint manufacturing, tanning and mixing with other oils. The remainder was dried and sold as fertilizer. A huge seine up to three-fourths mile in length was used for the catch. It required a group of fishermen in rowboats to set it, after which horses would draw it up on land. Plants for the processing of this oil originally were located all along the shore, but by the 1890s, they were reduced to two factories, one on Jamaica Bay. It became necessary by then to go far out to sea in large steamers for adequate catches, so that in 1899 even those factories were closed down and the great menhaden fisheries left this area.

Since colonial times, oysters had been

OPPOSITE:
Clamming in Great South Bay, Long Island, by Edwin A. Abbey, from Harper's Weekly, *September 8, 1877.*

gathered in the natural beds of Long Island waters. In the 1850s systematic farming of beds on both the south and north shores was begun. From that time forward, laws were frequently passed to regulate planting of beds and setting out differences between natural beds and planted areas. By the 1890s seed oysters were regularly planted to supplement natural beds. The business grew rapidly from the 1860s and large quantities were shipped to all parts of the country and even to Europe from the south shore communities of Freeport, Baldwin, Christian Hook, East Rockaway and Pearsall's Corner.

Menhaden fisheries as illustrated in Harper's Weekly, *1888.*

The barrier beach along the south shore was a graveyard of maritime wrecks, and lifesaving crews manned regular stations to be ready for rescues.

The Clam Fleet

Clammers Homes

Schooner Buying Clams

Clammers

Treading Clams

A Chowder

Hand-powered dredges greatly increased oyster harvesting.

Oyster Bay on the north shore was also a center of this harvesting. There 200,000 bushels of seed oysters were planted in one season. This was still an individual operation, although several men might work together off one boat. The oysterman had to obtain a town permit costing $5 per acre for the beds, which were predominantly town-owned lands. Some oystermen also owned their own beds of bay land, and the state began to lease its lands in the late 1880s.

Oyster growing had to be done in quiet bay waters which received a constant circulation of new water. Since the natural beds were limited, seed oysters were brought in from Chesapeake Bay or Connecticut. The latter did especially well in Long Island waters and were most generally used. Once planted, the seed oysters had to be thinned out and transported, as they grew fatter, to growing beds. When ready for market they were laboriously tonged up by hand, kept fresh in special houses along the inlets and shipped to market by the Long Island Rail Road, small sloops or overland by wagon.

In the late 1880s oysters valued at more than a quarter of a million dollars were shipped from the Town of Hempstead. Shipments from one small village, Inwood, amounted to 3,000 bushels a week. In 1901 an estimated total of 3,547,684 bushels of shellfish went to market from Nassau baymen with a value of $461,901. Oysters accounted for the major portion of this with other shellfish such as clams accounting only for $79,491.

However, by 1899, the industry was running into difficulties and it was estimated to be $100,000 short of a normal year. One of its problems was the introduction of the dredge, which led to an overworking of the small area available for oyster growing. Natural beds were very sparse and almost all production had to be cultivated by spreading seed oysters. This decline in the beds caused the organization of the Oyster Planters Protective Association in Nassau County to provide mutual protection against oyster thieves. Adding to these problems was the increasing

pollution of south shore bay waters by sewerage from Far Rockaway and Canarsie. The oystermen claimed this was also aggravated by the decreased flow of fresh water from streams in Nassau due to the increased pumping by the Brooklyn Water Company from its water supply reservoir system along Nassau's south shore. Lawsuits were filed against the company for damages and this continued to be a source of conflict in 1899 and 1900. It was clear, though, that never again would the local oyster industry be able to supply large quantities of the famous Blue Point and Rockaway oysters as it once had.

Historically a center of fishing activity in the county was Freeport Creek, but by 1900 all the main waterways leading into the south shore villages were lined with drying reels and racks for fish nets. Sailboats were used by both the skippers who concentrated on bay fish and those who ventured out to the deep seas. The major bay fish caught were fluke, flounder and weakfish, while deep-sea skippers brought back blues, tuna, sea bass, porgies and cod. Both net and hand fishing were employed. The catch was generally sold outright at the dock or held for later shipment to city or local markets. Statistics for the commercial catch are not complete because of the factors mentioned previously, but it is estimated that 974,366 pounds of fish were sent to market with a value of $49,444 in 1901.

In addition to the fishing and oyster activities, other commerce centered around the waterfront areas. Ports such as Roslyn, Port Washington, Oyster Bay, Freeport and Far Rockaway were active shipping points. Schooners and sloops plied back and forth to New York City and other island ports in a brisk traffic carrying sand, brick, lumber, coal, oil, manure and farm products. This trade was important to Nassau's development since roads were not yet adequate. Although Nassau had several east-west turnpikes, their condition was not good in bad weather, and traffic over them with heavy loads was difficult. Along the north shore the large steamboat landing docks were busy

The inlet at Freeport Creek was lined with baymen's buildings and it is evident that women also enjoyed boating activities.

The boat basin at East Rockaway, a busy coastal port.

areas handling the regularly scheduled boats and special excursion trips in the summer. Some of the steamboats were owned locally by the captains or small partnerships.

Each of the waterfront areas also had various maritime service industries. Throughout the county a number of small boat yards produced the boats needed for the fishing trade.

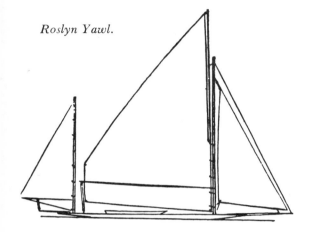

Roslyn Yawl.

Special skiffs, built along the south shore, were particularly suited for use on the Great South Bay. In Roslyn, Thomas Clapham, a builder and designer of merit, played an important role in the development of light-draft yachts. During the late 1800s he produced the famous Roslyn Yawl, which was noted as an extremely stable cruising yacht. By the 1890s he became interested in fast racing yachts and produced many of these. All his boats were made to order, running in size from fifteen to forty feet and priced from $100 to $1,500. Rope, marine stores, special blacksmiths, oyster storage and packing houses, seafood retail stores and other related businesses also were located along the waterfront.

A third major segment of the county's economy in 1900 was the large group of necessary retail services for agricultural, fishing and residential communities. Each local village supported a cluster of businesses around a major street intersection. A typical small community such as Baldwin had a blacksmith, mason, hotel, tin shop, oyster dealers,

insurance agent, dressmaker, carpenter, ice and coal dealers, shoemaker, livery stable, and drug, paint and paper, dry goods, ice cream and general stores. Other communities included additional businesses such as bakeries, harness and saddle makers, barbers, funeral parlors, feed dealers, stair builders, stationers, furniture and carpet stores. These merchants frequently had a valuable trade— Thorne's lumber and coal yard in Glen Cove grossed $50,000 per year. Such local businesses were a significant part of Nassau's economy, supplying the needed services to agricultural regions and beginning to develop the retail businesses required by the residential sections that were growing around the railroad lines.

Due to the general prosperity, needs of business and growth in the county, a strong local banking system was developing in the 1890s. The first bank in the area, the Roslyn Savings Bank, was opened in 1876, followed by the Hempstead Bank in 1887. During the 1890s banks were opened in Rockville Centre, Oyster Bay, Freeport, Glen Cove and Mineola. The Bank of Rockville Centre was typical of these institutions. Its stockholders were all local people; one third of them were either farmers or fishermen who raised $25,000 in capital. Business grew slowly but steadily and it began paying dividends in 1900. By that time most of the institutions were financially secure and a few had over half a million dollars in deposits. Total deposits of the seven banks were $1,851,662 with resources amounting to $2,295,648.

Nassau County also had a mutual insurance company. Founded as a result of the disastrous New York City fire of 1835, the Glen Cove Mutual Insurance Company provided insurance for local farmers, businessmen and homeowners. Operated by local men who were "safe and conservative," the company possessed total assets of $103,570 and carried insurance totaling $8,884,120 at the turn of the century.

A major development resulting from the utilization of electricity was the electric streetcar or trolley. Although Nassau had an

Most residents did their major shopping in Jamaica, Brooklyn or New York City. Abra- *ham & Straus, a large city store, provided a Long Island delivery service.*

First National Bank in Hempstead, 1890s.

extensive railroad system, there was still an enormous need for local transportation. Even horse and carriage travel was difficult, particularly between Hempstead and Freeport, both leading business and population centers. The old wooden plank roads, built in the mid-1800s as private turnpikes, had been taken over by the county government in the late 1800s. In December of 1897 the Queens County Board of Supervisors executed a tremendous number of road contracts in the three towns which were to make up Nassau County. Good stone roads were built covering sixty-nine miles in Oyster Bay, forty-nine and a half miles in North Hempstead, and fifty-seven and a half miles in Hempstead. However, despite this work there was still need for a faster transportation means between villages.

As early as 1895 professional men in the larger south shore villages gave serious consideration to the need for a local rapid transit line. Finally in 1898 the Nassau Belt Lines Traction Company, with an initial capital of $125,000, was organized by a

group of leading south shore businessmen and bankers. Its aim was to establish a trolley line between Hempstead, Freeport and Rockville Centre. Early in 1899, however, a rival company, the Mineola, Hempstead and Freeport Traction Company, was incorporated by a group of New York bankers. Both companies wanted to use the same right of way, so a bitter rivalry developed between them.

Throughout the rest of 1899 and 1900 the problem of which company should receive a franchise vexed the county, towns and various villages involved. Finally in December of 1900 the Nassau Belt Lines lost its franchise from the Village of Rockville Centre and thereafter a clear field was left for the Mineola, Hempstead and Freeport Traction Company. In 1901 it and several other companies began construction of an extensive rapid transit system in the county that provided additional local employment and stimulated the growth of retail business centers.

In addition to the retail businesses throughout the county, a considerable number of small manufacturers were located in this still rural area. There were 321 separate manufacturing establishments in 1900 with a

total capital of $3,433,224. The average number of wage earners was 1,675, and they received some $767,112. Of these employees 253 were women and 25 were children. Materials used by these establishments including transportation were valued at $1,895,-596. The value of their production was $3,369,973.

The largest industrial village was Glen Cove, the home of the Duryea Starch Company. This was an immense establishment on thirty acres of the waterfront which shipped its product, Satin Gloss Starch, throughout the country. It had a weekly payroll of several hundred people drawing $4,000 in wages. One of the major starch works in the world, it had received medals for excellence at international expositions from 1862 through the 1880s. In the late 1890s its operations became less steady and its factory was converted to other use in the first decade of the new century.

A sizable and growing industry, made possible by good local deposits of clay, was brickmaking. Several large brick factories operated in the county. The major one was the Stewart Brickyards at Bethpage, originally founded to produce material for homes at

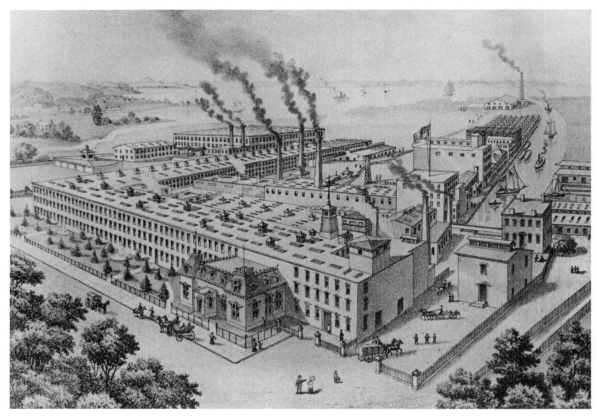

Duryea Starch Company, Glen Cove, in late 1800s.

Garden City. At times it employed a hundred men, utilizing the most modern methods and machinery such as a forty-ton press to produce bricks from the fine clay pits in the area. Another large brickyard on Centre Island produced about 5 million bricks yearly and employed forty men. Sand mining was also a developing business in the building supply field. Use of concrete was increasing and sand mining to supply the New York City market was begun in earnest in Port Washington and several other areas.

Small factories were scattered throughout the county. Lynbrook was a developing center. Here, Sherman Brothers had a factory which produced tin toys, ornaments and other goods with a work force of twenty. It also contained an ornamental iron works with forty employees. In nearby Rockville Centre, the Hicks Hammock Factory, established in the early 1880s by A. N. S. Hicks,

produced popular hammocks, tropical beds and fly nets and employed as many as seventy people. In 1899 it was working a ten-hour day, six days a week, to produce an order for 14,500 hammocks, and employed many knitters who worked in their homes.

Hicksville was the center of the traditional craft of gold beating, dating back to the town's original German settlers of the mid-1880s. The preparation of gold leaf sheets still continued there mainly on a home work basis. This was a pursuit requiring such special skills that it no longer attracted new workers. In several communities there were larger shops which made road carts and carriages. The principal ones were L. M. Hicks in Oyster Bay and the East Williston Road Cart Company. The latter produced the famous Williston cart, a highly desired and very serviceable light road vehicle.

An unusual establishment in Wantagh

*Factory of the famous East Williston cart,
Foster Oakley standing, William Griffin
seated.*

was William W. Wilson's taxidermy business. He employed more than a dozen men
and produced over fifty varieties of birds for
the popular Victorian parlor bird displays.
There were also several molding mills on the
north shore and a large picture frame factory in Farmingdale. These larger establishments and many smaller ones provided an
opportunity for industrial employment for
local people and greatly added to the county's economic well-being.

Residents of some Nassau villages looked
with envy on their neighbors and urged the
establishment of industry in their areas. Residents of Merrick proclaimed that it had
"an attractive location" and "as a possible
manufacturing centre" was "all that could
be wished for. It is within easy communication with the cities, both by rail and boat
and there is plenty of available land here for
the purposes of constructing factories . . .

The people in this section would heartily
welcome such enterprises, believing them to
be beneficial to any community." Such promotion was unusual in 1900, however, and
most villages did not desire the intrusion of
industry.

Village Life

The changes in the county's population
and economic structures were reflected in
other aspects of community life. Local education had developed gradually after the
establishment of the first school districts in
1812. By the mid-1800s when the common
school system was functioning effectively
throughout the towns, Hempstead had nine-

teen districts, North Hempstead eight, Oyster Bay twenty-one, and there were three joint districts. These fifty-one independent districts provided elementary schooling for children from five to sixteen.

Education was of major interest in local communities but its organization and administration slowly changed. By the 1880s professional direction in both local administration and teaching personnel had greatly improved. However, the small one-room schools of a rural area were not sufficient for the many growing villages, and the last decades of the 1800s saw drastic changes in local education facilities.

By 1900 the student population had tripled since the Civil War, with 10,188 pupils enrolled in the area's fifty-nine school districts. Providing physical facilities for this increase was a major task. Over one half the districts in the Town of North Hempstead erected new buildings after 1870. During the 1890s, school buildings were constructed ranging in cost from $4,000 to $85,000.

Improvements were not easily won and

advances were not made in many areas as rapidly as the increase in population made necessary. The residents, according to School Commissioner James S. Cooley, were "naturally conservative and slow to adopt new and untried measures." When Rockville Centre residents began to agitate for a new building, Board of Education President Francis F. Wilson reported, "The old school house, in which we formerly met, its confined space, close atmosphere and sombre coloring, dimly lighted by a few stable lanterns were all fit emblems of the gloom that pervaded our spirits."

Progressive elements in Rockville Centre and other districts fought for improvements and eventually won. School building propositions had to be approved by the voters of each school district, and the contests were bitterly fought. Often voters were apathetic and not interested, and construction plans failed by small votes such as 35 to 33 and 23 to 22. But supporters and education-minded school trustees persisted. Among the most vociferous supporters of better education was George Wallace, publisher of the weekly *South Side Observer*. Originally a district schoolteacher and later an influential political leader, he continually supported education improvements through the late 1800s. Gradually new buildings with adequate heating and ventilation replaced old one-room schools.

The need for physical improvement was paralleled by the need for more advanced educational training. In 1889 Rockville Centre District No. 21 decided to establish an academic department beyond elementary work. Such a department would provide high-school-level courses which were not available along the whole south shore of the island. Principal Frank Lindsley suggested the name South Side Union School and in 1892 a $20,635 high school was opened for 281 pupils from the district and 35 non-

One-room school at Herricks, T. B. Aldrich (the teacher) and pupils, late 1890s.

resident students. For several years it promoted non-resident use at a tuition fee of $20 a year.

As population increased, the need for such facilities spread and union free school districts were established in twenty-three districts, providing more flexible and efficient administration. By the mid-1890s Freeport and Great Neck also had academic departments. High schools particularly required better housing. In 1893 Freeport constructed a ten-room brick school at a cost of over $30,000. The construction of the nineties boosted the value of schoolhouses and school sites in the county to $541,080 by 1900.

The cost of new facilities and staff was a major obstacle to educational advancement. Originally the common school had been supported by a small state-aid allotment to each district, a matching town tax and rate bills by individual students' parents. By the late 1800s the rate bill was no longer in use.

Schools obtained state aid which supplied less than one fifth of expenses. Local taxes were raised in the district for the rest of the expenses. The union free districts received state aid of $800 plus a percentage according to population. Hempstead Town's districts were also fortunate since a special education fund had been set up with the money received from the sale of common lands to A. T. Stewart. As a result, more than $6,000 was distributed to the town's districts annually.

In 1900 the county's districts received a total of $26,008 in state aid and raised $167,255 in local taxes. Floral Park, which was a typical growing district, had an annual budget of $4,850 for 138 students. This provided salaries of $1,000 for a principal; $600, $560 and $550 for three teachers; $300 for a janitor; $200 for repairs; $500 for supplies; $300 for coal; $675 for interest; $150 for a truant officer; and $25 for the district li-

New Freeport High School at corner of Grove Street and Pine Street.

brary. Even in a bustling district the local schools were still rather modest institutions.

One of the continuing bothersome problems was pupil attendance. Although the percentage of school-age children who were enrolled had increased to 80 per cent, a considerable number were without schooling. Once students were in school, authorities found it continually necessary to stress the importance of good attendance. Even in the previously cited Floral Park district, a truant officer was required. Newspapers also commented upon tardiness, which "seems to be the great failure in our school. If parents could but see the need of establishing habits of promptness and punctuality in their children, some of the habitual cases might be overcome."

Another widespread problem, which, however, had been considerably improved from the mid-1800s, was teachers' pay. The average teacher's annual salary throughout the state in the 1890s was $467. Salaries in most of the union free districts in Nassau ex-

ceeded this amount. There were 249 teachers in the districts in 1899, of which only 35 were men. Teacher training had greatly improved; 169 had normal school diplomas and seven held state or college degrees. Principals received salaries in excess of $1,000 although sometimes, as happened in Rockville Centre, a principal who deserved a raise was dismissed since to raise him would have required raises for the other teachers.

The development of academic departments greatly expanded school curriculums beyond the common school triad of reading, writing and arithmetic. The first courses now appeared in higher literature, chemistry and other specialized areas. Instruction in fine arts including drawing, music and piano was also supplied in every school. The provision of free textbooks constituted a controversial program which slowly gained local acceptance. In 1901 Rockville Centre taxpayers held a public meeting to discuss the proposal. Taxpayers were told that the experience of other districts such as Baldwin,

Schoolroom in Port Washington District No. 4, early 1900s.

which had provided books for eight years, and Freeport, which began the program in 1886, indicated that costs ranged from $170 to $350 a year. Local pride was called upon to do the same, particularly since Hempstead had recently adopted such a measure. Local editorial comment also urged approval and reasoned that it cost parents three times as much to buy books for their children than if the school did the purchasing.

In addition to the public school system, local education was boosted by several fine but small private schools. Friends Academy in Locust Valley, established by the Society of Friends in 1876, had constructed a modern building in 1894 and offered an academic program. The Episcopal Diocese of Long Island operated St. Paul's School in Garden City, a preparatory school for boys planning to enter college or military school. Referred to as a "miniature West Point," it provided high-school-level training.

Local libraries also began to be established and provided a supplement to schools and educational resources for all local citizens, young and old. By the turn of the century, six communities had libraries, and in a few years this had increased to a dozen. The libraries were organized in various ways— the most popular method was as a public educational organization depending on dues and special fund raising. The Sea Cliff Library was organized in 1891 by the contribution of one thousand books from private citizens. It was managed by a board of library trustees and depended completely upon public contributions. Libraries were associated with the private schools in Garden City and Locust Valley, while Massapequa and Roslyn had libraries provided by the Delancey Floyd-Jones and Bryant families. Individual schools were supposed to maintain libraries but these were usually very inadequate so that frequently the public library was provided space in a school building.

As the three rural towns entered the new century, local education was in the midst of vital changes. New buildings were provid-

ing vastly improved physical facilities and the development of high school departments was broadening and improving the school curriculums. Educational quality varied greatly in the area, however, with many backward, small one-room districts alongside advanced districts with large high schools. Public library service was in its infancy and available only in limited facilities for short hours to a small portion of the county's population.

Religious activity was a major focal point of life in the small communities of the towns of Hempstead, North Hempstead and Oyster Bay. Historically the area's predominant denominations in terms of membership were the Presbyterian, Episcopal and Methodist churches. Established since colonial times, the Presbyterian and Episcopal churches had deep-rooted support among old-time families. The Episcopal Church had greatly increased in vigor in the late 1800s after the Cathedral of the Incarnation in Garden City was constructed in 1885. This beautiful building was built by A. T. Stewart's widow in his memory and became the cathedral of Bishop Abram N. Littlejohn. It was an accurate reproduction of thirteenth-century Gothic architecture with exquisite proportions. Built of pink sandstone in colossal blocks, its floriated spire rose gradually with precise symmetry to a height of 220 feet 6 inches. Many of the twenty-four Methodist churches had been established as small circuit churches in the mid-1800s.

The most vigorous growth in the area during the late 1800s was experienced by the Roman Catholic Church. The advent of new immigrant groups in the area prompted a demand for Catholic churches. These early congregations had a difficult time in obtaining the necessary resources. The first Catholic Mass in Rockville Centre was celebrated in a blacksmith shop before six communicants in 1887. This small group eventually grew into St. Agnes Church, later to become the cathedral of the Long Island Diocese. By 1900, twenty parishes had been established, providing a major force and new in-

Searingtown Methodist Church, a typical one-room church of the late 1800s.

fluence in local religious affairs. The older Baptist and Reformed Dutch churches and the Society of Friends had experienced little change, each maintaining a half-dozen congregations in 1900, a slight expansion beyond their size of the mid-1800s.

Religious activities were broadened considerably as church social activities increased on an organized basis. Ladies aid societies were organized in many congregations, and they became dependable sources of financial support for their churches while also providing a major means of social fellowship. Sunday schools expanded the activity of the churches, and their picnics and parades were major yearly events in all the small villages. Religious activities received extensive coverage in local newspapers, some weekly newspapers even running religious texts and stories covering a whole page every week. Church groups provided a major source of local social life, sponsoring suppers, lectures, musical entertainments, fairs and other activities. They were also greatly concerned with charitable projects and assisted in the care of the poor and needy.

In addition to church functions numerous social activities were available in the large villages throughout the area. Masonic lodges in Hempstead, Glen Cove, Oyster Bay and Rockville Centre had over 450 members. Royal Arcanum and Independent Order of Odd Fellows lodges were in the major villages, and three active Grand Army of the Republic chapters met in the county. These organizations and mutual benevolent associations, women's clubs and similar groups provided fraternal fellowship and supported local civic and philanthropic projects. The Hempstead Women's Club, founded in 1891, was principally interested in literary activities and greatly assisted in obtaining library services for that community. As the villages grew, the establishment of local promotional organizations such as boards of trade and village improvement societies provided social contacts for businessmen and a means

Cathedral of the Incarnation, photographed by George B. Brainard in 1888. Its floriated spire rises gracefully over 220 feet.

Matinecock Society of Friends meeting house built in 1725, a sketch by Richard Springsteed.

to direct or influence local community improvements.

Village social life was also influenced by the popular sports of the time. Bicycling was a great craze and organized races were held between local teams. Baseball was the major spectator sport, and a South Side League played regular games with teams from Bellmore, Baldwin, Rockville Centre and Amityville in 1900. Freeport also entered the league that year and lost its opening game to Rockville Centre by a score of 12 to 0. Water sports were a major activity with swimming, boat racing, duck shooting, clamming and fishing popular diversions. There was no greater treat on a hot Fourth of July than to go to Freeport and take the ferry over to the barrier beach for a day-long picnic. The ferryboats would be crowded and "all the yachts, sloops, naphtha launches and sailboats were employed, and it was a great day for pleasure sailing." Such a festive day was climaxed by displays of fireworks and the traditional piazza band concert.

Golf clubs at Cedarhurst, Oyster Bay and Meadow Brook provided courses for this fashionable sport. The Island Golf Links, a nine-hole subscription course, was opened in Garden City in 1896. It was enlarged and incorporated by 1900 as the Garden City Golf Club and no longer depended on two hundred sheep to keep the grass short.

In winter the many ponds and streams provided excellent skating, and iceboating was popular on Long Island Sound. Residents who had the means and time could enjoy yachting, tennis, shooting and almost every other sports activity. The easy accessibility to natural waterfront, streams and woodland made Nassau a sports paradise for all its people who enjoyed outdoor activities.

Charles Ransom, a leading county citizen from Sea Cliff, recalled those wonderful times when "no kids could have had a happier time than we who were carefree just before and after the turn of the century."

By 1900 it was evident that Nassau County's population and economic structure were undergoing significant change. Population was growing steadily through the promotion and development of resort communities along the railroad lines which acquainted city dwellers with the pleasures of country living. Local real estate developments and the railroad provided them with the possibilities of country homes on a year-round basis. Many did move out and the first commuter communities began to grow. The creation of large estates on the north shore brought an aura of glamour to Nassau and retained a considerable amount of land in undeveloped parcels.

The golden days of agriculture were also behind Nassau farmers by 1900. Dependent on market gardening, farm operations in the future would be under the shadow of increasing land demand for residential development. Fishing was also losing its economic importance, while the amount of manufacturing was not sufficient to provide extensive employment opportunities for local residents.

It was still possible to stand at most major road intersections in local villages and in one sweeping glance survey the entire community—an old-fashioned tavern, and small retail stores grouped around the railroad station with small houses and farms beyond. This rural quietude would soon be shattered in the rapid developments of the next seventy-five years as Nassau County became a bustling suburban area.

The rural quietude of the Hempstead Plains was broken by sounds of military activity *when Camp Black was established as an assembly place for the Spanish-American War.*

Benjamin D. Hicks, the father of Nassau County.

CHAPTER II

CHANGES IN GOVERNMENT

Creation of Nassau County

The small rural towns in Nassau County eagerly awaited New Year's Eve in 1899 and the beginning of the 1900s. Frank Margot of Plainview witnessed the great celebration as the new year was rung in and "the large pickle and cabbage salting factories set up a din with their whistles blowing a full blast and run by steam. There were whistles blowing at the brickyard and the church bells rang for hours." It was a particularly memorable time for residents of the towns of Hempstead, North Hempstead and Oyster Bay, since the end of the old year marked Nassau County's first year of existence as an independent county.

Less than two years before, on January 22, 1898, a public meeting had been called at Allen's Hotel in Mineola to discuss the creation of a new county. The hotel was crowded as P. Halstead Scudder called the meeting to order and indicated the alternatives that faced the residents of the towns. The possibility of annexation to Greater New York was dismissed, to the cheers of the audience, as entirely out of the question. Another, the idea of creating a new county by combining Queens County's eastern towns with different towns of western Suffolk, seemed unlikely of adoption. Scudder concluded that the organization of a new county was the only solution to the problem which confronted them.

Before the general discussion began, the meeting chose officers, headed by Benjamin D. Hicks of North Hempstead as chairman. Hicks had been a leader in previous attempts to create a new county. For his long years of work in striving for an independent county he deserves to be called the Father of Nassau County. A popular and successful Quaker banker, he was an intelligent and active participant in all types of community improvement. Archer B. Wallace, son of the assemblyman, was chosen secretary of the meeting.

Discussion began after J. B. Coles Tappen of Oyster Bay made the motion:

Resolved that it is the sense of this meeting that the towns of Hempstead, North Hempstead and Oyster Bay withdraw from the county of Queens, and that a new county to include the said towns be formed.

A few dissidents took up the question of alternative actions. North Hempstead resident W. W. Cock favored annexation to Suffolk County while John H. Carll wanted to join New York City, but neither proposal received support. Inclusion of Huntington and Babylon in a new county was urged by Fred Herzog, Sr., of Oyster Bay. General James Pearsall of Glen Cove, who had been a member of the assembly in an attempt twenty years before to create a new county, declared it would be impossible to get such a measure through the legislature.

Many of those in attendance felt, with Edward N. Townsend of Hempstead, that "the county would be an inexpensive one to govern." James H. Ludlam of Oyster

Bay also stressed the economy aspects, indicating people from his area wanted lower taxes. In appropriate Long Island fashion, D. N. Munger closed the subject by stating that "they should consider not what should be taken in but what barnacles should be taken off." The chairman called for a vote and Mr. Tappen's resolution was carried with only a few dissenting votes.

James Ludlam of Oyster Bay then offered a motion which was unanimously adopted, as follows:

Whereas, It is for the best interests of the citizens of the towns of Hempstead, North Hempstead and Oyster Bay to withdraw from the county of Queens.

Resolved that . . . Supervisors Underhill, Smith and Denton be requested to obtain authority . . . to expend a sum, not exceeding $250. for each town in defraying any expenses . . . in drafting and preparation of such bills as may be necessary to carry into effect the desire of the people to have a county free from entangling alliance with the great city of New York.

To pursue the action a committee was appointed composed of the following: P. Halstead Scudder of Oyster Bay, Lott Vanderwater and William G. Miller of Hempstead, Joseph H. Bogert and Wilbur Lewis of North Hempstead, James Pearsall and James H. Ludlam of Oyster Bay. The meeting closed with the proposal of several names for the county including Matinecock, Norfolk, Nassau and Bryant. Thus began the final and successful attempt to create Nassau County.

Previous agitation to institute a new county dated to 1859. In November of that year, the *Queens County Sentinel* suggested in an editorial that a new county, termed Nassau, be created out of the towns of Hempstead, North Hempstead, Oyster Bay and Huntington. It would reduce travel requirements and settle the long-standing dispute between the western and eastern sections of the county due to the Queens County Court House location in an unpop-

ulated spot in North Hempstead. As soon as the echoes of the Civil War had died down, the discontent in the western Queens towns over traveling to the courthouse in North Hempstead flared into the open again. During 1868 strong efforts were made to gain support to move the county buildings. A bill enabling the erection of a new courthouse was introduced in the state legislature in February 1869, with the powerful support of western Queens's residents.

The eastern towns were not to be defeated so easily. They began a counterattack on February 9, 1869, at a meeting held at Searing's Hotel in Mineola. William T. McCoun, a Republican leader from Oyster Bay, chaired the meeting which proposed a new county with the name Nassau to include Hempstead, North Hempstead, Oyster Bay and Huntington. Queens County assemblyman James B. Pearsall introduced the bill in the state legislature, including the towns of Smithtown and Islip in addition to those originally suggested.

Representatives from the Suffolk towns indicated that their residents were opposed to the bill and western Queens leaders fought it. Despite strong support by Hempstead town supervisor Carman Cornelius and other eastern county political leaders, the measure was killed by the state senate. The new courthouse measure also met defeat. The eastern towns' victory was only temporary. In 1871 a new courthouse act was passed and its location set in Long Island City. Opened in 1877, it signaled the political triumph of the increasingly urbanized western area of the county over the rural eastern portion.

After winning the supervisorship of North Hempstead and a state assembly seat in 1876, the Republicans began another campaign to create a new county. Benjamin D. Hicks was elected chairman of a citizens' committee and Assemblyman Elbert Floyd-Jones led the fight. A bill was introduced in the legislature providing for the creation of "Ocean County" from the three eastern towns of Queens together with Huntington and Babylon, towns of Suffolk County on the Queens boundary. Residents of North Hempstead led in supporting the new county so that they would not "have our rights trampled upon, our taxes unwisely and uselessly enhanced, our local government unscrupulously managed, our representation unequal." Although there was widespread support, Benjamin Hicks realized the extent of opposition and privately indicated to Henry Onderdonk that "I do not feel at all sanguine as to the success of Division. There are a few figures that stand in our way . . . We must not shout until we are out of the woods." The opposition lost no time and on February 13, 1877, the Queens Board of Supervisors, at a special meeting attended only by the western town supervisors, voted opposition to the division.

Again, despite strong support by residents of the eastern towns, the opposition of powerful Democratic forces in western Queens and the inclusion of the Suffolk towns spelled the doom of another attempt to create a new county.

In March of 1896, culminating a drive to consolidate New York City's government, the legislature passed a law creating Greater New York. The final boundaries of the act included all of the western Queens towns and a small part of Hempstead along its western edge. Since they offered little to the city but would require public spending, the consolidationists had left out the three eastern towns of Queens.

On January 1, 1898, about one third of Queens County became a borough of New York City. The three eastern towns were still part of Queens County but outside the city. This intolerable situation led to the citizens' meeting called in January of 1898. After the meeting the committee met at Pettit's Hotel in Jamaica on February 5, and adopted the draft of a bill. After spirited discussion the name Nassau, proposed by Archer B. Wallace, was adopted and the bill given to Assemblyman George Wallace. The Democratic leadership in Queens County could not reconcile itself to losing this large area from its control and moved to oppose the bill. The headlines in the *Long Island Farmer,* a newspaper representing Demo-

The residents of the rural eastern Queens towns enjoyed picking the famed Hempstead Plains violets, which spread across the plains.

cratic thought in Jamaica, protested: NEW COUNTY NONSENSE, SOME MORE FOOL BILLS. The newspaper contended that a number of prominent men desired to be taken into Greater New York and that District Attorney Youngs, a Republican, had expressed himself as opposed to the creation of a new county.

Assemblyman Wallace submitted the bill to the Statutory Revision Committee for an opinion on its constitutionality and then introduced it into the assembly on February 17. It was referred to the Internal Affairs Committee, which held a hearing on March 4, at which only supporters appeared. Assemblyman Cyrus B. Gale of Jamaica fought the bill bitterly when it was reported to the floor of the assembly in March during the last week of the session. It passed both houses and was sent to Governor Frank S. Black on April 26.

A Queens delegation opposing the bill and a delegation of citizens from the eastern towns met with the governor. Townsend Scudder, counsel to the Queens Board of Supervisors, argued against the bill, urging its defeat because it would be expensive. He also contended that Nassau County would have no public property and that the timing was wrong because of the Spanish-American War. Despite an agreement with Benjamin Hicks, he took up all the time allowed to the delegations. Hicks simply assured the governor it was a wise measure desired by the taxpayers of the territory included in the new county.

Governor Frank S. Black signed the bill into law and Nassau County would be created as of January 1, 1899. Since its government organization came under previous general county laws, the law only specified the six elective offices and provided that all the county records would be retained by Queens except those of the county engineer concerning the Nassau area.

In the spring elections of 1898, Republicans Smith Cox and Augustus Denton were elected supervisors from Hempstead and North Hempstead, while Oyster Bay elected

William H. Jones, a Democrat. These men would constitute the first Board of Supervisors but the remaining county officers had to be elected at a general election in November of that year. On October 4, both parties held nominating conventions at Mineola. The Democratic convention was harmonious and nominated for the most important offices: Robert Seabury for county judge and James P. Niemann for district attorney.

A fierce intraparty battle marked the Republican convention. Ex-Senator John Lewis Childs, chairman of the county committee, controlled the convention. His slate of nominations was vigorously opposed by William J. Youngs, Republican state committeeman and district attorney of Queens County. Childs's candidate for the county judge, George Wallace, won over Youngs's candidate on the first formal ballot, thirty-nine to thirty-three. Edward Cromwell, Childs's choice for district attorney, also won. Although badly defeated, Youngs moved to make the nominations unanimous. Nassau County's foremost resident, Theodore Roosevelt, had taken no direct part in this battle. After his election as governor, however, he appointed William J. Youngs as his confidential secretary.

This internal strife was the beginning of trouble for the Republicans. Queens county clerk John Sutphin would not accept their nominations until a favorable court ruling on Nassau's constitutionality. The election campaign was tightly fought with the Republicans harassed by the internal split in their party and also by a scandal that erupted in the administration of the justice-of-the-peace courts. Despite these handicaps, the GOP carried the majority of the county offices but lost the two important posts. James P. Niemann captured the district attorney office by seventeen votes, 4,749 to 4,732, and Robert Seabury won as county judge, 4,818 to 4,702.

Republicans captured the remaining four offices; Thomas Patterson as county clerk, Henry N. W. Eastman as county treasurer, William Wood as sheriff and George D.

Assemblyman George Wallace, a proponent of the new county.

Smith as superintendent of the poor. In this election voters also decided the location of future county buildings. They had a choice of a spot one mile from the station of the Long Island Rail Road in the villages of Hempstead, Hicksville or Mineola. Voters of the towns of Oyster Bay and North Hempstead supported Mineola, and it won, 5,280 to 3,396, over Hempstead.

Nassau County came into existence on January 1, 1899, encompassing an area of 274 square miles. At the first meeting of the new Board of Supervisors, the truck house of the Mineola Hook and Ladder Company was chosen as the temporary home of the county court. The colors of orange and blue were adopted for use in the official flag. The seal was a crest with the golden rampant lion of the House of Nassau on an azure blue field, encircled by seven gold bars. Sal-

aries were then determined for the various officials: the treasurer, clerk and sheriff were voted $2,000, the district attorney $1,500 and the superintendent of the poor $500. The Board chose J. Seymour Snedeker as clerk of the Board and Carrie Hicks as county stenographer and librarian. The Board also voted to accept land, which was within a mile of the Mineola railroad station but actually in Garden City, offered by the Garden City Company for county buildings.

After this initial meeting, the Board began to attack the various problems caused by the division from Queens. The first of these was the question of the apportionment of the Queens County debt. In 1898, after the establishment of Greater New York City, the Queens County Board of Supervisors and the municipal assembly had failed to agree on the apportionment of Queens's debt and as a result the matter had been thrown into the courts. Nassau County had legal representation at the hearings in 1899 and Charles F. Brown, the referee, rendered a decision in agreement with Nassau's theory that the apportionment should be made upon the basis of assessed values of the territory within and without the City of New York.

By now another complication had entered this specific problem. The original New York City consolidation had included a small portion of the Town of Hempstead. Energetic young assemblyman G. Wilbur Doughty introduced a bill in the 1899 legislature returning this portion, consisting of parts of Elmont, Foster's Meadow, Lawrence and Cedarhurst, to Nassau County. It became law on April 21. The apportionment of debt had to be corrected to include this area and the final settlement provided that Nassau would assume obligations of $1,011,-968—a staggering indebtedness for a new county.

The problem of the apportionment of personal property originally belonging to Queens County had arisen over Barnum Island. It was a large tract near Long Beach on the south shore where the Queens

Nassau County officers, 1899. First row, left to right: William H. Jones, Oyster Bay supervisor; Augustus Denton, North Hempstead supervisor; Robert Seabury, county judge; William Wood, sheriff; Henry Skinner, undersheriff; Thomas K. Patterson, county clerk.

County poor farm was located. On January 19, 1899, the supervisors of Nassau filed notice that they were going to sell the land. Immediately the Queens Board protested, contending that the personal property should be divided in the same manner as the debt, i.e., proportionally. Court judgment gave possession to Nassau but the supervisors were uncertain what to do with the property. On September 15, the poor farm was closed, and in April of 1901 the island was sold at public auction for $40,100 to raise money for new county buildings.

In December of 1897 the Queens County Board of Supervisors had executed a tremendous number of road contracts for county roads in the three eastern towns. Oyster Bay was to have sixty-nine miles

paved, North Hempstead forty-nine and a half and Hempstead fifty-seven and a half. The roads were to be graded and laid with stone six to eight inches thick at the center and four to six inches at the wings. The work was delayed, but by the time of Nassau's creation, $1,600,000 worth of contracts was nearing completion.

The inspection and payment for this work was still controlled by the Queens Board of Supervisors. On March 9, the Nassau Board of Supervisors passed a resolution requesting the Queens Board to appoint the Nassau supervisors as its agent to supervise the completion and acceptance of the roads being built in Nassau by these prior contracts. The Queens Board summarily refused and specifically directed its engineer to notify all

Temporary Nassau County courthouse in Mineola.

Original design of Nassau County seal, as emblazoned on old courthouse; in later use the lion was changed from the heraldic design to a more naturalistic shape.

contractors that they should proceed with such construction only at the times and in such order as would be indicated by the Board of Supervisors in Queens.

Warming up to the conflict, the Nassau Board directed Sheriff William H. Wood to take possession of steam rollers and other road equipment of Queens County in Nassau and started court proceedings to force the Queens engineer to turn over to the Nassau Board all plans, contracts, specifications and other documents referring to roads in Nassau County. A county road system was established and E. Harper Firth was appointed as Nassau County engineer to supervise all construction work and maintenance.

Although the Board of Supervisors had obtained temporary quarters for the court and arranged to board its prisoners with the New York City Department of Charities and Corrections, a pressing need was apparent for a county building. At the third meeting of the Board of Supervisors a bond issue of $150,000 was authorized for county buildings. The proposal met such an uproar of public disapproval that Chairman of the Board Augustus Denton indefinitely postponed it and promised "when it does take place the sum to be raised will not exceed $100,000."

A proposal of this magnitude shocked economy-minded residents and a press comment felt this amount was "amply sufficient to erect buildings that will answer every purpose for at least 50 years." The Long Island Farmers' Club objected to such an expenditure since Nassau County was a small county with limited wealth and already burdened with a large debt for stone roads.

The Board solicited architectural plans and in April accepted a proposal with the condition it be modified to enable construction for $100,000. This proved impossible. At the end of the summer a competition for the best plans was judged by a committee of representatives from the Architectural League, the New York chapter of the American Institute of Architects, and Beaux Arts.

In the meantime, $100,000 worth of bonds was sold.

Plans prepared by William Tubby were recommended by the committee but the cost was still excessive. The Board asked him and the architect whose plans won second place to submit revisions preserving the essential features of their plans but reducing the cost to $100,000. Builders' estimates on the new plans were still well over that amount so all the plans submitted were rejected. After considering the situation, in January of 1900 the Board employed Tubby as the architect to prepare plans and specifications for a county courthouse and jail to cost approximately $100,000. Three months later the plans were put out to bid and the contract for a new courthouse was awarded to Edward Roche for $105,137.39. In September of the same year Roche was the successful bidder on the county jail, to be built behind the courthouse for $99,982.

In addition to the settlement of problems arising out of the debt and question of buildings and roads, the county government also experienced some internal stress. Shortly after the county officers were installed, county clerk Thomas Patterson requested the Board to appoint another copyist. The supervisors objected since he had already hired one without consulting them. Patterson took the matter to court and obtained a ruling ordering the Board to recognize his appointments. Supervisors Cox and Jones finally voted for a copyist but only provided a salary of $52 a year. However, they conceded defeat at the next meeting and voted a salary of $611 for the additional copyist. They later also paid $50 for Patterson's legal costs in the action.

County government administration was simple and informal during its early years. The converted firehouse which was serving as the courthouse had only one rented phone, and five or six calls a day was normal business. In the first year about a hundred recorded papers of all kinds were registered with county clerk Patterson, and he collected $4,970 in fees. The county treasurer

Theodore Roosevelt at the groundbreaking of the old county courthouse, Mineola, 1901.

was probably the busiest official since he had the responsibility of meeting the payments due on the various notes. Besides the interest on the county's share of the Queens bonded debt, the county adopted the policy of short-term notes to meet expenses and obligations. The county's first budget contained $27,150 for salaries, $115,951 for loans due banks, $42,509 for interest on the Queens County debt, $6,780 for interest on loans and $25,357 for county bills and rent.

On July 13, 1900, a warm Friday, the permanence of the new county was symbolized by the laying of the cornerstone of the new courthouse. A large throng of prominent local civic and political leaders turned out to hear Governor Theodore Roosevelt dedicate the new building. He echoed the delight of all the citizens in the prospect of having a new building and reminded the audience that officials and residents must work together to ensure good government since "all free men are alike in privileges, duties and responsibilities."

During the next few years the county administration established routine functions. It concerned itself with the regular activities of the county—legal administration, records, elections, supervision of the poor and operation and maintenance of the county road system. In addition to these basic duties it also acted on new problems such as its local law in 1901 regulating the speed of automobiles on the highways of the County of Nassau. The provision limited speed to eight miles per hour within built-up areas and fifteen miles per hour elsewhere.

Another new responsibility in the early 1900s was regulation of the numerous trolley companies that had sprung up in the county.

First county courthouse used for administrative offices and courts; building to the left rear was the county jail.

The Nassau Belt Lines Traction Company and the Mineola, Hempstead and Freeport Traction Company vied before the Board in 1901 for a public use franchise to operate a street surface railroad from Mineola to Freeport. After extensive legal controversy, the Mineola, Hempstead and Freeport was granted the franchise.

Rural matters were also still important and the Board passed resolutions offering a $500 reward, which was later doubled, for horse thieves. A resolution prohibiting the digging of sandworms on shores and beaches of Long Island Sound, since this resulted in wholesale destruction and waste of soft clams, is indicative of the importance of maritime affairs.

The initial county budgets were not uniformly organized, therefore comparative statistics for different years are not precise. The budget of 1902 allocated the following expenditures:

County Buildings	$65,198
Interest on Bonds and Other Loans	65,000
New Roads and Bridges	56,831
Road Maintenance	43,397
Advertising and Printing	39,214
Salaries	39,000
Miscellaneous	28,000
County Poor	12,217
Total	$348,857

The county administration quickly settled into a pattern of operations that continued with little change until after World War I.

While these governmental changes took place, the private sector of life witnessed the beginning of corporations that were to provide major new public services. In the late 1800s, telephone service began on Long Island when a Glen Cove Central exchange opened in 1884. Shortly after, crank-operated phones for local service were installed in

Hempstead in the early 1890s. When the new county was created, telephone companies made application to the Board of Supervisors for permission to erect poles and string wires upon and over the highways of the county road system. Permission was granted to the South Shore Telephone Company in October of 1899 with the provision that "the company have installed and at all times maintain a telephone in the county court house . . . without expense to the county and service on which shall be at all times free to county officials upon county business." Unfortunately for future taxpayers, the South Shore Company was challeneged by a competitor, the New York and New Jersey Telephone Company.

The New York and New Jersey Telephone Company also received the right to install lines and rapidly expanded. In 1900 nine telephone exchanges in Glen Cove, Hempstead, Port Washington, Great Neck, Oyster Bay, Rockville Centre, Roslyn, Freeport and East Rockaway served 446 subscribers. Most of these telephones were in drugstores or other commercial buildings in each village. This initial service spread throughout the county and was stimulated by the increasing population. Technological changes enabled better service and in 1908 new phones which signaled the operator just by the lifting of the receiver were in use in the Freeport central office. A year later new quarters were obtained at Glen Cove, which alone had 575 telephones connected to its switchboard on a common battery.

Corporate changes accompanied the growth in service and the New York Telephone Company began its existence in 1909 and established more efficient operations. Garden City, Long Beach and Oyster Bay all had early central office buildings and by 1920 there were twenty-two offices servicing 17,564 telephones. The rapid population increase in the 1920s boosted residential usage to 34,236 telephones in 1925. In the late 1920s, new exchanges were being built in almost every major community, such as Floral Park with thirty-two operator positions and 10,500 telephones, and Glen Cove with

A utility line crew at work in the early 1900s.

twenty-two operator positions for over 5,000 subscribers. In 1930 the New York Telephone Company began construction of a ten-story operating and administration center, the tallest building in the Village of Hempstead, to service its over 70,000 telephone stations.

Under private enterprise, electric and gas public utilities also developed throughout the county except in Rockville Centre and Freeport. Just before the turn of the century, both these early incorporated villages began their own local municipal electric systems to provide service for their more densely populated villages. They each built power plants and distribution systems to provide residential and industrial power and street lighting. The administration of these plants and electric rates were a continual source of friction and dispute in the villages' politics. Nevertheless, the voters continued to sup-

port government operation and both became models of village-owned electric power systems by 1930. Elsewhere in the county electric power development was left to private enterprise and there were no efforts or demands to establish public utilities or government control.

Early in the 1890s, E. D. Morgan desired to obtain electricity at his estate in Wheatley and organized a local electric company beginning with four other wealthy estate owners as customers—Clarence Mackay, Dudley Winthrop, Foxhall Keane and W. C. Whitney. This original company, the Roslyn Light and Power, gradually extended service across the north shore. In 1904 it was renamed the Nassau Light and Power Company and constructed a new plant in Glenwood Landing to generate power. Gradually, under E. D. Morgan's presidency and Fred Maidment's management, it acquired other

Glenwood Landing plant of the Long Island Lighting Company in 1930s.

small local companies in Floral Park, Oyster Bay, Port Washington, Glen Cove and North Hempstead. It had over five hundred miles of pole lines in the county by 1920 and its network of lines extended all over the northern, central and southern parts of the county except Freeport and Rockville Centre. The main plant at Glenwood Landing was located on Hempstead Harbor and allowed cheap fuel delivery by water. From this 7,500-horsepower generating station, a network of transmission and distribution lines supplied the county.

In 1922 a controlling interest in the company was purchased by Ellis L. Phillips, who merged it into his Long Island Lighting Company which he had developed in Suffolk County. The stock issue of the combined companies was over $3 million. Fred Maidment continued to provide leadership in the new corporation, which quickly moved to increase its business capacity. Physical facilities were improved and a high-tension line was extended between the generating plants in Glenwood Landing and Northport to ensure more stable service. At this time the consumer rate in Nassau County was 12 cents per kilowatt, and almost all the service was used for residential lighting.

Gas supply facilities were also consolidated in the early 1900s. The Nassau and Suffolk Lighting Company was created out of the old Hempstead Gas Light Company, the Nassau County Gas Company, the Nassau Illuminating and Power Company and the South Shore Gas Company. It maintained a complete gas system with a manufacturing plant in Hempstead and high-pressure mains to Mineola, Baldwin and Freeport. The gas was used mainly for residential cooking purposes. The north shore was served by the Sea Cliff and Glen Cove Gas Company and the Public Service Corporation. In 1927 the growing Long Island Lighting Company acquired the Nassau and Suffolk Lighting Company together with all its subsidiaries and thereafter both gas and electric power were consolidated in this one large organization with headquarters in Mineola. Except

for the two villages, the necessary public utilities for the rapidly growing county were provided satisfactorily by private enterprise and service kept pace with increasing demands.

Home Rule Develops

The county government continued to be harassed by its building problems in the early 1900s. Large expenditures for the courthouse and jail received bipartisan criticism, particularly when a final accounting showed that county buildings had cost $319,622 by 1903. To make matters worse, the courthouse was plagued by falling plaster and newspaper critics reported that "every few weeks some ceiling either falls down or threatens to fall, until only a small portion of the original ceilings remain in the building." Building extravagance became a major political issue and two Democratic supervisors were elected to the county board in 1905 on an economy platform.

By 1911, however, the county government had already outgrown the courthouse and additional space had to be rented for county activities. Only one room was available for holding trial terms of the supreme and county courts so that alternate dates were necessary. In accordance with a new state law, a Board of Elections was created and, combined with personnel increases in the county treasurer's office, put additional demands on space. In 1916 wings were added to the original courthouse and in 1926 it was enlarged again.

Persistent disputes arose over the improvement of roads required by the increasing use of automobiles. Extensive improvements were undertaken in the road system of the county, particularly in the towns of the two Democratic supervisors who controlled the county board. County comptroller John Lyon, a Democrat, refused to issue construction bonds for roads in Hempstead, contending the roads were not "leading market roads"

Old county courthouse after addition of wings.

as the law provided. However, Hempstead fought his decision in the courts and he was not upheld. The bitterness engendered in residents of the Town of Hempstead over this road construction dispute led to a lawsuit by Hempstead against the other towns over tax equalization rates. In 1915 the final court ruling adopted different tax ratios than those in effect. Oyster Bay and North Hempstead had to refund Hempstead over $300,-000 it had paid in excess during the earlier years.

At this time there were four classifications of roads for purposes of construction and improvement. State highways were built solely at the expense of the state, while county highways were jointly supported by state, county and town. County roads and town highways were constructed and maintained by the respective governments. The county gradually began to take over main traffic routes and its superintendent of highways was the main source of direction in planning and building all roads in the county. The greatest proportion of the expense for these roads and two county bridges was obtained through bond issues. By 1930 a $20-million indebtedness had been incurred for highway construction.

Although bonds were issued for roads and buildings, every effort was made to keep county indebtedness low. After the end of

World War I, the great increase in population had boosted governmental demands and many new functions also required additional funds. County budget expenditures increased from $665,715 in 1911 to $2,058,418 in 1920 with over 50 per cent of the funds required for debt and capital improvements. These expenditures tripled in the next ten years.

The county government began to attack health problems as early as 1914, when a referendum was narrowly approved 6,796 to 6,643 to build a county tuberculosis hospital. The vote was only the initial step, as several years went by during discussion and planning over its eventual location. Finally in 1917 an unoccupied farm at Plainview was purchased as a suitable site. Architects were engaged and the first units were opened in 1920 with further expansion occurring in 1927, when a children's building was added. While the sanatorium provided facilities for treatment of the dreaded tuberculosis, other hospital care services for lower-income residents were needed. The Board of Supervisors proposed the establishment of a general county hospital in 1930. County residents approved by referendum the floating of a $2-million bond issue. Financial demands on the county government due to the Depression delayed the opening of the institution until the beginning of 1935.

Another important public health develop-ment was the establishment of the Nassau County Mosquito Extermination Commiss-sion in 1916. In that year there were over 475 cases of malaria in just four communities of the county. By 1920 the commission's ef-fective work in draining salt-marsh areas, preventing stagnant water accumulations, and house-to-house inspections had reduced malaria to a sickness of the past in Nassau County. The commission, which expended over a half-million dollars in its first ten years, maintained an active program of draining bay swamps by cutting ditches and educating citizens to destroy mosquito breed-ing places. It provided a significant public health service, materially increasing the at-tractiveness of living in Nassau County by ridding the area of the bothersome and deadly mosquito.

As population had increased, there was a corresponding increase in criminal activity and need for effective police protection. At the time of World War I, the sheriff had police duties throughout the county, but had only temporary special deputies to assist him. Each town had five constables who were peace officers authorized to make arrests, but mainly they prevented disorders and served court warrants. Most of the large in-corporated villages had their own police forces, such as Hempstead with five full-time patrolmen, watchmen who were partially paid by businessmen, and temporary patrol-men to help out with traffic on Sundays and holidays. Topping off this crazy quilt of pro-tection were five special process servers, at-tached to the county district attorney's office, who were actually motorcycle officers regulat-ing traffic and serving violators with tickets.

Village of Hempstead police force before World War I.

Nassau County policeman with new motorized equipment of the 1920s.

Lack of clear responsibility and little cooperation between the various police groups led to public demands to modernize the chaotic police system.

In 1921 the Board of Supervisors appointed a Special Citizen Committee for Police Protection to draw plans for improvement. It was composed of political leaders from all over the county led by Assemblyman Theodore Roosevelt, Jr., and Thomas McWhinney. The committee and county officials had to unravel a maze of conflicts and differences. A deputy sheriff then headed uniformed deputies who formed the county police force, while detectives were assigned to the district attorney's office. In 1924 Will T. Phillips, deputy sheriff in charge of police work, was convicted of ob-

structing justice in fixing traffic tickets, and action finally was taken on the committee proposals. A unified County Police Department was established and began operations on January 1, 1926, under Chief of Police Abram W. Skidmore. He instituted professional organization, and a well-trained department grew from fifty men to almost five hundred by World War II. Many existing village departments remained independent but within ten years the department covered 72 per cent of the county's area and 52 per cent of its population.

The county government during these years had surpassed the town governments and had become the predominant governmental organization in the area. Its budget in 1930 of over $6 million was ten times the total spent by all three towns and its scope of activities was continually expanding while the towns remained fairly static. As early as 1915 the county had almost as many regular employees as the towns combined. While the county was attacking the problems caused by the rapid suburban growth of the area, the town still functioned within its traditional rural concepts.

The problems caused by population growth, which fell within the geographical confines of the towns, were most often assigned to a special district. Since the county could not provide localized services and the towns were unwilling under their general tax base, special districts of a limited geographical area were set up by vote of the residents to provide a tax base and government organization for a specific local improvement. After 1915 such local districts for water service, street lighting, fire and hydrant service, sidewalks, drainage, etc. were extensively used in the unincorporated parts of the townships outside of established villages to provide many desired governmental services. From 1920 to 1930, the tax revenue of the 156 special districts in the county increased from $1.9 million to over $8 million. Since many of the districts were administered by the town boards, town governments had to expand physical facilities for these functions. In 1920 Hempstead opened a new town hall, which had to be further expanded in 1929. Special districts became the major public expense other than educational services, while the total revenues of the three town governments remained constant at a little over $600,000.

Another major governmental development of the early 1900s in Nassau County was the growth of incorporated villages. The Village of Hempstead predated the Civil War, and Sea Cliff was formally incorporated in 1883. Then in the 1890s, Freeport, Rockville Centre and Lawrence set up independent village governments. By 1910 only four other villages were incorporated—East Rockaway, Farmingdale, Mineola and Floral Park. The rapidly increasing population after 1910, due

to expanded real estate developments, influenced more and more areas to vote for incorporation. Independent local governments enabled residents to obtain needed local improvements and control further development of their areas.

By 1920, Bayville, Cedarhurst, Garden City, Great Neck Estates, Kensington, Lynbrook, Plandome, Saddle Rock, Sands Point and Woodsburgh had joined existing incorporated villages so that over one third of the county's residents lived within incorporated areas. Mounting governmental demands in the twenties caused the establishment of Bellerose, Centre Island, Cove Neck, East Williston, Great Neck, Hewlett Bay Park, Hewlett Harbor, Hewlett Neck, Island Park, Kings Point, Lake Success, Malverne, Matinecock, Mill Neck, New Hyde Park, Old Westbury, Stewart Manor, Valley Stream and Williston Park. Many of these villages were areas of intensive growth and urgently required local government improvements. Others with larger areas and small populations were created to retain an exclusiveness and strict control of development by the wealthy estate owners.

These governmental units ranged from small villages of a hundred people with part-time staff to large villages with regular departments to handle local record keeping, taxation, streets, water service, fire and police protection. The main problems faced by most villages were waste disposal, street paving and lighting. By 1925 the leading village officials had organized the Nassau County Village Officials Association as a central clearinghouse of information and means to achieve greater cooperation in attacking mutual problems. The original fourteen community members began work on sewerage, incineration and police problems and gradually the remaining villages joined in following years.

Between 1920 and 1930 the taxes collected by villages jumped from $534,280 to $3,075,-858 and their combined debt in Nassau exceeded $9 million at the end of the decade. Although greatly increased services were pro-

The Village of Freeport's new village hall.

vided, the average village tax rate decreased between 1920 and 1930. Many villages provided extensive services, such as Hempstead, which installed sewers by 1911 and electric street lighting by 1918. Rockville Centre completed a modern incineration plant for garbage in 1928 and a $2-million sewage system with disposal plant, trunk lines and pump houses by 1930. Freeport was a major progressive community, but even there village improvements were won only after constant effort. In 1906 night lighting was voted down but approved the next year, and after 1910 a fire alarm system and other extensive community improvements were made. Freeport welcomed 1930 with a spanking-new municipal building, an attractive replica of the original Independence Hall in Philadelphia.

Two local communities also took the option, under state law, to organize as a city instead of incorporate as a village. Glen Cove, one of the larger communities in the county with a population of over 10,000, was organized after an extensive campaign beginning in 1915. The local weekly newspaper and village improvement association urged city formation, which was approved in a close public referendum 720 to 713 in 1917. Glen Cove was promoted as the "model little city" and was a diversified community with some heavy industry, large estates, an active business district and growing residential areas.

Many of the buildings in Long Beach had a Moorish architectural flavor, including the city hall, erected before World War I.

On the south shore, a new real estate syndicate began to develop Long Beach as an elaborate waterfront resort in 1907. It obtained control over 1,000 acres and obtained an additional 100 from the Town of Hempstead after a public referendum approving the sale. Senator William H. Reynolds was the major promoter of the development, and he constantly sought publicity for the resort. Millions of cubic yards of sand were pumped in to fill in the marshes and add to the land area. Sufficient development had occurred by 1922 that Long Beach was incorporated as a city with Reynolds as its first mayor. In 1924, however, he and the city treasurer were charged with mishandling city funds. Although Reynolds was convicted, his supporters felt the action was politically inspired. The large hotels facing the boardwalk along the ocean at Long Beach became a favorite summer resort for city dwellers during the 1920s.

Village politics were generally very fierce and every small issue was contested by opposing factions. Traditionally local elections were not fought in Republican and Democratic party slates. Both major parties avoided village politics and left the field to local political parties formed in each village. G. Wilbur Doughty, GOP county leader, publicly indicated in 1929 that the Republican Party "has no interest in village elections" and "has always followed a hands-off policy in village affairs." When it was incorporated in 1919, Garden City, to free itself from the usual factional bickering, made a village agreement that apportioned its board of trustees among the three sections of the village with nominees to be chosen by the Property Owners Association in each section.

The development of village governments also led to a new general influence on public affairs—the local civic group. There were

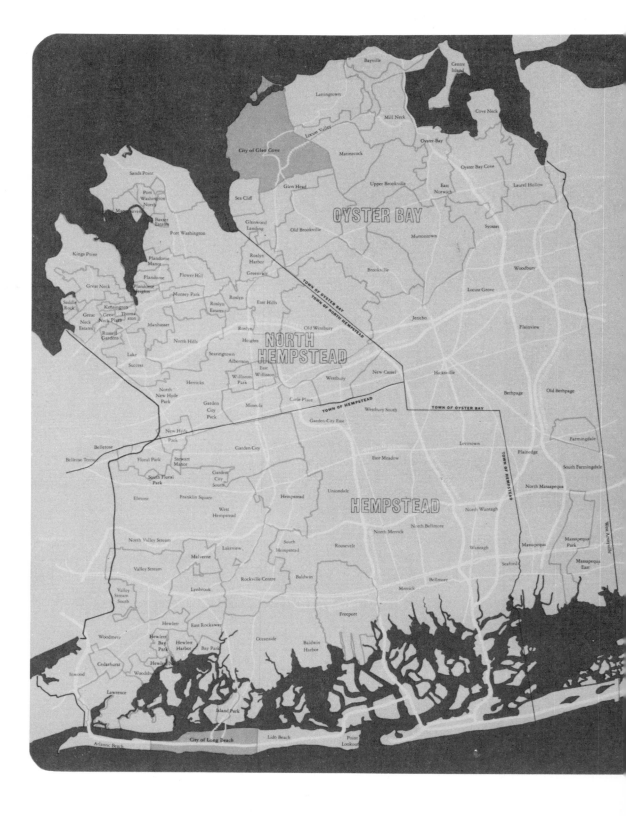

a few village-improvement organizations at the turn of the century. Civic groups became the major force in efforts leading to the establishment of villages from 1900 to 1930. Organized on a neighborhood subdivision development or community-wide basis, they were termed "the legitimate descendant of the old time town meeting."

Most had the same basic purpose as the Matinecock Neighborhood Association—to do "the things which should be done in every community, no matter how small, to make the neighborhood a better place to live in." Lack of roads, sidewalks, electricity, water, fire protection, transportation and street lights were common problems faced in all new areas of development, and the civic association became the most useful prod to obtain government action. Even after villages were formed, these associations continued to provide a collective voice for residents. Dr. J. P. Thayer, president of the Freeport Civic Association, indicated it performed the function of the old-time town meeting, bringing "matters of great importance before their members, debating them, deciding what in their opinion was the best course to take and letting their wishes be made known at the proper time."

Village government was accepted and firmly supported by residents and took a major role in the governmental structure of Nassau County by 1930. Almost 50 per cent of the county population resided within incorporated villages. Providing essential services and a government which was accessible and responsive to the resident and taxpayer, villages were a good influence, offsetting the general lack of planning in the county. The establishment of villages provided a focal point for local identification and residents developed and owed their allegiance to their village or community. This was the focus of their attention as homeowners and only slight interest or concern was evidenced toward the county as a whole.

Major party politics in Nassau centered principally around the county elections. Damaged by the charges of extravagance in county buildings, the initial Republican officeholders were hurt. In the spring elections of 1905, Robert Seabury was elected supervisor of the Town of Hempstead by five votes in an exceptionally close race. He was the only Democrat to win in the town but his election, coupled with that of William H. Jones as supervisor of Oyster Bay, enabled the Democrats to control the county Board of Supervisors.

Stung by the Democratic charges of extravagance, the Republicans began to impute an alliance between the Nassau Democratic Party and the Tammany organization in New York City. The residents were warned in 1904 that it would be "safer to keep the Tammany Tiger out of Nassau County." This war cry was continually given through World War II by the GOP, who contended that Tammany Hall wanted to bring Nassau under its control. They warned this would happen under Democratic leadership with the purpose "to annex Republican Nassau to Democratic Queens." To mitigate the effect of these charges and to capture more independent votes, the Democrats frequently supported "citizen" slates during these early years. Campaigning at this time was often rather personal and entailed little in the way of technique except a maximum of public exposure and voter contact. In 1903 supervisor Girdell V. Brower reported campaign expenses of $74, including $54 for cigars and refreshments, and the rest for carriage hire.

Although the Democratic Party lost control of the Board of Supervisors from 1907 to 1910, they were preparing for a grand effort. In the fall of 1910 they waged a vigorous campaign emphasizing the economy issue and swept all the county offices except county clerk. In this election the voters also defeated a $500,000 proposition to add to the courthouse. Invigorated by this victory, the Democratic Party captured the supervisorships of Oyster Bay and North Hempstead in the spring elections of 1911. Morris F. Craft held the Republican seat of Hempstead by a thin margin of 115 votes.

Nassau County GOP National Convention delegation, 1912. Left to right, first row: Smith Cox, Town of Hempstead supervisor; *U.S. congressman William Cocks; Theodore Roosevelt; and Charles F. Lewis, Republican leader from North Hempstead.*

The Republican Party's strength collapsed completely in 1912. Smith Cox, former supervisor of the Town of Hempstead, was a delegate to the GOP National Convention and indicated he would stand by Theodore Roosevelt since "He is from this county and a neighbor." However, in the final convention showdown, he voted for Taft. The local party immediately split and numerous "Roosevelt" Progressive clubs were formed in the county. There is no evidence they were stimulated by the national idealistic Progressive movement, but as one of the founders, Sanford Davison, indicated, "We joined the movement only because we felt Teddy had been cheated at the Republican Convention and many of us idolized the man." The new party soon had an impressive leadership including James L. Dowsey of Manhasset; Andrew J. MacElroy, publisher of a Rockville Centre weekly, *The Owl;* John Lewis Childs; and Elvin N. Edwards. All were leading Republicans, but they were also joined by some dissident Democrats, including W. Bourke Cochran, a former Democratic congressman.

In the election of 1912, Woodrow Wilson carried the county with 7,073 votes to Roosevelt's 6,563 and Taft's 4,608. Some members of the Progressive Party urged its retention on the local level, and party secretary Dowsey petitioned the Board of Supervisors to

Theodore Roosevelt, campaigning in Nassau during the 1912 election.

recognize it as the second-ranking party in the county. Such recognition carried with it the right to designate an official newspaper to publish county laws and legal notices. The Board resisted but was forced by court action to designate *The Owl* in 1913. Although the Progressive registration was only 893 in the whole county, they polled over 2,000 votes for their candidates in the election of 1913, indirectly helping the Democrats to victory. Elvin Edwards then took over as Progressive chairman and, in 1915 and 1916, backed local Republican candidates, who won all down the line. Early the next year he was appointed assistant district attorney and the Progressive

Party disappeared from the local scene.

In the years before World War I, Oyster Bay Town was the stronghold of the Democratic Party in the county. It had a well-developed organization headed by supervisor James H. Cocks, popular county treasurer "Honest Dan" Hegeman and state senator Frank Norton. Another Democrat, Philip J. Christ, represented North Hempstead for nine years on the county Board of Supervisors and was a leader in establishing needed health measures including mosquito control and a county tuberculosis hospital. He served five years as chairman of the Board of Supervisors and was regarded as a man of impeccable integrity. His position was based more

Philip Christ, chairman of the Board of Supervisors and popular Democratic supervisor from the Town of North Hempstead.

on personal competence and popularity than on party power.

In the early 1900s there had been no distinct Republican leader in the county. Supervisor Smith Cox of Hempstead had a great deal of power and generally represented the eastern section of the Town of Hempstead, but G. Wilbur Doughty of the western area was the rising leader. He emerged from the Progressive split as the countywide Republican leader in 1915.

In the fall elections of 1916, under unified command the Republicans carried all the county offices. The county judge and county surrogate races were especially close. James P. Niemann, the Democratic incumbent for judge, was defeated by Lewis J. Smith by 2,600 votes. John J. Graham, incumbent Democratic surrogate, lost a close contest to Leone D. Howell by 1,100 votes. In the spring town elections of 1917, the Republicans regained control of the Board of Supervisors by capturing the Hempstead and

North Hempstead seats despite opposition by a fusion candidate in Hempstead.

An interesting sidelight in Nassau politics during this period was the strong effort by local women in the suffrage movement. As early as 1908 they set up a booth at the county fair, and leading up to the election of 1915, the local suffragists planned a major campaign. They received excellent newspaper coverage, posted signs across the county, and leaders such as Mrs. Oliver H. P. Belmont, "General" Rosalie Jones and Mrs. Wilma R. Kearns promoted their cause at every possible meeting including the annual volunteer firemen's convention.

Many prominent political leaders from both parties gave their support and almost eight hundred delegates attended a local training meeting. Despite this coverage some of the support was halfhearted, like the newspaper editorial which indicated "that the people might just as well vote for it when it is up. Suffrage is coming some time in the near future." But the vote was no better in Nassau than throughout the state and suffrage lost by 3,338 to 7,079.

Defeat spurred the suffragists on harder and in 1917 they campaigned strenuously. A committee of women, headed by Mrs. Frederick Greene of Port Washington, petitioned the Board of Supervisors with 13,635 women's signatures asking for the ballot. The Board officially endorsed the suffrage amendment and many other prominent citizens voiced public support. Nassau County contributed a 1,500 vote plurality in the favorable vote for suffrage that fall, and the effects were felt instantly in the county, with 7,708 women registered as voters in 1918.

Nassau was also thrust onto the national political scene in 1924 when a resident was nominated for the presidency of the United States. After having served as solicitor general of the United States and ambassador to Great Britain, John W. Davis, a native of West Virginia, accepted a post with a Wall Street law firm. He purchased a gracious estate on Nassau's Gold Coast.

Suffragists on parade in Roslyn, 1914.

John W. Davis, Democratic presidential candidate from Locust Valley.

When he received the Democratic nomination on the one hundred and third ballot, Davis became the second resident ever nominated for the post. However, most people regarded him as a West Virginian and he had little local affiliation or affection.

After the Democratic defeat in 1917, the politically sagacious Wilbur Doughty planned a move that was to be a major influence in future county politics and government. In 1915, some 63,271 people, out of a total county population of 116,825, lived in the Town of Hempstead. The great population ratio and its larger assessed valuation caused Hempstead to seek a greater influence in county affairs and a reduction of the county government's favoritism toward the other towns. With a change in the Board's party alignment, Hempstead town leaders thought they would obtain more county services, but this was not the case. Therefore they sought greater representation on the county Board of Supervisors. Through the efforts of Assembly-

man Thomas McWhinney, the legislature passed an act in 1916 providing proportional voting strength for members of the Board of Supervisors according to population, and changing the town election from spring to the fall of the year. The act also established that no supervisor could have less than one vote or more than half the votes of the entire Board. The following year, special legislation allowed the Town of Hempstead to have two supervisors since it contained over half the population of the county.

G. Wilbur Doughty was appointed as the additional supervisor from the Town of Hempstead, and the four Republican supervisors were reelected in the 1919 fall elections. The Democratic organization was now suffering from apathy due to its frequent defeats and was conceded to be "shot to pieces." C. Chester Painter was able to overcome the Democrats in Oyster Bay, helped by Theodore Roosevelt, Jr., who ran for assemblyman on the Republican ticket. At the next election in 1920 Jeremiah Wood, chairman of the Nassau County Republican Committee, was elected lieutenant governor of New York State. In local races the Democrats ran mostly nonentities, and Republican supremacy was cemented.

An extremely capable leader, Doughty established good relations with the press and built up a strong party organization. His death in 1930 marked the end of the formative era when the Republican Party achieved superiority in Nassau County. Edwin Wallace of Rockville Centre assumed the GOP leadership after Doughty's death. A politician of the old school, he was a fiery speaker and controlled a well-disciplined organization in his home village.

However, a young leader and nephew of Doughty's, J. Russel Sprague, challenged Edwin Wallace for control of the county organization. Both were personable leaders but Sprague, supervisor of the Town of Hempstead, appealed to the younger men of the party, especially those interested in providing more energetic and dynamic lead-

G. Wilbur Doughty, founder of Nassau Republican power.

ership for the party and government. In March of 1934, his supporters initiated the appointment of a committee of five members who were to manage all campaigns for county, state and federal elections in the county and were to make all county patronage decisions. Members of the committee were Sprague, Wallace, A. Holly Patterson, James L. Dowsey and Leonard W. Hall. Sprague led the GOP ticket in the elections of 1934 and emerged as undisputed county leader.

Republicans had continued their superiority at the polls but Sprague realized they were running behind in percentage and stronger efforts were needed to ensure the conversion of the hordes of new residents. He set about to strengthen the party machinery and had the position of county leader created with his duties defined including the final approval on all patronage and management of all political campaigns. Sprague felt with these powers the county leader could build a mighty organization. He manned the government and party offices with active leaders who also supported him. The party became well disciplined with few primary contests and great emphasis was placed on getting out the vote. Party organization was intensive, concentrating on the individual committeemen in the local election district, and a firm financial base was obtained by contributions from party members and government employees.

The Republicans' test came in 1936. Although local Democrats made their strongest showing in twenty-five years, the GOP returns were more favorable than anywhere in the nation. J. Russel Sprague had created one of the major Republican organizations in the country and it would not be challenged again for several decades. Faced with such dynamic political opposition and with little opportunity to criticize the Republican governmental operations, the Democratic Party was moribund in the county. Many of its most attractive leaders were converted to Republican ranks and it could not generate any enthusiasm despite its national power.

J. Russel Sprague in center with Theodore Roosevelt, Jr., on left and Joseph Martin, GOP congressional leader, on right during Wilkie campaign, 1940.

Achieving Local Reform

During this period of Republican ascendancy, the county government attempted to answer the needs for increased public services. However, it became apparent that the organization of the government was not adequate for the task assigned it. Governor Alfred E. Smith, in a special message on the reorganization of county government, emphasized the situation in 1926:

Intelligent people generally agree in these two counties [Westchester and Nassau] that the existing form of government can not stand up much longer under the pressure of present day conditions.

We are living today as far as county and town government are concerned the same as under the Duke of York in 1676.

The first civic agitation for county government reorganization began with the formation of the Nassau County Association back in 1914. It was a general organization of residents formed to consider and act upon matters of public interest and see that the administration of town and county affairs was conducted on efficient and economic lines. Its committees urged governmental action in relief activities, sanitation, tuberculosis hospital, roads and public utilities, a farm bureau and county research. Secretary Rev. Dr. Maddaus indicated "we want to mobilize each person . . . make this the best livable county in New York State."

Investigation by the association revealed the need for so many changes in local government law that it decided to seek a completely new charter for government of the county. Through Assemblyman Leroy J. Weed, the enactment of a law was secured granting the Board of Supervisors the right to appoint a commission of seven to study the advisability of changing the form and method of the county government. Hiram R. Smith, Republican from the Town of Hempstead, James H. Cocks, Democrat from the Town of Oyster Bay, and Philip J. Christ, Democrat from North Hempstead, composed the Board of Supervisors in 1914. They voted to create such a commission and appointed Willard D. Straight, George S. Emory, William G. Miller, Frederick N. Watriss, Charles N. Wysong, Bronson Winthrop and Frank L. Crocker. All except Miller were nominees of the Democratic members of the Board.

The commission immediately went to work under chairman Bronson Winthrop. It found that Nassau was neither a rural, suburban nor a city county, but that it had characteristics of all types, as well as numerous large estates. There was no city within the county at this time. The local governments were the three towns and fourteen incorporated villages, only one, Hempstead, with a population over five thousand. The committee felt there was a unanimous demand for radical changes in the system of government in the towns and county, and in particular for a greater centralization of responsibility and authority. To assist its review, the commission had the New York Bureau of Municipal Research prepare a study of the government of Nassau County in 1915. The commission also cooperated with the Westchester County Commission, appointed to examine its local government and suggest improvements.

Both commissions reached a substantial agreement as to recommendations to be presented to the New York State Constitutional Convention in 1915. They favored a provision for optional forms of county government so that they could choose the form suited to their own needs. The convention approved most of the recommendations though a special committee of the convention found widely differing conditions and needs in counties such as Erie, Monroe, Schenectady, Nassau, Westchester and predominantly rural or forest counties of scattered population.

The voters' rejection of the constitution prevented any action and the commission issued a final report in 1918 which emphasized its conviction that centralization was the best method of securing good government. It contained a bill retaining the Board of Supervisors but placing all administrative functions, including those which could be transferred from the townships, under a single supervisor-at-large. The supervisor-at-large would function as chief executive with budget appointment and purchasing powers. Road administration, care of poor and health services would be consolidated under county government.

A city form of government had been considered but abandoned since there were strong sentimental reasons making it incongruous with Nassau's suburban and rural character, and considerable state aid received by the towns would have been lost. Just the rumor of this consideration caused opposition to appear since "many of the new settlers of this section have come out here from the city to avoid the high taxes of the metropolis."

The report was filed with the Board of Supervisors in December of 1918, and on March 24, 1919, the Nassau County Association asked the Board to recommend that the legislators representing Nassau submit the bill to the legislature. Although the Board majority was now Republican, the resolution was passed. The statute was not reported out of committee, however, and was permanently shelved in favor of a constitutional amendment.

In 1920 an amendment to the state constitution was proposed by officials of Nassau and Westchester counties which would permit the adoption of new forms of government in these counties. It passed the legislature in 1920 and 1921 and was submitted to the people that fall. The measure passed in Nassau by only 361 votes, even though it simply amended section 26–27 of article 3 of the constitution by empowering the legislature to provide new forms of governments for Westchester and Nassau counties subject to the approval of voters in each county by a referendum vote. The plan could include the transfer of town functions to the county and became the basis for the next attempt to change local government.

Little time was lost before a new attempt at reform was begun. On April 17, 1922, at the request of Assemblyman Thomas H. McWhinney and F. Trubee Davison, a bipartisan citizens' committee was appointed by the Board of Supervisors. It consisted of William S. Pettit, chairman; Augustus D. Kelsey, secretary; Philip J. Christ, Edward J. Deasey, George L. Hubbell, George E. Raynor, Thomas J. McLaughlin, Henry A. Uterhart, Arthur Brierly, A. Burnside Cheshire, William Cocks, Benjamin W. Downing, Carlton Macy, Floyd R. Stryker, Ernest S. Randall, Edwin W. Wallace and Mrs. Howard S. Kniffin.

Members attended many conferences with chairmen of committees of the Westchester County Charter Commission and members of the former Nassau County Charter Commission. They conferred with experts of state and national reputation and held some forty public meetings. These local meetings were well attended by town, county and village officials and civic leaders who thoroughly discussed problems. At the meeting concerned with road and highway organization, Archibald Patterson, Hempstead Town superintendent of highways, reported "the equipment which he uses is the equipment that was in use forty years ago." All the people present agreed there should be one engineering department in the county to supervise all road construction.

William S. Pettit of Woodmere.

Pettit worked endlessly on the project and researched all other forms of local government, even English, to obtain information helpful to Nassau. The commission found that the present form of county and township government was bound to be inefficient and wasteful, irrespective of the parties and personalities who provided direction. More important, the present government was absolutely incapable of dealing with the tremendous future problems of a community which was rapidly becoming urban in character and which adjoined the largest city in the country. The commission felt the problems of planning for the growth of Nassau County required a strong central county government.

Legislation was proposed providing a countywide elected president, a county budget, Departments of Public Works, Public Welfare and Public Health, county police and a County Planning and Zoning Commission. Strong executive functions were vested in the president, and the Board of Supervisors was given the planning and zoning power within the towns, outside of the limits of incorporated villages and cities. When the report was presented to the Board of Supervisors in 1923, approval of the proposals was voiced by many leading citizens as well as by the Nassau County Association. Former chairman of the Board of Supervisors Philip J. Christ believed "that it would add to the efficiency of our government . . . and was worthy of adoption."

Introduced in the legislature, the bill was enacted into law as Chapter 863 of the Laws of 1923 subject to adoption by the voters of the county in the general election of 1923. William Pettit waged a vigorous campaign for its adoption and received staunch support from the League of Women Voters and other women's organizations. However, strong opposition to it developed, with opponents charging that it would curtail home rule in the cities, towns and villages.

A change in the feelings of ranking Republicans ended its chances of adoption. County Attorney H. Stewart McKnight and G. Wilbur Doughty, county Republican leader, opposed the charter and argued that it would place Nassau County in line for annexation by New York City. At a public meeting of the Board of Supervisors, George Emory, president of the Nassau County Trust Company, urged its approval since the county needed a strong executive to conduct government as a business manager does a business. McKnight took sharp issue and contended the county was not a business and it was impossible for an elected government official to function as a business president in carrying out wishes of a Board of Directors. Despite Pettit's vigorous campaign for adoption, there was little agitation in the county over the proposed charter and it was defeated 18,507 to 8,654. Voter apathy is apparent in the fact that 23,720 blank votes were recorded.

Despite this stunning defeat, discussion over governmental reorganization continued. It began to have more partisan political overtones in 1929 when the executive committee of the Nassau Democratic County Committee had a Queens County Democrat introduce an act in the legislature calling for a city charter form of government for Nassau County. However, they were unable to obtain legislative support. The party then formed a Democratic Law Committee under the leadership of Supreme Court Justice Thomas J. Cuff, with members Ferdinand J. Haber, Martin P. O'Leary, Jeanne Marion Doane, L. Hamilton Rainey, Percy D. Stoddart, John G. Snyder and Jerome M. Hirsch. In 1932 it proposed a charter "to end duplication of services, overlapping of activities and lack of centered authority and executive responsibility." This charter provided for a single executive and a legislative Board of Representatives representing seven ward areas with most other features of a city government, abolished the three town governments and allowed other existing units to avail themselves of the new county departments and services.

The Democrats were successful in obtaining initial sponsorship of the proposal by the Village Officials Association of Nassau County. William J. Stratton, mayor of Malverne and president of the association, named a bipartisan committee to study the matter. Members included W. S. Pettit, H. S. McKnight, A. H. Patterson, L. H. Rainey, I. G. Hooley and A. C. Wysong. Republican opposition continued to be spearheaded by County Attorney H. Stewart McKnight, who charged that centralization of the functions and administration of local units of government would not provide better government. Due to the large amount of undeveloped land in the county, he advocated countywide districts (such as that for police set up in 1926) for sanitation, water and welfare.

The bill was submitted to the legislature by its sponsors in 1933 but the county supervisors refused to indicate approval and it died. As political battle lines were drawn, a

North shore GOP leaders gather at campaign clambake, left to right, F. Trubee Davison, Robert Low Bacon, Theodore Roosevelt, Jr., Marcus Christ, and Leonard Hall.

new committee was formed in May with McKnight replaced by W. J. Stratton, and a new educational drive was launched. The supervisors also acted and appointed a nonpartisan board of three authorities on constitutional law, including William D. Guthrie, Nathan I. Miller and John W. Davis, to survey the charter. In the beginning of 1934, the Republican leadership also had the Board of Supervisors engage Dr. Reed under the municipal consultant service of the National Municipal League.

Determined to continue the charter fight, the Democrats had the old proposal split into various bills. These were introduced by Kings County assemblyman McNamara in the Democratic-controlled legislature of 1935. Assemblyman Leonard W. Hall cannily fought the bill, charging the Democrats were trying to extend "Tammany corruption" into Nassau, and asserted that most of the McNamara bills were "ripper legislation." The Re-

publicans made such a vigorous attempt to stem the Democratic steam-roller tactics that Assembly Speaker Steingut was forced to recess for a special caucus to call in rebellious Democratic members from local hotels to vote for the measure.

Despite the GOP efforts, the Cuff-McNamara charter was passed and enacted into Chapter 938 of the Laws of 1935 subject to adoption by voters at the general election in November of that year. The proposition was strongly opposed by the Republican Party and was defeated 41,492 to 27,507. However, the voters did give approval to the so-called Fearon Amendment to the state constitution. This amendment authorized the transfer of certain functions of government to the county after approval by the voters.

After the election the Board of Supervisors then appointed an official Charter Commission. J. Russel Sprague, chairman of the Board, gave it full authority and completely

Chairman of Charter Revision Commission Earl J. Bennett.

supported its activities. Not only did he strongly feel that the present organization required improvement for better government administration but he also realized "that we had to do a real job of getting a good new charter or the Democrats would be back at it again with another of their own and we'd be on our way out."

Earl J. Bennett was chairman of the commission, which included the following civic leaders: Alfred Douglas Olena, vice-chairman; James N. Gehrig, secretary; Henry J. A. Collins, Elwood A. Curtis, Joseph Hewlett, Oscar R. Houston, Edwin Vandewater, Charles S. Wright, Edward S. Keogh, Ellery Mann, Lawrence E. Kirwin, Howard P. Kreutzer, H. Stewart McKnight, William S. Pettit, Henry R. Swartly, Jr., and Howard G. Wilson.

The commission organized early in January of 1935, and proceeded upon the theory that if an effective charter was to be drawn and adopted by the people, it must be based on a thorough knowledge of the general com-

position and functioning of the officers, boards, departments and agencies of the multifold separate units of government.

Discussions were held with all the supervisors, other local government officials, businessmen, community leaders and homeowners. Various reports were obtained and every effort was made to determine the areas in which change was needed. The commission determined two main objectives to be attained: first, to provide a means for obtaining county government services and county improvements at a reasonable cost; and second, to distribute fairly the burdens of cost.

With these objectives in mind, a theory of "two layers" of government was evolved. In the lower level villages, cities, towns and districts were to be retained providing community control and power over those functions of government which were closest to them, which they knew the most about and which they genuinely desired to have continued under the authority of the respective inhabitants.

The upper level was to be the county government, where advancement and reforms were to be made. This was to be designed to meet the needs and demands of a continually fast-growing population.

In drafting the charter the commission had given serious consideration to the fact that approval of county voters was required. They realized that:

Any new instrument which changes the administrative, legislative and judicial character of town governments, which have been in existence for more than two centuries, would naturally be accepted and digested by the people slowly and carefully and only then, without too radical an alteration in fundamentals . . .

Thus the charter was not revolutionary in character. It reorganized the county government without making changes in form and structure that would offend or violate local sentiments, traditions and associations. This "two-layer" theory was admittedly a compromise, but one that made for progress. Supervisor Sprague realized that the charter could have been written along more ideal lines but also knew that few such ideal governments exist. He felt "leaders of proposed changes and advancement should be out in front, but not so far out in front as to lose their following and thus fail in the accomplishment of proposed improvements."

The proposed charter abolished none of the existing independent units but did centralize services to allow more efficiency and economy. It provided for the creation of a county executive, a Board of Supervisors, a county budget, more responsible county departments, a countywide tax assessment board, a county health department, a county planning commission and a modernized local court system. Responsibility was specifically placed and duplication eliminated.

Of greatest importance was the provision for an elective county executive. The commission itself was split on this issue, some members contending that it would provide the voter with the opportunity to approve or disapprove county policy and would assist in developing a "county consciousness." However, a county manager to be appointed by the Board of Supervisors was also advocated, and Chairman Earl J. Bennett had to cast a tie-breaking vote in favor of an elective county executive.

Governor Herbert H. Lehman concurred with these thoughts and urged, in his legislative message of 1936, reforms of the county government including an elective county executive. The charter proposals were presented to the legislature at this session and enacted into Chapter 879 of the Laws of 1936. Assemblyman Leonard Hall guided the bill through the legislature with the political assistance of J. Russel Sprague. At the committee hearings, Ferdinand J. Haber of the Democratic Law Committee indicated he was in general agreement with the bill but suggested amendments to improve it. He pointed out that it would not cut out any units of government and opposed retention of the sheriff's office. James Gehrig, secretary of the commission, asserted that most of the

proposed changes were in the charter that had been defeated the year before.

Since the bill answered all the recommendations of Governor Lehman and in fact went further, there was little excuse for him to veto the bill. After signing the bill he made clear, though, that his signature should not be "construed as an endorsement of the new charter." The hardest hurdle ahead was approval by the people in the election of 1936.

During the fall of 1936, the commission worked energetically to educate the voters concerning the charter. It supplied speakers for civic meetings and issued a steady barrage of printed materials explaining the charter provisions. "True and false" speaker teams were organized under the leadership of Mrs. Genesta Strong of Manhasset. They debated before audiences to educate the public on pros and cons of the charter. Special emphasis was given to the benefits that would accrue from centralizing the numerous de-

Leading Republican women: Mrs. Genesta Strong on left and on right Mrs. R. Heidelberger, with J. Russel Sprague, who effectively harnessed women's support of charter reform.

partments of health and a single countywide tax assessment board.

The opposition soon took up the cudgels and a tax suit was entered by Lawrence A. Burket of Long Beach attacking the act as unconstitutional. The suit actually represented the attitude of the Long Beach Democratic organization. The court of appeals, however, ruled the legislative act was sound and that the people could vote on the measure. Initially the county Democratic Party did not take a stand on the measure. However, a strong undercurrent of opposition to the charter developed within other segments of the county. The Non-Partisan Civic Association of Oyster Bay sent out a circular attacking the charter and urging its defeat. Attacks on the charter's expansion of county power and diminishment of village home rule were also made by the Northeast Civic Association of Freeport and the Civic League of Nassau. Other active opposition developed in North Hempstead even within the Republican Party.

Gradually the campaign picked up momentum and in October Supervisor J. Russel Sprague began a strong drive to secure adoption. On the eighth he called a GOP executive committee meeting to approve the charter. Many district leaders thought he was not serious, because to cut out many of the existing political plums would seriously diminish political patronage. Sprague was determined to obtain popular approval and knew he would need the support of the powerful Republican organization. He even had readied an announcement indicating unanimous support directing all leaders to give their full efforts to the new charter and see that their workers pushed it through. The committee expressed approval and Sprague emerged satisfied that "the party had kept faith with the people by placing its unanimous stamp of approval on the proposed charter."

Assistance to the reform cause also came from an unexpected source. Both leading Democratic candidates came out in favor of the measure. Dr. Willoughby C. Pendill, candidate for state senator, and Gerald Morrell,

candidate for Congress, supported it as "a step in the right direction and undoubtedly the means of reducing taxes throughout the county and increasing the efficiency of officials and employees." Also throughout October the *Nassau Daily Review Star,* the only local daily newspaper, gave enthusiastic support and tremendous space to the advocacy of the charter.

Finally on November 1, John S. Thorp, county Democratic leader, broke his silence and attacked the charter. He called it "a tax eating Frankenstein that would push the county further back into the twisted maze of antiquated government . . . The Democratic Party . . . is definitely opposed to the county charter . . . [which] is merely a political gesture to fool the electorate in believing that something constructive or progressive is offered." Supervisor Sprague rebutted and urged the adoption of the charter as "not only the best document of the kind yet presented but as a positive guarantee against future annexation to New York City without consent of our own people." The result was left to the voters.

The election campaign of 1936 was disastrous for the GOP in almost all parts of the country, but Nassau stood out as a Republican stronghold. The county was easily carried by all Republican candidates and the charter act was approved. The earlier fears by Supervisor Sprague of opposition to change were proven correct. Only a tremendous majority in the Town of Hempstead enabled the passage of the charter. Majorities in North Hempstead and Oyster Bay opposed the act, but surprisingly Long Beach approved it. The countywide total was 57,-336 to 37,258 in favor of the charter.

After twenty-five years of sustained effort, Nassau County adopted a modernized governmental organization. Non-partisan and partisan attempts had failed to accomplish the goal. Utilizing fully his political organization, a farsighted political leader, J. Russel Sprague, led an educational campaign that enabled Nassau County to take "the first important step in the reorganization of county government in the metropolitan New York area." The new charter was the major governmental achievement in Nassau's short history as a governmental entity. Its adoption and subsequent speedy implementation assisted in solving the local Depression problems and enabled the county government to prepare for an unprecedented wave of expansion after World War II.

After the passage of the charter act and a slight amendment by Chapter 618 of the Laws of 1937, the county government had only a year to prepare for its new operation, which was to begin on January 1, 1938. Since Nassau County was the first county in New York State to adopt a charter providing a county executive, all the procedures and methods for the new operation had to be devised. In August of 1937, a charter organization bureau, under county comptroller Theodore Bedell, Jr., initiated plans for all the diverse administrative and physical changes that had to be accomplished, including preparation of the county budget for 1938.

Creation of the office of county executive was the most significant change in the county government. The county executive was responsible for the administration of all the departments of the county government and for preparation of the county budget. J. Russel Sprague fully utilized the powers of his office, instituting strict control of fiscal matters through approval of purchase requisitions and tight budgetary policy.

The other major area of change was the centralization into new county departments of services formerly provided by towns and villages. The most important was the consolidation of numerous welfare agencies into a county welfare department with divisions of family care, child welfare, medical care and accounting. The functions of numerous local health offices were also transferred to a county board of health, and a countywide health ordinance was established. Local justice-of-the-peace courts were abolished and a new district court system was instituted on a county basis. Judges had to be qualified at-

torneys and were not permitted to continue private legal practice. These district courts handled minor criminal cases and civil actions. The new charter provided for a county Board of Assessors, which began a program of reassessment by a professional appraisal company to rule out inequities between the areas of the county. Under the new assessment, Nassau County's total assessed evaluation was over $1 billion.

Local government in the 1930s not only had to contend with the problems of reorganization, but also was faced with severe economic stress. After the national financial crisis of 1929, the problems of unemployment and relief became acute in Nassau County and created a great fiscal and organizational challenge to the government leaders. At this time the county economy was in transition. Farming was declining and an increasingly large percentage of local inhabitants were commuters to employment in New York City. This latter group of clerical, industrial and mercantile workers was severely affected by the Depression.

The county administration quickly recognized the problem of unemployment and in November of 1931 established the Emergency Work Bureau of Nassau County. The bureau operated under the New York State Emergency Relief Act, which provided a 40 per cent refund by the state of all monies appropriated by the local government. The costs of field supervision, trucking, materials and supplies had to be borne by the county. Workers under this program provided the labor for countywide improvements of highways, lands and drainage systems. By the spring of 1933, some 23,000 families and single applicants had applied for work relief. As the Depression deepened, the character of applicants changed from mainly unskilled laborers to a large representation of office workers and professional groups.

On May 20, 1933, most of the work was suspended to recheck the program. By that fall, relief funds became available from the federal government and in November the Work Bureau became the Civil Works Ad-

MAP OF YORKSHIRE, OR LONG ISLAND

QUEENS COUNTY

SUFFOLK COUNTY

NEW YORK'S COUNTIES
WERE CREATED IN 1683
BY GOV. THOMAS DONGAN
(later Earl of Limerick)

ministration with state and federal support increased to 66⅔ per cent of the cost. Since the organization was now a federal agency, the loss of local policy administration caused a great deal of friction between the Board of Supervisors and federal administrators. From 10,000 to 14,000 people were given work under the program and were paid $3.20 and $4 a day.

The workers continued most of the previous public works projects and assisted in clerical duties, traffic accident surveys and road sign installation. Work projects included a historic survey of the county, resulting in several local histories; adult education courses; and staff assistance in the preparation of a lot and block map of the county. Relief workers also provided staffing for the establishment and operation of the Nassau Collegiate Center, a junior college–technical training center in the old Curtiss factory at Garden City.

Reorganization of relief activities in June of 1934 combined home and work relief under the Nassau County Emergency Relief Bureau. Its chairman, Lewis L. Delafield, estimated that 46,000 people were looking for work in the county. This would have been a peak unemployment of one out of six workers. Later that year, the Works Projects Administration (WPA) took over the bulk of work relief. Special public projects continued to employ three to six thousand workers yearly until the late 1930s, when the county's economy began to revive.

Extensive home relief expenditures were made by the county government until the war-related employment diminished welfare needs in 1940. The county provided local relief funds of more than $3 million annually from 1934 to 1938 for its share of all relief activities. Total costs exceeded $32 million for this five-year period with a peak of almost $10 million in 1935. Such large amounts were not available out of current

One of a series of murals in the old courthouse, which were completed as a WPA art project.

revenues and the county government assumed an indebtedness of over $22 million during the Depression to fund relief expenses. While costs were rising, the county was also faced with significant losses of tax revenue. Real estate tax collections were 20 to 25 per cent off the amount due and as much as $8 million a year was lost between 1933 and 1936. After the new charter act, the county established regular proceedings to sell off properties with unpaid taxes at sufficient upset prices to meet costs and the accumulated back taxes.

In addition to the local federally aided work projects, major public construction including large post offices in several communities and military structures at Mitchel Field were funded by the federal government and provided considerable local employment. In 1938 the Public Works Administration provided an outright grant of $1,192,500 and a loan of $1,457,500 to the county government for the construction of a new courthouse complex. The county had outgrown the original courthouse and required additional space for its increased functions. Surrogate Leone D. Howell, a member of the Queens-Nassau Agricultural Society Board of Directors, proposed to county officials that the society's fairgrounds in Mineola be purchased as a site for a county center where all county buildings could ultimately be grouped. The fairgrounds was only two blocks from the existing courthouse, and the society offered to sell its twenty-five acres for a nominal sum if the Town of Hempstead would deed its forty acres. In the election of 1937, the proposal was approved by the voters of Hempstead. Three structures were actually completed by 1940—the center one contained the district and county court, while the two flanking buildings provided administrative space for various county departments.

The new courthouse complex was indicative of the major changes and advances that had occurred in the county's local government from the turn of the century to the eve of World War II. Its three rural townships, providing very limited services, had been

Glen Cove post office, constructed in 1935—many local offices were built to provide building jobs.

During the Depression new brick buildings were constructed at Mitchel Field, including a large Bachelor Officers' Club.

New county courthouse with ornate art panels, another example of special art projects to provide employment.

transformed into a complex system of multiple governmental levels servicing the extensive and widely varying needs of different areas within the county. An overwhelming majority of residents gave their principal attention and concern to their local village and school district governmental boards. Concerned political and business leaders such as publisher James Stiles attempted to focus attention toward "the township and county . . . With other residents I have watched villages grow and expand until it is impossible to tell where one ends and the next begins. We must begin thinking of our township as a unit, instead of as a heterogeneous group of villages." It was a difficult task, however,

and reform of the town and county governments met indifference and disinterest.

The pressing governmental needs resulting from the dramatic growth of the 1920s and the support of farsighted political leader J. Russel Sprague finally overcame residents' apathy. This successful local movement to reorganize county government was a pioneer effort in the state and country to provide better control and more effective government for a rapidly growing suburban area. With little change, the new system continued for several decades and provided governmental needs during the spectacular growth of the years after World War II.

Glenn Curtiss' first flight on the Hempstead Plains.

CHAPTER III

AVIATION ON THE HEMPSTEAD PLAINS

A New Sport

The air was still as dawn broke over the Hempstead Plains on the morning of July 17, 1909. Heavy dew on the plains grass soaked the trouser cuffs of a group of men clustered around a strange machine. Valentine W. Smith, an old Long Islander, was among the crowd of spectators that had gathered, staring at this airplane that "looked like an enlarged boxkite. The driver's seat projected out in front and the engine with the propeller, set to push forward, was at the back." Even though it was 5:16 A.M., there were many spectators who had driven out by horse and buggy to this section of the plains near the county fairgrounds. Glenn Curtiss, the builder and flier of the aircraft, was surprised at the large turnout of residents, who were quite excited and skeptical.

After making ready, Curtiss wheeled his craft, the *Golden Flier,* to the east side of the fairgrounds, gunned the engine and slowly lifted off the ground. He flew only a little higher than the treetops but it was a thrilling experience for the spectators. One reported, "No motion is seen . . . the flight is never wavering, but steady and straight to the point . . . one holds the breath for fear it cannot keep up and that the flight will soon end." After this preliminary trial, Curtiss landed and then went aloft again with a more serious purpose. He wanted to win

the Scientific American Trophy which had recently been announced for the first flight of twenty-five kilometers (fifteen and a half miles) by an American.

A slight wind now rocked his craft and with this noticeable change "the flight took on the familiar freedom of the birds. The aviator boldly flew higher." He headed east toward Meadow Brook, banking around over Westbury, and returned to Mineola, covering twenty-eight miles in fifty-eight minutes, to win the trophy. Aviation had come to the Hempstead Plains. The local weekly newspapers hardly saw fit to give this interesting experiment a mention, but Curtiss realized, "This flight at Mineola gave that place a start as the headquarters for aviators, and it soon became the popular resort for everyone interested in aviation in and near the city of New York."

The flight actually had its origin in 1908 when the Aeronautical Society of New York City placed an order with Curtiss, who lived in Hammondsport, New York, for an airplane. It was delivered and tested at the Morris Park race track, but the grounds there proved too small for successful flights. After a thorough search of the New York area, Curtiss chose the large, level tract of land just outside Mineola as an ideal place for flying. The wisdom of his choice was continually proven since the flat plain enabled safe emergency landings, which were a regular occurrence in early aviation. Curtiss planned to demonstrate the machine thor-

Glenn Curtiss, second from right, with his Golden Flier.

oughly and sharpen his flying ability in preparation for competition at the forthcoming
Rheims air meet in France.

A flight course, marked by white flags,
was set up on the plains. It was an ideal
site, allowing the aviators to ascend or de-
scend without fear of wires, trees or any
hindrance. Curtiss was also to train some
members of the Aeronautical Society in
piloting their machine, but in a flight with
the first student he had a minor accident.
This did not faze the hardy adventurers interested in aviation, and he went on to
instruct his test pilot, Charles F. Willard,
in the mysteries of flying. On August 13,
Willard completed the first long-distance
flight on the plains, ending in a forced
landing at Hicksville. The Aeronautical Society quickly moved ahead and by the next
year had erected a 150′×48′ building which
housed seven aircraft.

From a distance the Garden City Aviation Field appeared similar to a large circus
ground with white tents and flying machines

on exhibit. Admission was charged for
special field shows, but most of the flying
was done during the period of least air tur-
bulence between 5 and 8 A.M. in the summer.
By now even the local press was proud that
the "part Long Island has played in the
development of aviation will go down in
history. It is a fact that in this country the
enthusiasm over flying was born and waxed
strong through the feats performed on the
Hempstead Plains." From this adventure-
some and experimental beginning, aviation
began to grow as a major activity in Nassau
County.

In the fall of 1910, international attention
was focused on Nassau when an International Aerial Tournament was held at Belmont Park from October 22 to 31. The
greatest aviators came from America, France
and England to compete in several major
races. Two courses had been laid out on the
spacious race track grounds, and a fence
restricted close view except to visitors who
paid a $2 entrance fee. Most of the events,

INTERNATIONAL
AVIATION
TOURNAMENT
BELMONT PARK
OCTOBER 22ND TO 30TH
1.30 P. M. DAILY

OFFICIAL PROGRAM 1910

Observers at the International Aerial Tournament, Belmont Park.

however, could be seen from outside the grounds, and large crowds witnessed one or more of the races, which were surprisingly free from accidents.

The galaxy of attending aviation pioneers, such as Glenn Curtiss and Wilbur and Orville Wright, was overshadowed by the novelty of the planes themselves—particularly the monoplanes, which were the center of spectator interest. There were daily altitude contests, distance runs, cross-country races, a mechanic's prize of $1,000 and countless other events with a total of $74,800 in prizes for the tournament. The daily altitude contests for a $5,000 prize between Arch Hoxsey and Ralph Johnston, both skillful fliers of Wright planes, captured the public's imagination, and the "Stardust Twins" thrilled the crowds in their quest for the large prize. Their planes would spiral upward higher and higher till out of sight. Late in the afternoon of the last day of the meet, they both took off again in the final contest. Spiraling upward in the calm air, they continued climbing as the sun went down. Neither daring flier would stop until

his gas tanks were dry. Unable to see them, the spectators heard the engines sputter, and soon the aviators had glided to safety on Long Island's soft fields. Johnston had won and established a new world's altitude record of 9,714 feet.

At the end of the week, the meet's highlight occurred in two major races, the Gordon Bennett Trophy and the Statue of Liberty. The Gordon Bennett speed race was over a 100-kilometer distance and on the final lap Alfred Le Blanc of France, who had averaged sixty-eight miles per hour, ran out of gas and crashed. England's Claude Grahame-White, flying a borrowed Blériot, won the $5,000 contest with a sixty-one-miles-per-hour speed. The Statue of Liberty race attracted a tremendous crowd on October 30, when over 75,000 packed the track. Large crowds watched from the city and island as the planes made their flight around the famed lady in the harbor. The contest was somewhat confused since it was on an elapsed-time basis. By 4 P.M., it seemed that Claude Grahame-White had won with a time of 35 minutes and 21.50 seconds for

Preparing for the first U.S. airmail flight in 1911 from Garden City.

the thirty-three-mile course. But the American flier John B. Moisant took off late in the afternoon and returned at four-thirty, winning the race by 43 seconds. A bitter controversy arose and Grahame-White unsuccessfully challenged the judges' decision.

Despite this note of discord, the meet was a great success. It showed, to the technically minded, that French and American airplane designers were equally talented. The meet focused public attention on aviation and stimulated people to talk and think about the future of the airplane. Lieutenant Governor Timothy Woodruff, Thomas Ryan, Clarence Mackay and other society and industrial leaders were eager visitors to the meet. Hereafter the airplane could not be dismissed as a mere toy. The many records and solid performances at the meet had made many in the crowd feel that it was "veritably the dawning of a new era."

Cross-country flight now became a major aviation interest. On September 17, 1911, Calbraith P. Rodgers left Mineola Field on the year's outstanding flight. For forty-nine days he flew his Wright airplane cross-coun-

try, reaching Long Beach, California, on December 10, completing the first transcontinental flight. Despite the many forced landings and even some time in the hospital, Rodgers' flight was a portent of things to come.

That fall, Long Island was chosen as the site of the Second International Air Meet. A new field on the western edge of Garden City, the Nassau Boulevard, was used for the meet. Again, it was a very colorful affair with long lines of hangars and tents with each contestant's national flag flying over his hangar. Although there were many contests, the lack of large prizes limited the excitement of the meet. Several insignificant happenings at this meet were forerunners of future aviation activities. The Aero Club had arranged with Postmaster General Frank H. Hitchcock for a temporary mail station on the field. Hitchcock designated Earl Ovington, a popular local flier, as airmail pilot number one and on the first day of the show handed Ovington a bag of letters and postcards. Ovington flew in his Blériot-type monoplane to Mineola, dropping the bag at the post office six miles from the field. These 640 letters and 1,280 postcards are highly desired postal rarities —the first airmail in the United states.

Another special occurrence at the meet was the first official appearance of Army aviation. At the previous Belmont Park meet, Lieutenant B. D. Foulis, the only qualified Army aviator, was present but only as an observer. Army aviation had advanced rapidly and was well represented at the Nassau Boulevard meet by two fliers, Lieutenant T. D. Milling and Lieutenant H. H. Arnold. They piloted Burgess-Wright machines in a demonstration of the military use of the airplane, which was conceived at the time to be mainly for reconnaissance use. The two lieutenants flew out over the countryside to locate several groups of troops which had been concealed in nearby woods. Thus air power was demonstrated publicly for the first time by the United States Army.

These meets greatly stimulated interest among many young men such as Grover Loening, who later became a leading aeronautical engineer. Feverish with excitement, Loening was able to obtain two rides at the boulevard meet and exulted, "I was a seasoned airman. I had flown twice and already been in an accident." This intense spirit of excitement and challenge of adventure stimulated both aviators and the pioneer airplane builders.

Aviation slowly grew in technique and facilities during these years. New fields in Nassau were established at Nassau Boulevard, and in 1912, the Aero Club of America established the Hempstead Plains Aerodrome as its official field. Off Clinton Road to the east of Garden City, it encompassed 1,000 acres and had an elaborate entranceway leading to a fully developed field. Four grandstands, twenty-five hangars and a regular course with pylons made it one of the finest flying fields in the country. It bustled with activity as lessons were given each morning and afternoon, and the air was filled with every type of plane.

Flying was still regarded by people as entirely an experimental and exhibition activity. Aviation pioneer Casey Jones recalled that "it was not considered to have any particular commercial value." In 1911 Alfred Moisant opened the Moisant School at the Hempstead Plains Aviation Field and began a sizable operation with six monoplanes, five hangars and a workshop. The usual five-week flying course cost $750, "with what breakage the pupil causes additional." Giuseppe M. Bellanca, an instructor at the Bellanca Aeroplane School, taught eleven pupils to fly each year from 1912 to 1916. These schools at the fields and exhibition flights provided an income source for the new industry. Nassau's significance in early American aviation is indicated by these activities, which trained 30 per cent of the first one hundred American fliers.

Local citizens were now interested in aviation, and crowds regularly gathered along Washington Avenue and the other main roads near the fields to watch the flights. Ten thousand people would frequently collect on Saturdays and Sundays. Fred Baldwin, a frequent spectator, wrote they "would toot their automobile horns vigorously whenever a daring airman would make even the briefest flight. If a flier bobbed his plane up and down in the air in daredevil fashion, the crowd would applaud vigorously. The feat was looked upon by the throngs and newspaper writers as something to talk about for some days."

Local men became deeply interested and provided much of the manpower, both paid and unpaid, for the infant industry. Some designed and built their own craft, like Arthur and Albert Heinrich of Baldwin, who successfully flew their own monoplane in 1910. Others assisted the leading aviators, and gathered to relate events of the day at the Gold Bug Hotel operated by Pete McLaughlin opposite the fairgrounds.

But aviation was not for the fainthearted and its progress was materially hampered by the great danger a flier faced. Accidents during flight were very frequent, and airplanes were ususally unstable and treacher-

The Heinrich Bros. hangar at Roosevelt Field.

Peter McLaughlin's Gold Bug Hotel, a popular rendezvous for aviators.

Flying required a special courage due to the many accidents.

ous even to the experienced aviator. Since many pilots attempted to earn a living by stunt flying, the hazards were doubled. Well-known fliers such as Johnston, Hoxsey, Beachey, Ovington and many others were killed during these years. The dangers continued up to World War II. Aviation executive George Dade, who first saw Roosevelt Field in 1921 as a boy, remembered "keeping a list of those who were killed in air crashes. Before I graduated from high school that list numbered over 150." The experimentation in flights continued, however, and these fearless airmen who flew on the Hempstead Plains made possible the continued improvememt and development of aircraft.

World War I

An important development in local aviation took place in 1915 when the New York National Guard organized an active aviation unit at the Hempstead Plains Aviation Field. A year later, Colonel Walter C. Kilmer and Major Raynal Bolling took over opera-

tion of the field as a regular military post and named it after Sergeant Hazelhurst, the first non-commissioned officer killed in an aviation accident. A special flying school was set up there, one of four Army aviation schools in the country. A select squadron of men recruited from eastern colleges, many of them local Nassau boys, was organized as war clouds darkened Europe. When America entered the war, the base expanded greatly and became a major military installation.

The war in Europe became a major concern of all Americans after 1914. This was particularly true in Nassau County due to the influx of many residents of German descent in the early 1900s. Local attitudes were cautious toward the war in the beginning. Early in 1915, George Wallace indicated that though his "sympathies are not with Germany in the present European War" he would not care at all if it was against Russia and had no feelings for the British. But slowly local attitudes changed, and his newspaper found it hard to remain neutral. After two American ships were destroyed in February of 1915, the alarm was sounded that "we are not prepared for war. The United States will have to provide a much larger Army and Navy and thus make ready to protect its people anywhere in the wide world."

It was both alarming and distressing to local residents to have this European conflict involve the United States. The sinking of the *Lusitania* confirmed the need for preparations in the event America was drawn into the hostilities. When President Wilson moved to prepare the country, he received local support for essential war appropriations. At Locust Valley, Yale sophomore F. Trubee Davison, who later served as Assistant Secretary of War for Air in the late 1920s, and a number of his fellow students joined a group formed by his father to learn flying in preparation for military duty. The Yale crew began training that summer at their own expense in Nassau County and went to service the next year as naval aviators. In the spring of 1917 when war was declared Nassau residents were ready to take their share of the burden.

Patriotic spirit quickly took hold in the county and the war effort became the major concern of everyone. As soon as the draft regulations were established, local exemption boards were set up throughout the county. On June 5, the first day of registration, a public holiday was declared in Freeport. A spirited parade was held and patriotic speeches filled the air as Nassau men prepared to go to war. Many had already volunteered or had been called up through their National Guard units.

Most of the initial Selective Service calls were filled with volunteers, such as the first group that left from Board No. 4 in Lawrence. The day before they left on September 9, a gala parade with bands led to a decorated grandstand and long patriotic speeches filled the air. "Over There" reverberated throughout the community, and that final evening every man was feted and partied at a local clubhouse and given a comfort kit to remind him of home. This scene was repeated in one community after another as Nassau's finest manhood left for the Great War.

Out of 29,245 men registered in the four

Quentin Roosevelt in training as an aviator at Mineola Flying Field.

local draft boards in the county at Glen Cove, Mineola, Freeport and Lawrence, 3,302 were inducted for service during the war. They manned heavy machine guns as members of the Hempstead Gun Company of the 10th Regiment, sailed the convoy ships to Europe and flew airplanes over the lines in France. As is so often the case in wars, those who did not return were most noticeable. Young Quentin Roosevelt was among the first group of college students trained as aviators on the Hempstead Plains, even before the war began. He was a member of a United States squadron in France and lost his life in combat over German lines on July 14, 1918. That next Sunday in all the Protestant churches in Oyster Bay and St. Dominic's Roman Catholic Church, prayers were offered for Quentin and the other three Roosevelt boys in France. The town's service flag with 321 stars now had a gold star in its border to remind every citizen that one of them had, as his father said, "died as the heroes of old died; as brave and fearless men must die when a great cause calls."

Quentin Roosevelt and many of the other local heroes still are remembered through the various community American Legion posts which were named in their honor after the war's end. Garden City was the home of Nassau's most highly decorated soldier, William Bradford Turner. Commissioned in April 1917, he was a lieutenant of the 105th Infantry, 27th Division in the assault on the Hindenburg line. His heroism there was not revealed until some captives returned through the German lines. Advancing with his men, he discovered they were surrounded but valiantly continued to clear machine gun nests and trenches of the enemy. Lieutenant Turner was posthumously awarded the Congressional Medal of Honor, one of seventy-eight awarded in the whole war. The call of military service wrenched the bayman, farmer and commuter from his small village in Nassau to strange places in Europe and the daily discipline and uncertainty of military life.

The rumble of motor lorries painted in camouflaged earthen tones or sporting the blue, red and white cockade of the Air Service was a common noise in Nassau villages throughout the war years. From the very beginning of hostilities, the Hempstead Plains seethed with Army and aviation activities. In July of 1916, carpenters, plumbers and mechanics began to set up hundreds of tents and other temporary camp facilities on the entire area north of Hempstead Turnpike from Clinton Road to Meadow Brook. The tract had been obtained by the Army for the establishment of Camp Mills.

Supervised by young officer Douglas MacArthur, the Rainbow Division was organized and moved into the installation in August. The camp had grown so rapidly by Decem-

Congressional Medal of Honor winner William B. Turner of Garden City.

ber that 4,200 tents were blown down during a terrific storm. Thousands of soldiers were trained at the camp, and it became a principal embarkation center for troops going to Europe. The tremendous numbers of soldiers created major problems for the surrounding communities. Merchants were pleased since business had boomed to unthought-of heights, and the village of Hempstead became such a busy town it resembled the city. Accommodations for visitors were scarce and "every boarding house is crowded, hotels are filled and private families are renting their rooms." Local families responded generously and tried to assist servicemen and their families in every way. Hempstead was warmly thanked for its hospitality and the Rainbow Division had such close ties with Garden City that after the war it placed a monument to its 2,950 dead and 13,290 wounded in a small park on Clinton Road south of the railroad tracks. Residents not only opened their homes but spent many hours at YMCA, Red Cross and other facilities providing fellowship and special services for members of the armed forces.

There were other problems associated with a large military camp that were not so easily handled. After several bad fights and disturbances, the use of local taverns by servicemen became a major problem. Many local residents feared that the presence during the evenings of so many soldiers on Hempstead's streets might "in absence of careful oversight be a menace to the morals of some. Young girls should not be permitted to mingle with the crowds without proper chaperonage." The danger was removed on December 14, when all the troops were pulled out of Camp Mills, and ten thousand left in one day. In the next summer when troops returned the military authorities closed all bars within a five-mile zone of the camps to all service personnel.

In 1918 plans were made to make Camp Mills into a major installation, and it was merged with Aviation Field No. 2, which was directly south of it. During the summer there was constant activity as troops were processed through the camp. Endless construction work had created over seven hundred barracks, officers' quarters, lavatories, a post theater, post exchanges, mess halls, laundries, complete water and sewer systems with pump buildings, stables, hay sheds, delousing plants, quarantine huts, a library and administrative buildings. The base hospital No. 2 had 2,500 beds and the old fairgrounds buildings were taken over in April of 1918 for use as a convalescent hospital for soldiers.

Aviation facilities for military use were also rapidly expanded. Hazelhurst Field, founded just before the war, was renamed Roosevelt Field in honor of Quentin Roosevelt after his death in July of 1918 and was

Camp Mills during World War I: setting up facilities, the 165th Infantry arriving, and life in camp.

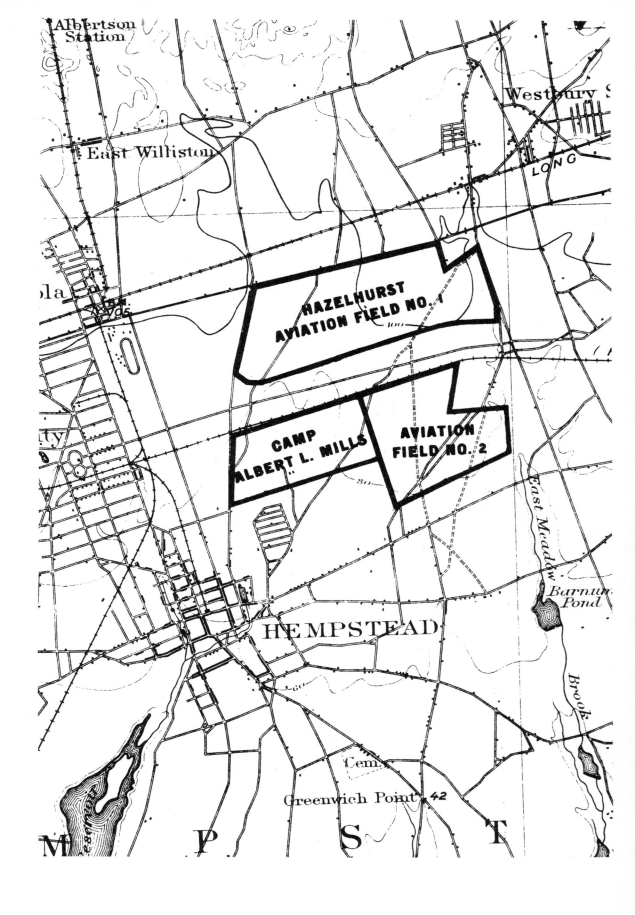

Hazelhurst Field with JN-4 training airplanes lined up.

used throughout the war to train aviators. Additional land was leased from the Hempstead Plains Company in July of 1917, and the Aeronautical General Supply Depot and Concentration Camp was established. It was used initially to receive and distribute supplies to the nearby training fields and was reorganized later in the year as Field No. 2, Mineola, as part of Signal Corps Aviation. Then in July of 1918, it was renamed Mitchel Field in honor of former New York City mayor John Purroy Mitchel, who had been killed during aviation training in Louisiana. Thousands of aviators were trained at these facilities, and the sight of airplanes overhead was a commonplace view for local residents. In September of 1918, a formation of over sixty airplanes flew over Hempstead, the greatest concentration of aircraft ever seen over Nassau. Aviation still was extremely hazardous. Almost every week there was a fatal accident—these took a constant toll of both experienced and novice fliers.

By early fall of 1918, plans had been prepared to train thirty-six squadrons of aviators on Long Island. Roosevelt Field was to be the main base with units at Mitchel, Lufbery Field (a new installation under construction at Wantagh) and seven other new fields. The sudden armistice canceled these developments.

In addition to the Army aviation training activities on the Hempstead Plains, the Cur-

tiss airplane factory opened there at the southeast corner of Clinton and Stewart avenues in the fall of 1917. It expanded very rapidly, and its employment shot up from five hundred workers to three thousand employees engaged in experimental development and fabrication of Curtiss airplanes by the end of the war.

From the winter of 1918 through the summer of 1919, Camp Mills served as a major demobilization camp for the Army. The rail lines to the camp were jammed with units arriving and being discharged. By fall the base was abandoned. Within a year after the armistice, peace also came over the Hempstead Plains. Nassau County could return to normalcy.

In addition to all of the military activities, the wartime home front had seethed with citizen effort. Early in 1917, a Home Defense Committee was organized in the county. One of its major activities was the formation of a Home Defense Corps to take the place of the nationalized National Guard. Over 1,500 men were enrolled in the county and paraded before former President Theodore Roosevelt on the fairgrounds in Mineola in July of 1917. They were fitted out with regular military uniforms frequently supplied by the local community, such as Freeport, which expended $3,000.

Residents were caught up in the many home-front efforts. Liberty loan drives were

Meadow Street Canteen was manned by local volunteers.

enthusiastically supported and millions of dollars were subscribed by residents—the Hempstead district alone selling $1,125,000 of bonds in 1918. People were urged to grow home gardens and to conserve food. The newly created county Farm Bureau assisted farmers in raising their production, and 1919 was a peak year for potato production. The most impressive home-front work was the entertainment and assistance given to the thousands of soldiers who were stationed at the military bases in the county. The YMCA and other service organizations set up information centers, kitchens and social centers. Local women in Garden City established the Meadow Street Canteen, which through private and government assistance provided wholesome relaxation and food for off-duty aviators and soldiers.

The Red Cross became a major local service organization. A Nassau County chapter was formed in 1916 by Mrs. E. D. Morgan to support national activities and supply local facilities. Its unit covering the Hempstead

Plains area kept careful records of military personnel, assisted in operation of the great field hospital on the fairgrounds, maintained centers for soldiers and provided a diversity of services. As one worker indicated, "Individuals entertained the officers while the Red Cross looked after the privates." Throughout the war women knitted socks and gloves, made surgical dressings, Christmas boxes, and in hundreds of ways through the Red Cross provided things which eased the serviceman's life.

In May of 1917 Henry Pomeroy Davison of Locust Valley was appointed national chairman of the Red Cross. Davison immersed himself in directing the Red Cross activities beginning with the great $100-million War Fund Drive that year. The success of the Red Cross wartime effort was due in large measure to his capable efforts. Walter Hines Page also left his local home on Cathedral Avenue in Garden City to serve with distinction during the war period as ambassador to Great Britain.

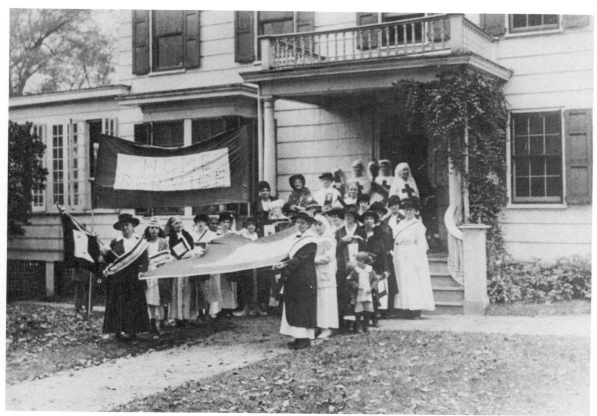

Red Cross volunteers in front of Roslyn headquarters.

The great victory ball at Camp Mills.

The wartime atmosphere of Nassau was joyfully broken when the war ended on November 11, 1918. Every village burst into excited celebration—greater than any ever seen before. When the news was announced, the air in Hempstead was filled with the sound of church bells, whistles and automobile horns. Thousands of workers from the Curtiss factory came parading down the main street beating old tins and shouting themselves hoarse, the beginning of almost continuous street parading throughout the day. The war to end all wars was over, and Nassau citizens could take up their peacetime pursuits.

An Infant Industry

Aviation on the Hempstead Plains between World Wars I and II was marked by a succession of record-breaking flights from local airfields. The flights illustrate the progressive development of American aviation during its adolescent years and are indicative of the extensive aviation experimentation initiated by local aviation pioneers. In addition the events focused attention on the area and thereby acquainted many people with suburban life and its diversified interests in Nassau County.

The first great flight took off on May 8, 1919, but originated during World War I. During the war the Navy organized a program to build a gigantic anti-submarine airplane that could also fly across the Atlantic. The Curtiss Aeroplane and Motor Company at Garden City was awarded the contract and undertook the project in secrecy. In early August 1918, assembly of the NC1 began and was completed in January of 1919. The work was delayed due to the war's end, but it was decided that four planes should be assembled and work went ahead on an overtime basis.

The great ships were partially disassembled and shipped to the Naval Air Station at Rockaway Beach for final assembling and testing. Three of the big three-engined flying boats were ready on May 8, and began the first leg of their flight to Trepassey Bay, Newfoundland. From there they set out on May 16 across the Atlantic Ocean. Mechanical troubles caused the NC1 and NC3 to land in the ocean before reaching Europe, but the NC4, commanded by Lieutenant Commander Albert Read, reached Horta, Portugal, on May 17. This dramatic flight of over 4,500 miles was the first successful transatlantic air crossing.

Only a month later, Great Britain reversed the pattern and sent the great dirigible R-34 across the ocean in the first transatlantic lighter-than-air-ship flight. The huge hydrogen-filled airship, powered by five 250-horsepower engines, came non-stop from Scotland, and as its fuel was running low planned a landing at Montauk Point. However, at the last moment fresh tail winds enabled it to make Roosevelt Field. A squadron leader parachuted from the dirigible and supervised the landing arrangements, which had become confused due to the anticipated Montauk landing.

Since there was no hangar large enough for it, the R-34 was moored in the open and required constant attention due to the different condition of the ship's weight during the sunny daytime and at night. A new sight to Americans, the dirigible attracted a great deal of attention. Throngs of people drove and bicycled out from New York City to Roosevelt Field. The long ship was illuminated at night and the crowds of admirers surpassed those of any other single aeronautical occasion. After a short stay, weather conditions became favorable and the great silver ship left at night on July 9. It was lit up by three giant searchlights, and as it circled New York City in a farewell gesture,

The British dirigible R-34 drew thousands of spectators from New York City to Roosevelt Field.

The NC-4 flying boat is readied for flight at Rockaway.

Long Islanders once more had a ringside seat to aviation history.

Long-distance flying was now a principal interest of aviators. At dawn on June 23, 1923, Army Lieutenant Russell L. Maughan took off from the plains. It was one of the longest days of the year, and he raced the sun across the continent, arriving at San Francisco at dusk of the same day. The 21-hour, 48½-minute flight was a new record but thereafter almost every year there would be a new record established for a transcontinental flight. In 1929 Captain Frank Hawks set new transcontinental records by flying round-trip between San Francisco and Roosevelt Field in 35 hours, 46 minutes and 38 seconds. These were record years in almost every category, and fliers continually tried to improve performance of aircraft. Solo duration flights and altitude records were set many times from Nassau, and Elinor Smith, a local girl, set new endurance and altitude records for women.

The great long-distance challenge was the Atlantic. In 1926 Captain René Fonck, the leading French World War I ace, and a crew of three with a Sikorsky biplane came to Roosevelt Field. He announced plans to fly non-stop to Paris to win the Orteig prize of $25,000. This almost forgotten prize had been posted in 1919 by wealthy hotel owner Raymond Orteig for the first non-stop airplane flight between Paris and New York. Loaded heavily with gas, Fonck's ship crashed and burned at takeoff with the loss of two crew members. Although the attempt failed, many others made preparations for a transatlantic flight to win the prize money.

Soon plans were under way on both sides of the ocean for attempts at the prize. Roosevelt Field was the headquarters for most of the American contenders. Commander Richard Byrd, flushed with a successful flight over the North Pole, began to prepare his Fokker tri-motor airplane, the *America*. Byrd had an excellent crew and was methodically planning and preparing for the flight. Clarence Chamberlin was also there with a Bellanca airplane owned by Charles Levine.

Experimenting with its endurance, Chamberlin and Bert Acosta circled over Long Island for two days, staying in the air 51 hours and 11 minutes. Convinced that they could win the Orteig prize, Levine had Chamberlin prepare for the flight.

Stimulated by the intense rivalry, public interest began to rise to a high pitch. It was increased after May 7 when the French war aces Charles Nungesser and François Coli took off from Paris in their airplane *White Bird*. They departed over the ocean and no trace was ever found of them. This tragic element of danger added to the careful preparations, now in their final stages, of Byrd's *America* and Chamberlin's *Miss Columbia*. Then out of the west came the unexpected news that another American, young airmail pilot Charles A. Lindbergh, was flying east in a new Ryan monoplane, the *Spirit of St. Louis*. On May 12 he arrived over the island and inspected its fields from the air in anticipation of his future takeoff. Mitchel looked better kept but its sod seemed rough. Curtiss was too small for a heavy-load takeoff, but he saw that "Roosevelt is large enough, and it's the only one that has a runway—a long, narrow affair, laid out approximately east and west." Lindbergh landed on a field crowded with photographers and newsmen and for the next few days his every action was relayed to a waiting America.

Could this modest young man, without mechanics or crew, really succeed? Lindbergh checked his engines himself, and a crack in the propeller spinner was generously repaired by the Curtiss corporation. For days he waited at the Garden City Hotel for good weather, and the suspense grew. The widespread radio and newspaper coverage brought crowds of people including thirty thousand on Sunday out to Curtiss and Roosevelt fields in hopes of seeing the competing aviators. Finally on May 19, despite

Charles Lindbergh and Clarence Chamberlin discuss flight plans at the Garden City Hotel.

Charles Lindbergh and the Spirit of St. Louis *at Curtiss Field while awaiting good weather.*

the falling rain, the New York City weatherman Dr. Kimball indicated to Lindbergh that it was clearing over the Atlantic.

Early on the morning of May 20, Lindbergh had his plane towed from Curtiss to Roosevelt Field. It was dark and overcast with a slight rain and very muddy on the ground. The *Spirit of St. Louis* was heavily loaded with gas as Lindbergh slowly took off into the gray sky at 7:52 A.M. The drama of this lone man flying off with quiet confidence in himself and his machine captivated the hearts of Americans. They waited with charged suspense and burst into great joy when word was flashed back that Lindbergh had made it to Paris, landing at Le Bourget Field after 33 hours and 30 minutes of flight. This dramatic achievement was the highlight of aviation on the Hempstead Plains and had a significant influence on the advancement of aviation.

The tremendous public attention given the flight created a new awareness of the potentials of aviation. Until this flight, aviation was regarded as an entertaining but dangerous sport by most Americans. Hereafter, its commercial and military possibilities were given increasing consideration. In the next month, Chamberlin succeeded in flying to Eisleben, Germany, and Commander Byrd reached the coast of France, landing in the water at Ver-sur-Mer. Long-distance flights were not unusual after this and aviation pioneers moved to consider the techniques and design changes required for commercial flights.

There was an unknown sidelight to this flight which would later have immense importance. Lindbergh had met Harry F. Guggenheim, who was greatly interested in aviation's potential, at Curtiss Field before his flight and Guggenheim told him to look him up when he came back. Upon Lindbergh's return, Guggenheim made good on the casual invitation, and the flier stayed at Guggenheim's Sands Point estate, Falaise, and wrote his account of the flight, *We.* A friendship developed between the men, and two years later Guggenheim suggested that Lindbergh discuss the work of an unknown

After his transatlantic flight, Charles Lindbergh frequently returned to Roosevelt Field.

George Dade assists him with his parachute during such a visit.

rocket experimenter with his father Daniel Guggenheim. Lindbergh had been impressed with the work of Dr. Robert Goddard and obtained the senior Guggenheim's financial support for Goddard's pioneer rocketry work.

On May 15, 1918, the first aerial mail route between New York and Washington was begun by Army aviation fliers. Operations were transferred in August to the Post Office Department. The eastern division headquarters was initially at Hazelhurst Field but later Belmont Park became the New York terminal. On July 1, 1924, transcontinental service between Curtiss Field and San Francisco was initiated. Night flying was inaugurated on this run and the average trip took 39 hours and 49 minutes. But airmail was not a self-sustaining project and,

Lieutenant James Doolittle, pilot of the first blind flight, who later became a leader in American aviation development.

due to the delays because of inability to fly in bad weather, it could not develop greater patronage.

At this point the growing aviation industry on Long Island attacked the threat posed by bad weather and long-distance flying. Harry F. Guggenheim provided funds for a project to study blind flying and blind landing. Lieutenant James Doolittle was selected to carry out the flight experiments at Mitchel

Field. He worked with the Sperry Gyroscope Company of Brooklyn, the country's first aviation instrument makers, and the Pioneer Instrument Company of Brooklyn. Paul Kollsman, a fine instrument maker in Elmhurst, Long Island, also contributed a highly sensitive altimeter. By the summer of 1929, Doolittle had equipped his plane with instruments never seen before, including Kollsman's altimeter, a gyro-horizon and a directional gyro made by Sperry.

Before a small audience of interested engineers, Doolittle climbed in his plane on September 24, 1929, and drew a black hood over the cockpit. He climbed off Mitchel's runway and, as aviation leader Preston R. Bassett wrote:

. . . flew down wind several miles; then he turned toward the field and carefully let down on a long slanting approach, using only his radio direction finder and his flight instruments. It was a long minute both for him and the observers as he cautiously felt for the ground . . . Finally the wheels touched and he rolled to a stop. A new chapter in aviation had started.

Only two years later, Wiley Post and Harold Gatty equipped their plane, the *Winnie Mae,* with the new blind-flying equipment. Planning an around-the-world trip, they took off from Roosevelt Field and raced across the world, traveling 15,128 miles in less than nine days. After 1930, scheduled flying at night became a reality through the manufacture and improvement of these instruments.

Due to aviation's impact, Nassau was never to be the same again. The great expansion of flight activities on the plains and the increased usefulness of the airplane had firmly implanted aviation as an integral part of the Nassau County scene. A significant portion of the center of the county, covering several

An aerial exhibiton at Mitchel Field in the late 1920s.

thousand acres of flat land, was created as an aviation center with several airfields. This development provided facilities for aviation and stimulated Nassau's major industry. Since this land area was also excluded from residential development, it provided a major unused land resource after World War II.

After the long period of troop disembarkation, the government reviewed the status of all the installations in Nassau and decided to retain Mitchel Field as an active flying field. It became the home base for observation, bombardment and pursuit groups of Army aviation. The base had not received much permanent construction and was in bad repair after World War I. Low budget appropriations cut maintenance to the bone so that "there were no sentries for the gate, and the field became a favorite parking place by day and night." The runways then were loose dirt with only one having a hard-packed surface.

Gradually, as aviation achieved more military status in the 1920s, improvements were made at the base. Sidewalks and paved roads were installed, but still there were only old frame buildings for officers' quarters. In 1926 the field's status was changed to the Bombing Unit of General Headquarters Air Force and funds were appropriated to improve and extend the runways to 2,700 feet. Mitchel Field was the only regular Army post in the northeastern United States and the main air defense point for New York City. The garrison consisted of eighty-three officers and eight hundred enlisted men with over fifty planes housed in metal hangars. In the early 1930s military appropriations for the base were increased to stimulate employment and permanent structures were erected on the base including concrete and steel hangars, multistoried brick and concrete barracks, administration buildings and officers' homes. All this construction was in a pleasing Georgian architectural style and the field became one of the most attractive military bases in the country.

Mitchel Field became a center of military aviation activities and a major base for avia-

tion experimentation and development. Four Army airplanes, under the command of Captain St. Clair Streett, flew to Nome, Alaska, and back to Mitchel in 1920. The trip covered 9,327 miles over a one-month period and provided considerable data on navigational problems of distance flying. In November Lieutenant Corliss Mosely established an American speed record of 156 miles per hour, winning the first Pulitzer Trophy race at the field.

A great series of war games capped a busy year in 1922. Artillery and infantry units participated and giant searchlights pierced the skies over Nassau in simulated warfare. Aviation's risks continued, and a bomber crashed during the games with a loss of six lives. In August the first planned air route, known as the Model Airway, was established by the Army Air Corps between McCook Field, Ohio, and Mitchel. Emergency landing fields, markers, beacons, coordinated weather reports and radio communications were established to enable regularly scheduled cross-country flights. This airway was a helpful example to the post office, which was preparing to set up the first regular airmail across the country. In the same month, pilots from Mitchel demonstrated the power and capabilities of aerial bombardment. Three Army de Havilland planes flew from the field to attack warships off Sandy Hook. Two of the airplanes dropped ten bombs from an altitude of three thousand feet and were successful in sinking a naval target.

Aerial exhibitions were held at the field to stimulate public interest in aviation and provide entertainment for the airmen. A large program was held in 1923 with an exhibit of various aircraft such as the DH-4-B; Sperry Messenger; JN-4-H; a triple-engined heavy bomber, the Owl. One of Glenn Curtiss' original biplanes, which had first flown on the plains only fourteen years before, was exhibited as a historical wonder! The Navy dirigible *Shenandoah* flew in for the program and the day was crowded with events—skywriting, acrobatics, formation flying, speed tests, bombing and smoke screen demonstra-

Preparations being made at Mitchel for first non-stop transcontinental flight in 1923.

tions, parachute competition and a trophy race. It was an impressive display of the ability and versatility of Army aviators.

The outstanding aviation event of 1923 was the first non-stop flight across America. Lieutenant J. A. Macready and Lieutenant O. Kelly took off from Mitchel Field on May 2, in a large single-engine Fokker airplane. Flying through the night, they landed in San Diego, California, in 26 hours and 50 minutes. This record would not stand long but it was the pioneer non-stop transcontinental flight.

Mitchel operations had now begun to settle down in a regular pattern. Major William Hensley, Jr., the commanding officer, broke down activities at the field into two phases: "the summer season of training . . . and the winter season when the maintenance work and the overhaul of equipment is done." There was one final burst of excitement in October of 1925 when the National Air Races, including the Pulitzer Trophy race, were held at the base. Lieutenant Cyrus Bettis established a new world speed record of 248.975 miles per hour in a Curtiss pursuit plane over the 200-kilometer course.

In addition to the significant physical improvements made in the late 1930s, Mitchel Field began to experience an increased tempo of activities as national defense efforts were expanded. When World War II broke out, Mitchel was made headquarters of the First

Air Force and was responsible for the air defense of the New York metropolitan region. Patrol planes from the base surveyed large areas over the ocean to detect German ship movements. The base was a major training installation for Air Force personnel and in 1943 became a reception center for returning wounded GIs from the European theater of operations. It served as headquarters of the Air Defense Command for the entire United States in 1945 and seemed to be slated as a major Air Force installation when the adjacent Meadow Brook Club was purchased and a 6,627-foot runway constructed for jet aircraft.

However, only a few years later in 1949 all tactical aircraft were shifted from Mitchel Field to other air bases due to the increased danger of flying missions over the heavily populated areas of Long Island. Several accidental crashes of military planes in Nassau had created public calls for reconsideration of the base's operations. The development of jet aircraft and the piercing noise of their operations aggravated the situation. Flying operations after this time were mainly administrative and training. In October of 1960, the Defense Department announced that Mitchel Field would be closed by June of the next year.

The last aircraft were gone by April 15, 1961, and most of the base was declared surplus property by the federal government.

Mitchel Field in late 1930s with new brick buildings.

This was the end of airfield operations in Nassau County and provided a massive section of highly valuable land for future development at a key location in the county.

In addition to the military flying operations, a variety of private airfields provided facilities in the county. There were several small fields in Wantagh, Freeport, Baldwin and other areas which were little more than pasture areas that barnstormers or private fliers used. A regular commercial seaplane base was operating in Port Washington in 1920 and continued to be used by various commercial firms developing flying boats. The first scheduled transatlantic passenger service began there in 1939.

The original Curtiss Field, established in connection with the Curtiss plant in Garden City, was operated for company use and as a private field for other commercial users after World War I until its sale in 1929. A new

Curtiss Field was then built south of Sunrise Highway in Valley Stream. A $4-million aviation center was planned for the 270-acre site, which alone was reputed to have cost over $1 million. The initial plan envisioned four runways from 2,800 to 3,600 feet long, able to handle large airliners. A combination casino and embarkation building, an exposition and technical building, an aviation school and seven large hangars were to provide extensive public and trade facilities. The sudden economic depression prevented this development and the grandiose plans were scaled down.

The most exclusive flying field on Long Island opened in June of 1929 on ninety acres of close-clipped grass around a $300,-000 country club clubhouse. Forerunner of similar units throughout the country, the Long Island Aviation Country Club at Hicksville was established to provide facili-

Pan American Airways operated its international seaplane flights from this base at Port Washington.

Curtiss Field in Valley Stream.

The elite Long Island Aviation Country Club headquarters for private fliers.

ties for the socially elite to fly or lounge in an atmosphere of aviation activity. Many aviation notables were officers and frequent users of the club, including Amelia Earhart, Chance Vought, Charles A. Lindbergh, Harry Guggenheim and Alexander de Seversky. The opening of the club was a gala occasion with spectators enjoying the performance of fifty planes including five Army Falcons from Mitchel Field and fearless feats by a young Army stunt flier, Lieutenant James Doolittle. Local resident F. Trubee Davison, the Assistant Secretary of War for Aeronautics, arrived from Washington with the Japanese ambassador in a tri-motored Fokker monoplane.

These gay festivities highlighted a year during which much expansion of commercial airfields in the county was planned, including major changes at Roosevelt Field. Originally Hazelhurst Field, Roosevelt was abandoned by the Army after World War I and converted to peacetime use. It was operated as a private commercial airfield with many airplane hangars, shops, flying schools and other aviation maintenance facilities. Flying lessons were a major activity. One school alone, the Roosevelt Aviation College, gave 2,129 hours of student instruction and 1,286 hours of student solo lessons in one year for a gross income of $75,000.

Suffering from a lack of capital to develop

proper facilities, the base was menaced by the desire for land during the real estate boom of the 1920s. In June of 1927 a local committee, headed by District Attorney Elvin N. Edwards, attempted to raise sufficient funds to preserve the field as a memorial to Charles A. Lindbergh for his transatlantic flight from there. This plan failed, but the field continued in operation under the Aerodrome Development Company. Richard Reynolds, heir to the tobacco company fortune, was the actual owner at this time.

In 1929 a syndicate headed by Seth Low purchased it and the adjoining Curtiss Field with plans to create a modern airport. The new Roosevelt Field Inc. quickly moved ahead with a modernization and expansion program. A new lighting system was installed for the two all-weather fields with 5,000-foot-long runways. Eight large steel and concrete buildings providing hangar, shop and office space were erected along Old Country Road. The field at this time included over fifty buildings with some 150 aviation enterprises including repair and supply businesses, aerial advertising, airplane taxi and corporate aviation services. There were several hundred planes based at the field, and the Roosevelt Aviation College, at its peak enrollment, had 1,500 students.

Large crowds gathered every weekend at

Roosevelt Field had extensive aircraft facilities in the late 1930s, including large concrete hangars which stood on Old Country Road until 1973.

the field to watch its spectacular aviation shows. Thousands of visitors paid admission to these air shows, which provided a display of many different types of aircraft and their stunt abilities. The shows were usually climaxed by a delayed-opening parachute jump. Visitors could also take a ride to see the Long Island countryside from the air and a "joy hop" to Jones Beach cost $5.

In 1935–36 the eastern 260 acres of the field were leased for an auto race track. This land was eventually purchased by Roosevelt Raceway for its operations. At the beginning of World War II Roosevelt Field was possibly the largest private airfield in the world, with over 270 airplanes based there. The corporation was one of the few airfields to pay a dividend in 1940 and continued to earn divi-

Roosevelt Raceway with its enormous auto racing track.

dends for several years. During World War II its aviation training facilities were extensively used for military instruction.

However, the development of La Guardia Field as a public airfield on Long Island and the increasing residential development around the field ended any chance for its continued development as a public aviation facility. In 1949 after the aviation school closed, the field lost its main economic resource. Its sale to Webb & Knapp, Inc., a large realty concern for industrial and commercial development, was announced in August of 1950. Webb & Knapp acquired the 250 acres of the field and an additional 110 acres of the adjacent Westbury Golf Course for construction of a major shopping center and industrial park. On May 31, 1951, a large twenty-foot-long white X was painted over the main runway at Roosevelt Field, ending the era of private aviation activity in Nassau County.

Aviation on the plains was more than just the fields and spectacular flights—an infant industry was also growing in Nassau County. From the time of the first flights, local residents established small shops and built experimental aircraft. The Heinrich Brothers of Baldwin constructed and flew several monoplanes before World War I. Stimulated by military orders in 1918, Glenn Curtiss established a major industrial plant at Garden City. It was smaller than his upstate New York facilities and provided a place for experimental work. Curtiss built laboratories and a factory with a great number of special facilities including three wind tunnels, a model shop and chemical and metallurgical research laboratories. The company instituted a personnel policy of utilizing women in production work.

Curtiss himself worked at this engineering facility on the original designs and development of a secret World War I project—the NC flying boat. After the war, the plant served as a parts and service facility for the many Curtiss JN-4 Jennies produced for the military. They now were widely available to

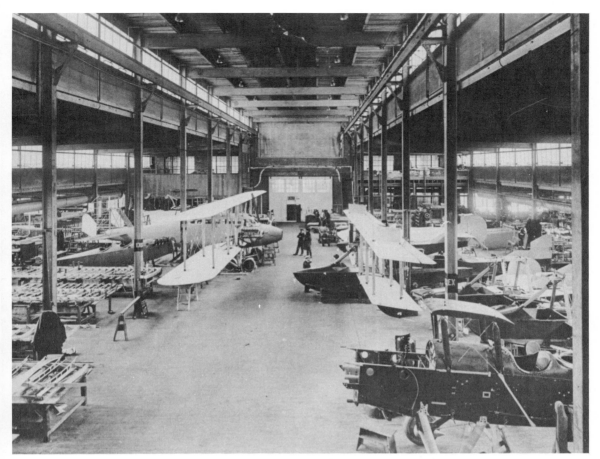

Interior of Curtiss factory at corner of Clinton Street and Stewart Avenue, Garden City.

the public and the military declared so many surplus that Curtiss repurchased them to provide some price stability and protect his local dealers. The factory built speed triplanes and biplanes, K-6 and K-12 motors. Curtiss continued his experimentation in 1922, working on a wood, duralumin and silk glider weighing 150 pounds. The famous Curtiss racers produced here won Pulitzer prizes each year from 1922 to 1925. By 1929, the factory had developed and produced the initial models of the Condor, an eighteen-passenger transport plane, one of the largest planes built in America. Although Curtiss activities were growing, the company's facilities were centralized in Buffalo and the Garden City plant closed in 1931.

Many smaller aircraft companies started in the county after World War I. Young Lawrence B. Sperry founded the Lawrence Sperry

Aircraft Company in a factory at Farmingdale. It produced the Sperry-Verville, a speedy low-wing monoplane with the first retractable landing gear. The Sperry Messenger, a small general-utility biplane, followed. It was so easily handled that Sperry flew from his home in Garden City to the factory, taking off and landing on a vacant field. Lawrence Sperry and his father Elmer had experimented in World War I with the development of an aerial torpedo. In 1918 they constructed pilotless planes fitted with aerial torpedo gear and a radio control system. Unfortunately Sperry met an untimely death in 1923 and his company was dissolved.

Throughout the 1920s a host of smaller aviation companies attempted to design and produce new models or adopted existing airplanes for special uses. Several local concerns, including the American Aeronautical

Corporation in Port Washington and the Ireland Amphibian Company at Roosevelt Field, constructed flying boats and amphibians. Other companies, including the Kirkham Products Company, the Ordnance Engineering Company, and the Cox-Klemmin Aircraft Corporation, made various aircraft for a few years. Russian aircraft designer Igor Sikorsky also produced airplanes at Roosevelt Field during this period. None of these small companies were able to enter into full-scale production although several other firms emerged as major manufacturers.

In 1925 Sherman Fairchild incorporated the Fairchild Airplane Manufacturing Company and three years later moved its offices and factory to Farmingdale. The factory, with a steel and brick hangar, dope shop, heat-treating plant and metallurgical laboratory, had 150,000 square feet of floor space and a 100-acre flying field. The company made a monoplane for use by corporations and executives. It had a seventy-five-man engineering and experimental staff and soon developed a line of aircraft, from its two-place training monoplane to an eight-place cabin cruiser for commercial air transport lines. In 1928 it produced 138 planes with sales of $1.9 million. Its activities began the development of Farmingdale as an airplane-manufacturing center. In 1931 the firm moved its airplane division to Maryland, but the engine division continued as the Ranger Aircraft Engine division, which produced engines and components through World War II.

Military Aircraft Production

Several small aircraft concerns had existed in Baldwin, and on December 29, 1929, Grumman Aircraft Corporation was begun in a small rented garage. Leroy Grumman was born and raised in Huntington and had been among the excited spectators at the famous Belmont meet of 1910. He entered the aviation industry and rose to general manager of Loening Aero Engineering Corporation in New York City. There he met Leon A. (Jake) Swirbul and William T. Schwendler. They decided to establish their own small shop, repairing and making parts for the Loening amphibians as their first job. Soon they won their first contract with the Navy for a pontoon with a retractable landing gear for converting scout planes into amphibians.

As orders increased, Grumman moved temporarily to Valley Stream in 1931, and the next year took over the old Fairchild plant in Farmingdale. The corporation continued its work in the development of naval aircraft and began to construct a series of Navy fighter biplanes and amphibians in the 1930s. In 1937 it constructed its own plant and also produced its first civilian aircraft, the twin-engine Grey Goose amphibian. It also worked on a small Navy fighter, the Wildcat, with a thirty-eight-foot wing span for use on aircraft carriers.

Only a few short miles from the Grumman plant in Farmingdale, the great aviation inventor Alexander P. de Seversky had established his plant in 1934. The Seversky Aircraft Corporation was founded in 1931 and its president's aim was to design and build high-speed fighter planes for the Army Air Corps. Supported by small Army purchases, the Seversky company was able to produce a series of planes which broke existing speed records. In 1939, as the storm clouds of war were appearing over Europe, the corporation was reorganized and refinanced as the Republic Aviation Corporation.

The worsening international situation caused the United States to begin military preparations in 1939, and the production of military aircraft became a priority objective. The aviation corporations in Nassau County were available and had developed the necessary skills and techniques during the 1930s. Republic Aviation received a $3-million Army contract in 1939 and in 1940 began the regular production of the P-47 Thunderbolt,

Grumman Aircraft Corporation FF1, built in 1933.

Production line of Seversky-built BT-8 trainers.

The famed Thunderbolt, rugged Republic P-47 fighter plane.

a powerful and strong Army fighter plane. Republic produced over fifteen thousand Thunderbolts during the war, with nine thousand manufactured in the Farmingdale plant. At its peak during the war, Republic employed over 25,000 persons on its 560-acre field. A massive plant was established with over 2 million square feet of building space.

The Thunderbolt became the principal aircraft of the Army and took a terrific toll of enemy planes and equipment in the European theater of action. In his book *Thunderbolt,* American ace Robert S. Johnson praised the rugged plane which was nicknamed the "Jug" by its pilots after he survived a vicious air battle: "The Thunderbolt has brought me home . . . and this airplane is not a pretty sight. My awe and respect for the fighter increase as I walk around the battered machine. There are twenty-one gaping holes and jagged tears from exploding 20 mm cannon shells . . . my count of the bullet holes reaches past a hundred . . . Every square foot, it seems, is covered with holes . . . The airplane had done her best."

Grumman Avengers in flight.

Grumman F4F Wildcat, backbone of World War II naval air forces.

At the Grumman plant, the impact of Navy wartime orders was immediate. The seven hundred employees of 1939 were rapidly increased and moved into an enormous new plant in December of 1941. Regular production of the F4F-4 Wildcats with folding wings for carrier duty began. In the first year of the war, Grumman produced 426 planes including two amphibians, the Widgeon and the Duck. Its employment reached a height of 21,000 employees in 1944 when it was averaging production of over five hundred planes a month. *Fortune* magazine observed that Grumman "got going faster and stayed ahead of schedule more continuously than any other aircraft plant working for the

Navy . . . At the same time, Grumman kept changing and improving its planes just enough throughout the war to keep them superior to enemy aircraft." The Wildcat was succeeded by a series of other carrier-based planes including the Hellcat, the Tigercat and the Bearcat just before the end of the war. It also produced the Avenger torpedo bomber and other minor models for a total of over seventeen thousand aircraft during the war.

Grumman established a strong liaison with the Navy and became a trusted producer of its aircraft. A naval aviator observed, "The F-6 [Hellcat] would stand terrific punishment and still get home and . . . it could equal or outdo the most recent Zero in everything except maneuverability. The Zero fell

apart when hit." One naval squadron destroyed 187 Japanese planes without the loss of a single Grumman Hellcat.

Since both Grumman and Republic had only a small staff of employees at the beginning of the war, an enormous recruitment and training program was necessary to staff the wartime factories. Long Islanders from all areas, including a great number of housewives, were trained to man the production lines in special classes held in local high schools and private training centers.

Local residents also provided the production personnel for a huge plant built in 1941 at Lake Success by the Sperry Gyroscope Company. Elmer Sperry's old company had evolved into a major airplane-instrument producer. Some 16,000 Long Islanders were

Machinist at work in Sperry Gyroscope plant, Lake Success.

Republic Aviation's F-84, Thunderjet, production line during the Korean War.

trained to make the most advanced type of instruments, and the Sperry Gyroscope factory produced automatic pilots, bomb and gun sights, and radar components essential to military success. At its peak in 1943, the company employed over 32,000 employees at the Lake Success plant, a radar factory and laboratory in the old Curtiss factory at Garden City, and other facilities.

In addition to these major aviation corporations, the war stimulated the growth of a vast number of subcontractors and suppliers to the major contractors. The Fairchild Camera and Instrument Corporation employed over 4,400 workers at its World War II peak. Liberty Aircraft Products Company was founded at Farmingdale and became the largest subcontractor, with over

The clean room at the Grumman plant with Lunar Module No. 5 in final assembly.

A LM on the moon—a tranquil scene of the CBS television model in simulated moonscape at Grumman plant.

several thousand employees during the war. Curtiss Field in Valley Stream provided quarters for the Columbia Aviation Corporation, which produced military amphibian planes.

At the end of the war, the local aircraft industry was instantly shattered by the cancellation of military aircraft production. Grumman Aircraft Corporation immediately laid off its entire work force of 25,500 employees and, after considering its future develop-

ment, rehired 3,500 for permanent staff. It continued research and planning for better Navy aircraft and began to produce the F-9F Panther in the late 1940s. Grumman also began production of civilian aircraft, but military business still accounted for 80 per cent of its income during this period.

In the early 1950s, the landing field requirements for jet aircraft caused Grumman to establish a large field and plant at Calverton, Long Island, but its Farmingdale plant continued as a major production and research facility. The Grumman F-9F Cougar jet made the first transcontinental flight in less than four hours in 1954. The next year Grumman, which had produced 23,000 airplanes from its inception, celebrated its twenty-fifth anniversary. Although Grumman's employment was stimulated by the Korean War, it continued operations at a moderate level, with sales of $225 million in 1958 and a staff of over 14,000 employees.

The new cyclical nature of the aircraft industry on Long Island was evident in the experiences of Republic Aviation after the war. Dependent completely on military orders, Republic quickly developed a jet-engined successor to the Thunderbolt after the war. The F-84 Thunderjet became the basic Army fighter-bomber of the Korean War. Once again Republic had to create special training centers throughout the island to provide over 29,000 production employees in 1954. It received the first contracts that year for the F-105 Thunderchief, an enormous jet fighter-bomber. Although the largest producer of jet aircraft in the free world, Republic's business was completely dependent upon military needs and, by the early 1960s, production of the F-105 was phasing out. Republic was unable to acquire any other prime contract from the military services, and the staff was reduced in 1964 to 5,000 employees. The corporation was acquired by the Fairchild Hiller Corporation and reorganized to provide major subcontracting services to other principal aircraft contractors.

The Grumman Aircraft Corporation, which had consistently applied efforts to diversification and civilian business, turned toward the new exploration of space. In 1962 the National Aeronautics and Space Administration (NASA) announced that Grumman was selected as a prime contractor for the Lunar Excursion Module for the Apollo space program. Grumman's diversification had paid rich dividends, and it now became a major contractor for America's space exploration. The construction of the LEM vehicles at the Grumman plant instituted a new era in its operations. By 1965 over 27,000 employees were at work on various naval aircraft production lines and its enormous space program. Through media coverage of the various flights, national attention was focused on the Grumman plant and the exacting technology that was required to produce the Lunar Module. This program was completed in the early 1970s and the corporation was unsuccessful in its attempt to obtain contracts for new space station vehicles. However, it began production of a new commercial executive fan jet and, after several years of uncertain negotiations, initiated a major production run of another naval carrier aircraft.

Grumman Aircraft Corporation's success in coping with the vagaries of military aircraft production was due to a combination of exceptional executive leadership and an outstanding staff. The corporation was noted for its unusually low labor turnover, which was half the normal industry rate. Company policies, particularly developed by president Leon Swirbul, had emphasized the incentive system for employees and provided many special personnel services including recreational programs, distribution of holiday turkeys and special cash bonuses. This created a very cohesive work force and, despite numerous attempts, unionization of the Grumman plant was never achieved, although most of the aviation industry on the island was unionized after World War II.

In a period of less than seventy years, aviation had grown, matured and declined in Nassau County. From a dangerous sporting venture, aviation grew through its experimental years on the Hempstead Plains into an infant local industry. The numerous early exploits and records established by aviators from Nassau's flat fields had provided national attention and increased interest in aviation. The significant activities and improvements of aviation technology developed here have earned the county the appellation "Cradle of American Aviation."

By 1930, early aviation pioneers and supporters including Glenn Curtiss, Elmer Sperry and Daniel Guggenheim had died. A new generation took their place and created an industry that was a key component in the production of military aircraft so essential to America's victory in World War II. This new aerospace industry was a principal economic stimulant to the growth of Long Island in the 1950s.

The rapid pace of aviation development was climaxed by Grumman's production of the space vehicle used in man's first landing on the moon. From a simple biplane fluttering over the grassy plains to the fabrication of a spaceship in a "clean" room at the Grumman factory, the evolution of aviation in Nassau County has been an incredible technological accomplishment, unequaled in mankind's history.

Edward, Prince of Wales, at Meadow Brook Club.

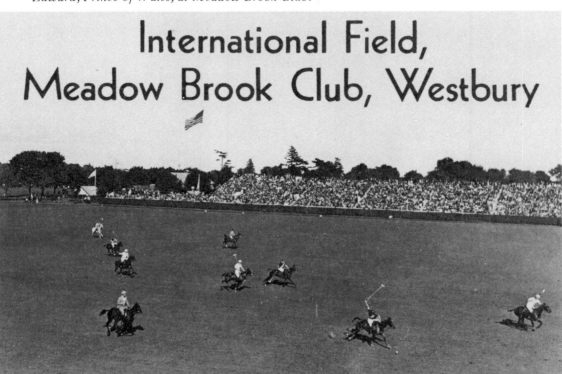

International Field,
Meadow Brook Club, Westbury

CHAPTER IV

THE ROARING TWENTIES

The Gold Coast

It was the social highlight of the nineteen twenties in the United States. A week never to be forgotten in high society—when the world's most eligible young bachelor captured the hearts of American womanhood. The frantic week began on August 29, 1924, when the Prince of Wales was met by sixty reporters upon arrival in New York harbor, and concluded after a Long Island stay with every minute detail recorded as front-page news. He immediately slipped away to Long Island on the yacht *Black Watch,* owned by Robert Graves. Since no one knew where he would land, the whole north shore was lined with people, boats, welcoming banners and bunting, and even an Italian band. The prince disappointed the crowds, however, and landed on a private float off the Pratt family estates at Glen Cove and sped by car to James A. Burden's 140-acre estate in Syosset, where he stayed for the coming week.

Ostensibly the prince was on the island to attend the International Polo Matches at the Meadow Brook Club, but to the public his stay was the epitome of the luxurious, carefree and exciting dream world the very rich could live on Long Island. After streaking off on a fast rail trip to Washington, D.C., the prince returned to be caught up in a never-ending whirl of activities. He sped across Long Island Sound in a motorboat, played polo on Nassau's lush green fields and cheered the races at Belmont Park. He was wined and dined at exclusive lawn par-

ties, luncheons, polo dinners, masquerade dances, and at a Piping Rock Club dinner attended by Will Rogers. Over a thousand dogs paraded before him at J. S. Phipps's beautiful estate during the annual dog show of the Westbury Kennel Association. He attended the International Polo Matches at the famed Meadow Brook Club, which had freshly painted its stands a beautiful piazza blue.

The exciting week ended in a great reception and dinner for 1,200 society leaders at Clarence Mackay's great estate on Harbor Hill. Guests entered up the long, winding entrance road dazzled by thousands of blue lights strung through the trees, and the Stars and Stripes in electric lights towering above the mansion were visible for miles along the shore. The great reproduction French chateau mansion, with its fabulous medieval armor and processional flag collection, was the perfect setting to end this social triumph. There was little doubt after these thrilling days that this "part of Long Island contests with Newport for the honor of being the social capital of the United States."

The great estate era had reached its highest point in the 1920s, and as Edwin D. Morgan pridefully indicated in a masterly understatement, the area had become "one of the most delightful and unusual suburbs in any part of the United States." It was certainly an area unlike any other in the country, with an unmatched concentration of wealthy families, beautiful homes and landscaped estates. A bucolic, rural setting of rolling countryside with narrow roads

Clarence Mackay's great estate house on Harbor Hill, Roslyn.

shielded by enormous trees and varied woodland, the north shore was an exceptionally beautiful area. The way of life of its inhabitants was unlike any other—money was expended lavishly on the Gold Coast. The most highly sophisticated recreations were developed, and life centered around the great entertainments at the estates and activities at the private clubs. All of this social whirl was generally conducted, though, with a restraint and good taste that excluded inelegant excesses.

Edwin D. Morgan's estate of 666 acres in Wheatley Hills had been considerably improved since its inception with a lodge, chapel, indoor squash court and its own private reservoir. In 1907 fourteen grooms had to flee for their lives as the 300-foot stable burned, destroying ten coaches and several automobiles. Morgan, in addition to playing polo and yachting, was a member of the New York Racing Commission and master of hounds at Meadow Brook. Clarence Mackay had also added to his estate and built a tremendous casino and clubhouse designed by Stanford White in 1907. It had, in addition to the popular squash room, a main salon, tennis court, pool, showers, steam rooms and a special ladies' bath.

Elaborate estates now stretched all along the edge of the Sound. In 1924 Marcus Loew purchased Pembroke, a forty-six-acre waterfront residence near Glen Cove with a seventy-foot mosaic circular swimming pool and a garage for twenty cars. Much of the prime estate lands in that city had been taken over by members of the Pratt family. Charles Pratt, co-founder of Standard Oil of New Jersey, purchased the original lands before the turn of the century. By 1920 over three fourths of a mile of Sound frontage and some 1,000 acres with 125 buildings were held by members of the family. Harold I. Pratt developed his home Welwyn; Herbert Pratt, The Braes; and John T. Pratt, the Manor House. The estates had their own private water works, a prize dairy herd and over four hundred day laborers to maintain the meticulous grounds.

A 257-acre island off Glen Cove known as

Meadow Brook hounds leaving entrance to the Hudson estate, Muttontown, late 1920s.

East Island was developed by J. P. Morgan into his own self-contained community. Over a hundred employees ran the self-sustaining operation including a creamery, gardens and greenhouses. Peacock Point at Locust Valley was purchased by Henry P. Davison in 1909. Its charming beaches, polo field and tennis courts and the hospitable Davison family made it a center for young people's activity.

Large estates took over all the area around Oyster Bay. Various members of the Roosevelt family occupied Cove Neck, while Mortimer L. Schiff and the great glassmaker Louis C. Tiffany also developed large holdings nearby. William K. Coe imported the magnificent early-eighteenth-century Carshalton Gates made in England for the entrance to his 435-acre estate, Planting Fields. C. Oliver Iselin and Joseph H. Harriman occupied estates in Brookville.

A great complex initiated by E. D. Morgan grew within the Old Westbury-Wheatley-Jericho area. There, alongside old Quaker farmsteads, stood the great estates of Alicia Du Pont, Edward F. Hutton, Arthur S. Bur-

den, Elbert A. Gary, F. Ambrose Clark, Virginia Vanderbilt and Bronson Winthrop. The Whitneys had several holdings; both Cornelius V. and his son Harry Payne had a strong interest in thoroughbred horses and built huge stables and a private race track. The son's home was an exact copy of a French chateau outside Paris. Just to the north, John S. Phipps had built a typical eighteenth-century English manor home designed by a London architect with interior furnishings of the Georgian period. Its grounds, shaded by majestic beech and linden trees, were actually a well-developed park with sumptuous landscaping, special children's, rose and Italian gardens, pools and other features.

In 1915, when real estate was reassessed throughout the county, Oyster Bay Town was raised from 25 to 35 per cent of market value, which greatly increased the assessments and tax load of the estates. The Pratt family holdings, which increased from $608,700 to $1,527,550, were indicative of the monetary value of the great estates. In North Hemp-

Estate buildings reproduced all the great traditional European architectural styles, even the feeling of an Irish castle in Castle- *gould, the garage and stables at the Guggenheim estate in Sands Point, now a county park.*

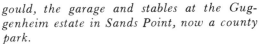

stead the same process jumped Isaac Guggenheim's $300,000 value to $465,750 and Howard Gould's $500,000 to $675,000 even greater than Clarence Mackay's $540,000. Estate development continued actively through the 1920s with improvements to established properties and the creation of many new smaller estates for children of original Gold Coasters.

These were the great years of the estates and probably none anywhere in the United States was finer than financier Otto Kahn's mansion overlooking Cold Spring Harbor. Every weekend guests streamed in to lunch and play croquet and golf at their host's genial bidding. On one such occasion, the noted wit Franklin P. Adams effectively punctured the splendid Byzantine air of the grand dining room when he turned to one of the numerous footmen behind the table and asked, in a moment of silence, "Can I order from the menu, or do I have to take the blue-plate lunch?"

The magnificent estates were a world of their own, of European splendor, rural Long Island quietude and a life of leisure. At their height in 1930 they occupied a sizable portion of the land area of the towns of North

Landscaping and gardens were a spectacular part of the estate scene and none surpassed the Italian garden at Phipps's estate.

Hempstead and Oyster Bay, and retained a completely rural atmosphere in this area despite a great decrease in farming.

North shore life was also stimulated by many people in the theatrical and literary fields who discovered the allure of suburban life within easy commuting distance of their Manhattan employment. An unofficial colony existed in Great Neck, Port Washington and Roslyn. Author Will Durant expressed the sentiments of some, indicating, "We wanted a quiet place, hygienic, with a good school, preferably public, and good air. We got it all." And so they joined the moving throng of new suburbanites: Ring Lardner, P. G. Wodehouse, William Rose Benét, Frances H. Burnett, Charles and Kathleen Norris and, in 1914, Sinclair Lewis. Lewis, as the others, commuted to the city writing feverishly in every spare moment. His wife Gracie took up the newly emerging role of suburban woman shepherding campfire girls, campaigning for woman suffrage and working for the Village Welfare Association. Theatrical luminaries who settled in Great Neck included Ed Wynn, Donald Brian, Jane Cowl, Olga Petrova, Ernest Truex and Sam Harris. Much of the music that stirred Americans in the early 1900s emanated from George M. Cohan and John Philip Sousa, both north shore residents.

But of all those who came, it was Scott Fitzgerald who left the most indelible record of life during the roaring twenties. He and Zelda had moved out to Great Neck to be near his friends Ring Lardner, Lillian Russell, the great Ziegfeld and the other actors, song writers, comedians and producers who kept the colony humming. Fitzgerald claimed that you "couldn't live in Great Neck on anything under $36,000 a year," but then his style of living was exceedingly high.

During his stay in a rented house on Gateway Drive in Great Neck, he wrote *The Great Gatsby* from his observances and experiences during the evenings on the Gold Coast. The house at East Egg, "a cheerful, red and white Georgian Colonial mansion, overlooking the bay," could have been no-

Louis C. Tiffany's estate, Laurelton Hall, near Oyster Bay reflected his exotic artistic talent, with a dragon alongside the pool. In the Hall's entrance court there was a pool with flowing water that filled the center vase, changing its exquisite color but also causing it to explode occasionally. Courtesy of Tiffany and Co.

THE GOLD COAST   125

Greatest American band leader, John Philip Sousa, a resident of Port Washington.

where else but on Long Island, where "the lawn started at the beach and ran toward the front door for a quarter of a mile, jumping over sundials and brick walls and burning gardens." Fitzgerald's pace was too frantic even for this fast area—his neighbors often found him in the morning asleep on his lawn—and he soon left for Europe.

There was another prominent show business colony on the south shore in Freeport. Leading actors in musical comedy and vaudeville congregated there weekly. Some moved into the community, others came out for a weekend of fun at the Lights Club. The Long Island Good Hearted Thespians included Victor Moore, Frank Tinney, Eddie Foy, George McKay, Jack Diamond, Thomas Duggan, George "Spider" Murphy and Fred Stone. Each weekend they gathered in the clubhouse and gave great impromptu performances for their own enjoyment, and

they could always cool off in the nearby bay. Undoubtedly on their drives out from the city, they stopped at the roadhouses and gambling places along Merrick Road in Lynbrook, where blond and buxom Texas Guinan greeted customers at the Blossom Heath Inn with her hearty and unforgettable, "Hello, sucker."

The gay and light times of the postwar years reached their zenith in the "gleaming and dazzling" Gold Coast parties that Fitzgerald described so well, when "a crop of caterers came down with several hundred feet of canvas and enough colored lights to make a Christmas tree of Gatsby's enormous garden. The lights grow brighter as the earth lurches away from the sun and now the orchestra is playing yellow cocktail music and the opera of voices pitches a key higher." Such an evening of entertainment by the very wealthy was unforgettable even to as widely feted a man as Charles A. Lindbergh. After his famous flight, Lindbergh was honored at a dinner of eighty of New York's most prominent people at Clarence Mackay's beautiful Roslyn estate, and he saw a place "transformed into a fairyland of colored Japanese lanterns, fountains, and illuminated shrubbery."

Sportsman-journalist Herbert Bayard Swope's parties often concluded with midnight croquet games illuminated by car headlights for $2,000 stakes. There was also no better party spot than Gene Buck's home—a wag described Ziegfeld's right-hand man's place as "the Yale Bowl with lamps." In 1929, partying even took to the water when the *Amphitrite,* a former Navy monitor, was brought up from Palm Beach and its five decks converted into a floating country club in Hempstead Harbor. The gaiety and laughter that rang out over Long Island in the twenties when "the moon had risen higher, and floating in the Sound was a triangle of silver scales, trembling a little to the stiff, tinny drip of the banjoes on the lawn" will never quite be matched.

Playground of the East

With the increased standard of living and shorter work hours nationwide, all Americans were spending more time in recreational activities. This trend was particularly evident in Nassau County, which was promoted as a suburban area abounding in recreational possibilities. Local boosters showed no shyness and proclaimed that "as the Playground of the East, Long Island is synonymous with outdoor sports at their best." Its unexcelled climate was continually praised and all were informed that "only two places upon the American continent have as much sunshine as Long Island." The existence of a wealthy segment of population with a great deal of leisure time led the way in this development of recreational activities.

In the 1890s polo became a new sport on Long Island, with a vigorous rivalry springing up between the teams of the Meadow Brook Club and the Rockaway Hunting Club. As the north shore increased in afflu-

ence, polo became increasingly a prominent recreational symbol of the wealthy residents. By the 1920s, the game reached its greatest heights in the United States and the great Meadow Brook Club with its six fields was the "Mecca for players from all over this country as well as from every part of the world where the game is played."

Harry Whitney had formed an American polo team in 1909 consisting of himself, Larry and Monty Waterbury and Devereux Milburn, which went on to win the International Challenge Cup that year. They successfully defended it in 1911 and 1913, and by then the championships and even regular games drew large crowds of spectators to the robin's-egg blue Meadow Brook grandstands. By the twenties, Nassau had over thirty polo fields, from Sands Point to the Fort Neck Polo Club in Massapequa. Activities became so intense the Piping Rock Club and the Roslyn Polo Club layouts included two fields, and the Phipps family also owned two private fields. Devereux Milburn, Louis Stoddard, J. Watson Webb and Thomas Hitchcock, Jr., had regained the International Cup in 1921 and the same team,

Sketch by noted Garden City artist Paul Brown of exciting Old Westbury-Greentree match Stewart Iglehart with good sportsmanship hands mallet back to Jock Whitney. Courtesy Charles Scribner's Sons.

with the substitution of Malcom Stevenson in place of Stoddard, participated in the 1924 contest before the Prince of Wales.

Polo had caught on with the younger members of the wealthy set and G. H. "Pete" Bostwick, Raymond and Winston Guest, John Schiff, W. Averell Harriman and D. Stewart Iglehart greatly improved the game. The game required great skill but participants did not have to be strong athletes. Of prime importance was the mount, and desirable polo ponies became a very expensive purchase as competition for them drove prices to dizzy heights. The great concentration of energy on polo in Nassau County produced some of the greatest players in the world, and Foxhall P. Keane, Thomas Hitchcock, Sr. and Jr., Harry Payne Whitney and F. W. C. Guest rank among the world's polo greats.

Yachting closely paralleled polo develop-ment in the early 1900s as a major activity of the new wealthy residents. The north shore of Long Island, with its many protected bays, was geographically ideal for boating. Although sailing was a great recreational activity, the yacht clubs organized in the late 1890s also emphasized competition races. There were many classes of boats, with probably the best-known being the 1911 Star Class, which was a 22 foot 8½ inch boat. Whole families such as the Morgans, Roosevelts, Pages, Stevens, Vanderbilts and Astors participated in yacht racing and centered their leisure activities around the clubs. Their financial resources made large crafts over fifty feet long a normal size. The New York Yacht Club established its Station 10 at Glen Cove in 1904 and it served thereafter as a major rendezvous for the finest and largest yachts in the country.

Racing on Manhasset Bay.

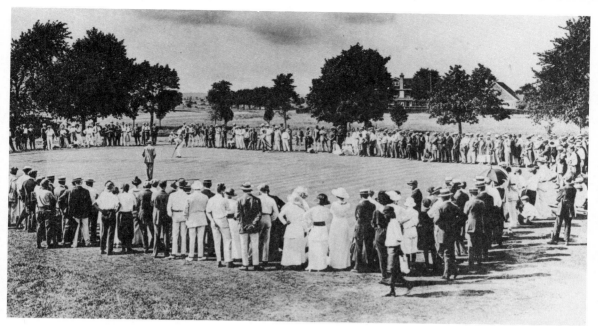

A golf match at the Garden City Country Club in the early 1900s.

The development of smaller yachts was helped by the racing programs of the Manhasset Bay Yacht Club, which began junior yachting activities in the 1920s. The Seawanhaka Corinthian Yacht Club also assisted this development and its Seawanhaka-International Challenge race for small yachts was the next best-known race to the America's Cup. Begun in 1895, this race played a leading part in the improvement of racing yachts of a modest size.

Golf was also a recreational activity fostered by the county's new wealthy residents. By 1920 over fourteen country clubs had golf courses in the rolling, wooded countryside on the north shore of the county. The National Amateur Championships were held in Nassau three times at the Garden City Golf Club and other local clubs. A young woman, Helen Hicks of Hewlett, became one of the stars of golf during this period. Golf continued to expand mainly as an activity of the higher-income residents, and there were thirty-six clubs by 1930. Most of these clubs also had well-tended tennis courts.

Horse racing has been a sport on the Hempstead Plains since the early colonial races held by Governor Richard Nicolls. Around 1900 the Westchester Racing Asso-

ciation, led by August Belmont, Jr., and William C. Whitney, decided on a site of 650 acres in Elmont for a major new race track. By 1903 over five hundred immigrant Irish, Italian and Polish laborers were at work creating the new Belmont Park. Surrounded by miles of ornamental iron fence, the huge track had a grandstand for nine thousand people, a separate railroad station and two thousand stalls in its barns. It opened to the public on May 4, 1905, with spring and fall meetings in the grand fashion, racing clockwise as in England. The track closed temporarily in 1911 and 1912 due to anti-betting laws passed by the state legislature, and its grandstand and many other buildings were destroyed in fires aided by wind and low water pressure on April 7, 1917. A new and larger grandstand seating twenty thousand was built, and the track reopened in 1920 in time for the Belmont Stakes, which was won by Man o' War. Famed for its beautiful and meticulously landscaped grounds, the track was the scene of many great races, including the Belmont Futurity of 1929 with a purse of $105,730, won by Whichone, owned by Harry Payne Whitney.

A newer racing sport also was on view for Nassau residents in the early 1900s. The

Automobile Club of America, a national organization promoting that new device the horseless carriage, staged a fifty-mile point-to-point race between Springfield and Babylon over the old Merrick Road, then among the better highways in the east. In 1904 William K. Vanderbilt II, who wanted to advance American prestige in world automobile circles and stimulate American efforts to match European standards, offered an impressive silver trophy as the prize for the first Vanderbilt Cup race. Vanderbilt had a luxurious estate, Deepdale, at Lake Success inside the western edge of Nassau County. He loved to race his motorcars around his estate and Long Island roads with a daring skill.

Vanderbilt was an ardent motorist and spared no pains or money in producing a major attraction. There was some opposition to the races by more conservative citizens, who did not like the idea of the great mechanical monsters tearing around local roads, but they were outweighed by the $5,000 Vanderbilt spent to improve the local roads making up the course. A grandstand and special press and parking facilities were set up for the race, and its safety features were proclaimed. Excitement over the contests built up to a feverish pitch with extensive newspaper coverage of the various European racers and their awesome machines with massive engine blocks. Great crowds choked the roads out to the island on the day of the race, October 8, and they overran the track in excitement after George Heath's victory.

The next year the event was definitely a major international sporting feature, and the famous turns on the course at Jericho and East Norwich were known by all car buffs. The economic benefits of the race now appealed to local residents, and Congressman William Cocks proudly proclaimed to the Southern New York Volunteer Firemen's Convention that "we have the best roads and don't forget we have the automobile race . . . A great deal of advertising has been

The exciting steeplechase course at Belmont Park.

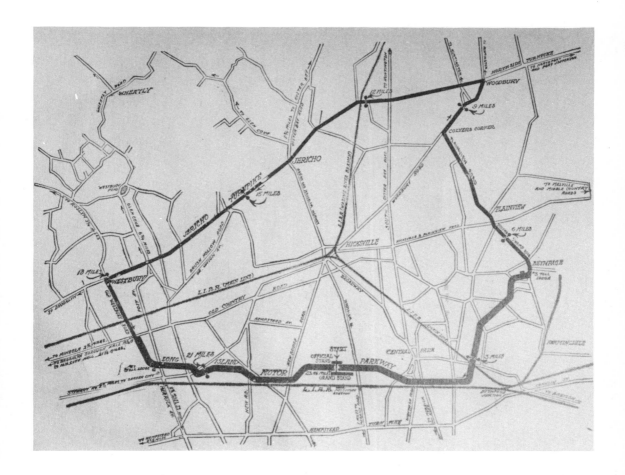

made out of the race and a great amount of money has come into Nassau County on account of it, and all are looking for their share, I hope the business men will profit by it."

There was so much advertising that over 200,000 people, "a frenzied, jovial exodus . . . from New York alone, by ferry, train, auto, wagon and bike," jammed local inns and farmhouses the day before the race. There was considerable difficulty in controlling the great masses of people over such a long course, and the next year when they became completely uncontrollable, the danger of a serious disaster caused the temporary end of the races in the county.

Vanderbilt was now at work, however, on one of the first really modern roads in the United States—the Long Island Motor Parkway. It was the first concrete non-stop ex-

clusive automobile road in the country, and he provided special racing facilities such as sunken pits to attract the race back to the island. In 1908 the race was held over nine miles of the parkway and fourteen miles of public roads. George Robertson, driving a 120-horsepower American-built Locomobile No. 16, won the race with the then dazzling average speed of 64.39 miles per hour. The next year the route covered twenty-two circuits of a 12.64-mile stretch with carefully controlled access to handle crowds. Crowds diminished in 1909, and in 1910 the last great speed extravaganza was held. That year two deaths and numerous injuries to foolhardy spectators caused the race to be shifted out of the area. These celebrated races stimulated American interest in the automobile and acquainted thousands of people with the north shore of Nassau County.

Crowds lined the country lanes of Nassau to view the famous cars during 1908 Vanderbilt Cup race.

Although the exclusive recreations received great publicity, only a limited number of residents could participate. Of more direct impact on the average resident were the numerous participant sports and activities. Organized sports began to play a pronounced role throughout the county as high schools were established and scholastic athletic programs were initiated. By 1917 a Nassau County Scholastic Baseball League was in operation, with teams from Freeport, Rockville Centre, Lawrence, Hempstead, Lynbrook and Woodmere. Local athletic clubs for young men became very prominent, such

Sea Cliff baseball team, 1912 Nassau County champions.

as the Dragon A.C. of Rockville Centre, which had one of the county's first basketball teams in 1910 and semi-pro baseball teams which, by the 1920s, played games in local villages. These local contests were a focal point of community competition and fostered development of village pride and neighborliness. A. Holly Patterson, who later became county executive, was a feared spitball pitcher in those games and recalled that on the game day, "all the merchants and businessmen in Hempstead would close down."

Football also began as a scholastic sport just before World War I, with Freeport High School playing Oceanside in 1915, and Glen Cove beginning a schedule in 1917. Traditional rivalries in football quickly developed between different communities, and the scrappy games during the fall became major centers of community interest far beyond the scope of mere school activities. By 1930 when Great Neck achieved recognized status as the championship team in the county, foot-

South Side High School football team of early 1900s.

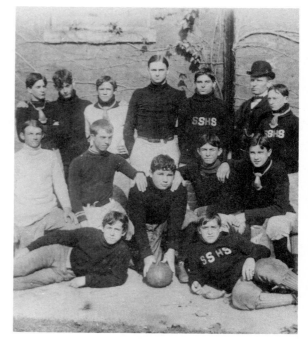

Ellison's ferry from Freeport to the barrier beach.

ball was the predominant school sports activity, with seventeen schools playing seven-to-eight-game schedules.

Track and field sports had also developed and a countywide championship meet was held in 1930. When Ray Barbuti of Lawrence brought home two gold medals from the 1928 Olympics in Amsterdam, interest was stimulated in track. Barbuti, a rugged football player at Syracuse, was not favored in the 400-meter race but won by inches with a final lunge through the tape. An anchor run in the 1,600-meter relay gave him a second gold medal for the only American bright spots in the field events at that Olympics.

The expansion of school athletics was so great that a committee of fifteen school superintendents was formed in 1929 to supervise all scholastic sports activities. Up to this time there was no formal procedure to handle disputes over game protests, assignment of officials and other problems of organized athletic activities. In the short period from 1915 to 1930, school athletics had grown quantitatively so large that there was a pressing need to provide an organizational structure for future development and control.

Boxing was also a major sport that flour-

ished in the 1920s. Originally programs were held in a converted warehouse at Mitchel Field which seated about 1,500 spectators. Although the programs began as entertainment for the military base personnel, their popularity spread and some of the finest fight cards on the East Coast were held at an outdoor stadium seating six thousand. Local residents such as Harry Ebbets and Lew Primavera became crowd favorites, and there were many exciting contests with other fistic notables such as Sergeant Sammy Baker and Kid Chocolate.

The attractions of boating, fishing and bathing at the nearby seashore became a major leisure activity. Excursions to the barrier beaches along the south shore were especially popular. Usually an all-day outing, and frequently an overnight sojourn, sailboat trips to Jones Island would take from an hour to three hours, depending on the wind. This was greatly shortened after naphtha launches came into regular use in the early 1900s, and soon there were regularly scheduled ferries to carry people to the barrier beaches such as High Hill.

In 1925 the newly formed Long Island State Park Commission, under Robert Moses' guidance, became interested in future de-

The greatest surf bathing beach in the world crowded with sun-worshipers.

velopment of this prime natural resource of the island. The commission requested the Town of Hempstead to turn over its interests in the outer beaches and a right-of-way access across the bay so that a major park and parkway could be constructed there. Since these were common lands, the town's residents had to make the final decision.

Opposition immediately arose, stimulated by landowners in other sections of the county where the park commission was taking land for a major parkway construction program. The opponents could "see no reason for turning this immensely valuable property over to the state to exploit and mismanage," but wished to keep it in local hands and control. Stimulated by the vision of being engulfed by visitors from New York City, the voters rejected the proposition in the 1925 election.

Moses did not give up, however, and persuaded the town to set up a special Hempstead Development Commission to obtain

Opening ceremony at Jones Beach, Robert Moses on far left, James Farley, Governor Franklin Roosevelt and W. Earle Andrews, deputy chief engineer of the park commission.

citizen support. Thomas McWhinney, Robert L. Christie and George L. Hubbell were commissioners and worked hard to obtain public approval of the plan. G. Wilbur Doughty, supervisor of the town, was won over and his efforts were the deciding factor. The next year Hempstead voters approved the land transfer.

Work began on the project immediately, and in 1927 the Town of Oyster Bay also conveyed some of its common lands in the High Hills beach section to the commission. Over 1,500 acres of land at Jones Beach and Gilgo Beach were developed, with a causeway built across the meadows from the beaches to Wantagh in 1929. Jones Beach State Park opened on August 4, 1929, with ex-governor Alfred E. Smith and Governor Franklin Roosevelt as principal speakers. A howling windstorm blew sand over everything, clogging car radiators and carburetors. Robert Moses afterward recalled that many said, "The whole thing was a fiasco and . . . nobody would ever come there again."

Despite the inauspicious beginning, the great vision held by Robert Moses of a simply developed beach began to take shape. Beach grass was planted to stabilize the dunes and the clear, smooth, white beaches and sparkling surf provided a major recreational resource for people throughout the New York region.

The Long Island State Park Commission was also pushing other park development within Nassau County. Moses' persuasive powers convinced New York City to turn over 2,500 acres of city water supply lands in Nassau for park and parkway purposes. Hempstead Lake State Park, with over eight hundred acres, was planned and other areas were set aside for future park development in Valley Stream, Wantagh and Massapequa providing picnicking, playgrounds, boating, swimming and skating. To provide a separate funding source, the Bethpage State Park Authority was created in 1933. It acquired extensive acreage and opened three golf courses and a clubhouse two years later.

This extensive program of parks was due to the exceptional leadership of Robert Moses and the Park Commission, despite the reluctance of many residents to support parks when there was so much rural land in the county. Only thirty years later, however, these same parks are the only green areas along a densely populated south shore.

To satisfy residents' hunger for recreation, business began to provide outlets for leisure time. A giant amusement park, Playland, was opened in 1923 on the Freeport waterfront. It had numerous rides, a dance hall and salt-water swimming pool. The Freeport Theatre, with an eighty-one-foot-wide stage, was a center for vaudeville and photoplay shows. Almost every village had a small meeting hall for dances and social parties.

Neighborhood taverns had always served as local recreational resources providing meeting facilities, food and drink for residents. With the coming of Prohibition in 1919, the speak-easy took over the normal activities associated with the neighborhood tavern. As elsewhere in the nation, the Prohibition laws were honored more in their breach than observance. Clandestine bars were everywhere and it was easy to make a nightly circuit of them and rub shoulders with the most substantial citizens. A local wag even suggested that realtors should advertise "For sale, fine bungalow, 7 rooms and bath, near water, cellar stocked with summer's supply of scotch and rye." There was considerable truth in this mirth, however, for probably nowhere in the nation was illicit alcohol so available as in Nassau County.

Immediately after Prohibition began, Long Island became the center of extensive rumrunning operations and a major portion of the action was in Nassau County. Large boats with cargoes of alcohol would anchor in the Atlantic outside the three-mile limit and unload to smaller craft, which then sped into hidden docks along the small creeks lining the south shore. Federal agents who covered "every foot of the coast" knew that contraband goods were pouring into the

The development of motion pictures, particularly talkies, led to the end of live performances and the building of theaters such as the Fantasy in Rockville Centre in almost every village before World War II.

area and being transported by truck to New York City, but the Coast Guard did not have enough men and ships to cover the miles of waterfront.

From April 1921 to June of 1923, these activities were under the state Mullen-Gage Act, and local officials attempted enforcement. District Attorney Charles R. Weeks obtained indictments on 249 rumrunners in this period. Convictions were made in 77 per cent of the cases and fines totaled $17,-610. After Governor Alfred E. Smith obtained repeal of the state legislation, local police officers, including the sheriff, did not feel they could act under the national prohibition act and thought federal officers should do the enforcing. By now, rumrunning had become a highly profitable local business.

Runners used very speedy boats such as Sea Bright dories with eight-cylinder Banfield motors capable of forty miles per hour. Some had two boats, a powerful one to bring alcohol in from the larger ocean-going vessels and a lighter speedboat with a silent motor to distribute rum to shore resorts and landing points. Most of the action was clock-like in precision as the local baymen and fishermen would speed out to unload a large ship and discreetly deliver the cargo to waiting gangsters and bootleggers, who distributed the illicit alcohol. Despite nightly Coast Guard patrols, only occasionally would they be caught. The sixty-foot motorboat *Krazy Kat II* was captured in one of these incidents when she ran aground in choppy seas on the Jones Inlet Bar off Freeport with three men and $10,000 worth of whiskey.

*Cargo on the deck
of a rumrunner.*

The local Coast Guard crew rescued the men after residents saw its distress rocket, and found a cargo of one hundred cases and twenty-five burlap bags full of whiskey, a typical way of packing bottles to enable easier transfer between boats.

Enforcement was so lax that the going price of scotch on the local market was openly quoted. When bad weather prevented normal operations, a local newspaper quipped, "occupants of Rum Flow have not had a thing to do but eat three square a day." About thirty boats, all scattered far apart so that one did not know what price the other was quoting, had broken the local market in whiskey and the article lamented the lack of future in the rumrunning business. There is little doubt that a great deal of collusion between local village officials, heads of police departments and local speakeasies provided a ready local market for the rumrunners. District Attorney Elvin N. Edwards campaigned hard against the speakeasies in the late 1920s but was unable to make any real dent in their activities due to this local laxness.

A final ironic note to the area's role as a major source of bootleg alcohol occurred in 1928. William F. Varney, who moved to Rockville Centre as a boy, had become chairman of the national Prohibition Party in Nassau County in 1911. A local businessman, he eventually devoted himself full time to Prohibition activities and moved to New Jersey as a field secretary in the movement. In 1919 he returned to Rockville Centre and entered the insurance business. He was nominated as the national Prohibition Party's candidate for the presidency in 1928 and ran a quiet campaign from his home in Rockville Centre. Since he was not on the ballot in New York State, local residents were not even able to vote for him.

Community Activities

As the county's population had spurted ahead in the first three decades of the 1900s, its social life became increasingly complex. From small communities with few non-religious organizations, by 1930 Nassau's villages were crowded with a host of fraternal and civic community organizations. Some of the civic groups were created mainly from political impetus, but they still served as social meeting grounds for neighbors. The great proliferation was in basically social organizations, most of which usually engaged in educational, community betterment or welfare activities, but these programs were carried on in a context of providing expanded social relationships for members. The membership of these organizations usually cut across social class lines.

Volunteer fire companies were significant organizations throughout the county. Although providing a necessary public service, they also had a major social and political role. The first volunteer fire company was formed in Hempstead in 1832, and by the turn of the century a dozen communities had volunteer departments. Relying on horse-drawn apparatus with animals supplied by a local stable or a member, these groups were an ideal example of men voluntarily banding together for community good. As the villages grew in size, greater demands and needs for fire protection began to exist. Although volunteers were respected

Official Program

1913

Parade and Tournament

Nassau County Firemen's Association

At VALLEY STREAM, L. I.

WEDNESDAY, JUNE 25, 1913

Parade Starts 10:30 A. M.   Tournament Starts, 1:45 P. M.

Hempstead Village firehouse, late 1800s.

and admired, citizens couldn't help but suggest, after a particularly disastrous fire in Rockville Centre, that the firemen improve their discipline and teamwork, obey the chief and improve "in working on interior fires."

. Leaders of the volunteers recognized the need for more skilled and well-trained men and in 1903, Thomas A. McWhinney, Floyd Weeks, George Finley, Edward Aldom and William P. Horton organized an advisory committee of firemen from the various towns of the county. They established the Nassau County Firemen's Association and elected McWhinney as president. The 746 members organized "to protect and promote the interests, welfare, amusement, maintenance, equipment and discipline of Volunteer Firemen . . . and to promote the efficiency of [the county's] fire service." A principal method of firemen training was the preparation for fire tournaments, which also provided communication and comradeship with other departments. Tournaments had been held even before the turn of the century, with full schedules of contests testing various fire-fighting skills. In 1901, a new contest was of great interest at the Town of Hempstead tournament—a hook-and-ladder contest. The firemen were to run their trucks three hundred feet to an arch, raise a ladder, form a bucket line and fill a tank on top of the arch and return to the starting line. Obtaining proficiency in such an event developed the skills needed in fighting fires, and, as a contemporary indicated, these events "create a great deal of amusement, as generally several men get ducked with water."

The original 52 companies in the county grew to over 194 by 1940, including some 6,674 volunteer firemen throughout the county. There were 68 departments, some consisting of a half-dozen companies. Freeport's department was the largest in the county, with 7 companies and 350 men. Only Garden City had any paid firemen. Major changes took place in this growth, enabling the volunteer service to keep pace with the growing needs of the county. Better

firemen training was initiated and the regular schedule of tournaments was a competitive stimulus. Tournaments provided competition between villages and the rivalries between neighborhood companies, common before 1900, were diminished. Fire companies still pridefully retained their individuality, but increasing allegiance was directed to the village department. The better discipline and training enabled chiefs to direct efforts more effectively at conflagrations.

In 1926, the chiefs in the county organized a Fire Chiefs Council of Nassau County and established procedures for cooperation between adjoining fire districts. When the reorganization of county government was studied in the 1930s, an Executive Council of Firematic Associations was formed to coordinate the efforts of county firemen and provide citizen suggestions for the new county charter. The charter created a Nassau County Fire Commission in 1938 which divided the county in nine districts to be represented on the commission. The commission was responsible for the establishment of a countywide fire protection ordinance, enforcement of the ordinance and investigation of fires. It also developed a cover-up system of fire protection in which areas provided standby protection for others when they were engaged in fighting a fire. A separately administered training school for volunteers had previously been established, funded equally by the state and county. The commission's high standards and the cooperation of local departments created an ideal example of a locally administered volunteer public service reaching high quality through area-wide standards and training.

Since fire companies were private-membership organizations, fire protection districts were gradually formed throughout the county providing a tax base to raise funds for equipment and fire hydrant service. Companies still frequently raised their own funds to purchase equipment and houses, such as the Salamander Hook and Ladder Company of Oceanside, which obtained, through contributions, a new truck with a

Nassau County Fire Tournament at Great Neck, June 16, 1926.

A firemen's parade at Great Neck, 1928.

Horse-drawn hook and ladder of Freeport Excelsior Company.

New motorized equipment of Freeport Fire Department in 1920s.

thirty-five-foot ladder. In the 1920s regular aid began when a 2 per cent state tax on fire insurance premiums of out-of-state companies was returned to local fire companies.

Originally all these companies depended on horse-drawn equipment, and one of the major problems was acquisition of motorized equipment. By World War I, departments were beginning to acquire such vehicles, but not without some resistance. Hempstead had a new Ford chemical truck on order in 1915 when a bad fire hit the business district. Within twenty minutes two motorized hose wagons from Freeport were assisting them at the scene and "they came up so fast in their motors that . . . even old timers who had opposed a motorized department fell in line and begged for motors." Hempstead went on to obtain a splendid American La France pumper for $8,000 and three combination chemical and hose wagons. By the 1920s there was a definite rivalry between communities in obtaining superior equipment, and motorization quickly spread throughout the county. In 1928, at the annual Nassau County tournament, new records were set by Mineola, Westbury, Malverne, Syosset and Port Washington companies in motor hook-and-ladder, hose and pump contests.

While the companies were supplying good fire protection, they also functioned as active local social groups. Volunteers attended weekly meetings and socialized over good food, such as, in Hempstead: "When caterer Coles Johnson announced the stew as ready to be served, they fell to and ate everything in sight except Mr. Johnson and the dishes." The 1903 annual ball of the Lawrence-Cedarhurst Fire Department was attended by almost nine hundred people. President Theodore Roosevelt addressed the South New York Volunteer Firemen's Association meeting at Sigmond's Hall in Freeport in 1910, and the frequent tournaments were always major community events.

In 1922 the golden jubilee of the New York State Volunteer Firemen's Association was held at Freeport from August 14 to 19.

A great parade was held on August 18, with over five thousand fire fighters and equipment passing in review. The East Rockaway Department, resplendent in all-white uniforms, twenty-five bands, three drum corps, and the 116-piece New York City band were part of the five-hour parade that was one of the greatest gatherings of volunteer firemen in the United States. At that grand meeting, "Uncle Billy" Patterson, Freeport's oldest volunteer at a young seventy-nine years, reminisced: "In the old days they called us vamps because we 'vamped' a fire, that is, we ran after it. Nowadays they call the women vamps if they run after the fireman."

Besides the good fire protection these volunteer companies provided, the close contacts they afforded between neighbors and the interest in community affairs created an *esprit de corps* that was a major influence in the civic spirit of local villages. Due to the strong lines of communication between the great numbers of volunteers, it was almost mandatory for political leaders to have close ties with local departments. By 1940 fire protection in the county was provided by some 68 departments with 194 companies and almost 7,000 volunteers.

The years after World War I were marked by the creation of various community social organizations. Over thirty-four American Legion posts were organized after World War I by returning veterans. Literary societies, mutual benefit associations, the Odd Fellows, the Knights of Columbus, the Order of Mechanics, the Lions and Masonic lodges spread across the county. The Floral Park Women's Club was typical of the many women's groups, with activities which included literary evenings, charity fund raising, civic improvements, musicals, gardening, card parties, teas, luncheons and lectures.

Children were not overlooked and by the 1920s the Boy Scouts had become an outlet for young boys. F. Howard Covey, executive secretary of the Nassau County Council of Boy Scouting, which was chartered in Feb-

Boy Scouts from a Lawrence troop met with Theodore Roosevelt at Sagamore Hill. F. Howard Covey, long-time Scout leader, *second from left, and Scoutmaster Charles Hewlett to the right of Roosevelt.*

ruary of 1917, directed the activities of some 90 troops with 2,500 boys. The council conducted a summer camp on a six-hundred-acre tract at Wading River in Suffolk purchased for $180,000. Even Theodore Roosevelt had participated in local Scout activities and was a committeeman of Troop 39 at Oyster Bay. Girl Scouting also developed in the twenties after the first troop was created in Glen Cove. A Nassau County council was set up in 1923 under the leadership of Mrs. Ervin D. Johnson. However, due to organizational troubles in 1928, separate area councils were established for over five hundred girls in the Five Towns, south Nassau, central Nassau and north Nassau areas.

The new $200,000 clubhouse of the Freeport Lodge of Elks, constructed in 1925, was indicative of the great influence and scope of activity a club could wield. Organized in 1911 with 30 members, it had grown to over 2,500 members including the cream of the county's economic and political leadership.

A great many business and professional organizations were also formed in the 1920s, ranging from the Hempstead Town Liquor Dealers Association to the Empire Poultry Association. Almost every community had a local board of trade. The Nassau County Bar Association in Mineola provided social contact for lawyers, as the Long Island Real Estate Board Nassau Chapter, the Long Island Chamber of Commerce and the Long Island Society of Architects did for other professions. Many cultural groups were initiated, including women's clubs and the Nassau County Art League, which organized in 1926 with seventy-six members. An abortive attempt was even made to establish a county historical society in 1915, but residents were too busy building to be concerned with preserving the past.

The increasing organizational base of the county was apparent in the development of private welfare and health organizations. Community leaders actively supported such non-governmental attempts to assist directly less fortunate citizens and provide opportunities to broaden their knowledge and abilities. Several neighborhood associations were established in 1915 to provide a variety of local services. The Nassau Cottage Association, an outgrowth of the Nassau County Association, established a home for unwed mothers, and the Roslyn Neighborhood Association acquired the Valentine House in that community for programs ranging from adult classes to infant care and art.

Glen Cove's Neighborhood Association opened a community social center for over one thousand members with a full range of activities including Scout troops, cooking classes and a kindergarten. Late in 1920, the Lincoln Settlement House for blacks and the Orchard House for Italian residents provided additional social and recreational facilities in Glen Cove. In 1916 YMCA activities began, and the Red Cross, which had been chartered in May 1917, continued to function in many fields after the war. It provided nurses in public schools, clinics, disaster relief, junior activities, and opened a permanent headquarters in Mineola in 1928. A temporary home for children had been established in Mineola before the turn of the century, and in 1929, a new children's shelter was opened by the Nassau County branch of the Society for the Prevention of Cruelty to Children.

Private hospital facilities were first available in the county in July of 1900, when Nassau Hospital opened at Mineola. It was considerably expanded in 1926 with construction of a private pavilion and nurses' home to handle 175 beds. Glen Cove Community Hospital had been established in 1920 after a bad winter showed the need for closer facilities and opened in 1922 with nineteen patients.

The next year, the Nassau County Medical Society conducted a study of hospital needs in the county and showed the serious need for additional facilities. A fund of over $1 million was raised, and Glen Cove Community was expanded into an eighty-nine-

bed institution in 1927, with its name changed to North County Community Hospital. South Nassau Communities Hospital was opened the following year in Oceanside with seventy-six beds for south shore residents. From its beginning, the hospital depended upon extensive support provided by women's auxiliary units throughout the county. Long Beach Hospital, with forty beds, and Mercy Hospital for Roman Catholics were also established by 1930.

Even prior to World War I, the National Tuberculosis Association began to promote the sale of Christmas seals and one of its first areas was Nassau County. In 1913, Edward L. Bernays, one of the pioneer public relations men in America, "set out along cold, windy and empty Long Island roads, persuading ministers, doctors, social leaders and housewives in Nassau County to accept stamps for resale to the public." By the late 1920s, the Nassau County Tuberculosis and Public Health Association had successfully obtained public tuberculosis hospital facilities and was actively promoting programs to find early cases of the dreaded disease.

In 1922 the Welfare Federation of Nassau County was set up by over seven hundred members to make a countywide group appeal for charity funds. It had a goal of $80,000 and was to distribute its funds among the Scouts, the Wayside Home for Girls, Nassau County Association welfare work and various other charities. Lack of response, however, caused the agencies to rely on individual fund drives in future years. The proliferation of both social and welfare organizations had provided a complex structure of activities throughout the county by the 1940s. These private community-minded efforts characterized the developing suburban villages and were a principal means of developing neighborliness and community identification in addition to alleviating social problems.

A disruptive element entered the social scene on September 8, 1922, when a *Daily Review* banner headline screamed out, KU KLUX KLAN ORGANIZED. Hooded and white-robed members of the notorious KKK had held a meeting before over 150 people at Freeport. The principal speaker was a strange Southerner who allowed guests to stay for one half of the meeting. In a ranting speech, he attacked the politics, habits and method of living of Jews and predicted dire consequences from their ownership of the motion picture industry and control over newspaper advertising. The remainder of the meeting was secret. Thus began a nightmarish period when secret meetings and strange parades brought the specter of bigotry to Nassau County.

The Klan was immediately attacked in a vigorous editorial by the *Daily Review:*

. . . heads of Freeport's organizations admit that the Klan had no place in the life of that village or in fact anywhere in this county as its doings in other localities in the past have proved it to be un-American and made up of only persons of bigoted minds . . . Every man, woman or child, Protestant, Catholic and Jew should openly challenge entrance into their community of any organization such as the Klan.

However, the organization secretly continued to grow throughout the county, its activities reaching a height in the summer of 1924. For a whole week that warm August, the Klan held meetings on its own large lot on Prospect Street in Hempstead. Rev. William Hayward, a Klan organizer, spoke to six hundred people at the opening session and explained the organization's nature as a secret, religious order for Protestants. Carnival booths were well attended and special meetings were held nightly. Paul W. F. Lindner of Malverne, Exalted Cyclops of the local Ku Klux Klan, presided at the meetings. In a short talk, Lindner indicated the Klan's principles were free public schools, free press and reading of the Bible in public schools.

These surface aims of the group were innocuous and the general community disposition hoped the Klan would gradually fade away. The conclusion of Hempstead activi-

ties came on September 9, when in an evening ceremony lighted by a burning cross, the Klan presented an American flag to the Hempstead Methodist Church. Later in September a parade was held in Freeport with seven hundred Klansmen and numerous floats in the line of march. The night before, a women's meeting had been held with the New York State Kleagle and other notables presiding before an estimated ten thousand people. The Klan was now recognized as an important factor in the organization life of the village. Another large rally was held in Hicksville in 1925. Several thousand people viewed the hooded and masked paraders who marched as local groups, many carrying banners, although places of origin were not indicated. Stringent security precautions were taken at the meetings.

With only meager information about its activities available, it is difficult to ascertain the complete aims and results of the Klan in Nassau County. Shortly after its formation, Freeport village president Robert L. Christie received a complaint that black residents were being discriminated against and being prevented from renting or purchasing property on the north side of Freeport. Ku Klux Klan influence was alleged in confining blacks to the Bennington Park section of the village. There was also a cryptic suggestion in the 1924 school board election that the Ku Klux Klan should be credited with victory, although only one black was running out of nine candidates.

Although it reinforced undercover discrimination, the Klan did not make any open physical attacks. Its mysterious Konklaves, burning of crosses, and hooded parades were sufficient non-physical methods of harassment. There was one open incident on August 14, 1924, that received considerable publicity. Several Klansmen kidnapped Ernest Louis, a Jewish druggist in Freeport, and took him for a long drive out on the island and warned him to leave town. The same week he was charged with molesting a small girl and left the village under a cloud of suspicion.

Since Nassau's black citizens had increased less proportionally than any other segment of the population, they were probably less disturbing than the greatly increasing number of Jewish families that were moving into the area in the 1920s. Thus the Klan bigotry in Nassau was oriented against both blacks and Jews. Despite the flashes of vigor it demonstrated, the Klan received only a passive submissiveness from local residents and its general lack of support prevented any major disturbances or activities by its more rabid supporters. Under the glare of the unfavorable publicity engendered by national leaders, the local organization faded away although a hard core of Klansmen burned a cross in Roosevelt on the Fourth of July, 1928.

Nassau's social life in the early 1900s illustrates an increasing range of activities and change as varied as its extensive physical development. From elite parties for the Prince of Wales, to Boy Scouts meeting with Theodore Roosevelt on the lawn at Sagamore Hill, to a cross etching race hatred in a summer sky, the social structure of the county illustrated the best and worst of American society of the day. Due to the area's unique physical assets and the presence of many high-income families, special recreational pursuits were highly developed. Although participation in many of these activities was greatly restricted, the life-style of the wealthy was a forerunner of a new leisure-oriented population. The great increase in community service organizations fulfilled public needs and provided a medium for social interaction between recent and old residents. Their social life revolved around the newly developed village institutional structure of educational, civic and social organizations.

From polo action to a day at Jones Beach, (following page) Nassau life before World War II provided a wide variety of experiences.

Assemblyman Thomas McWhinney.

The old Merrick Road in the late 1800s.

CHAPTER V
THE SUNRISE HOMELAND

Transportation Influences Growth

There were no brass bands or great crowd of cheering citizens; only a few local businessmen and governmental officials gathered at a small luncheon to celebrate the opening of the first stretch of Sunrise Highway on November 1, 1928. The bright new ribbon of concrete from the city line to Lynbrook was only the beginning of this major highway's thrust across the south shore of Long Island. Residents gazed in wonder at the enormous concrete mixers and road-building equipment working alongside steady teams of horses drawing scrapers to prepare the road bed. There was little doubt in all minds that the automobile would play a major role in Nassau's future.

An aggressive community leader and assemblyman from Nassau County, Thomas McWhinney was hailed at the small gathering as "the father of Sunrise Highway." Constructed over the right of way of the New York City water conduit line running from its Long Island reservoirs, the highway's original name was to be Pipe Line Boulevard, but the Rockville Centre and Lynbrook Exchange Clubs boosted the name Sunrise due to promotion of the island as the "Sunrise Homeland." McWhinney was responsible for pushing the state legislation to construct the roadway. As Robert Moses recalled, it was McWhinney who "counted a quorum in the Assembly when the un-

practiced eye could discern only thirty out of some one hundred and fifty members in their seats . . . the clerk, a friend of Tom's, and a devotee of progress, read the title of the bill in Choctaw and it went to third reading without objection."

As early as 1907, the *South Side Observer* had suggested the need for such a parkway along the south shore to provide access to the many developing villages there. By World War I, Merrick Road, the old colonial post road along the waterfront, was highly congested and on fair-weather Sundays was jammed with vehicles. The straight, wide, pipeline right of way was an ideal route for a new roadway since it extended across the length of Nassau County from Brooklyn. Public meetings were held urging that a new highway be built in 1916, and optimism was high when Hempstead town supervisor Hiram R. Smith indicated he was in favor of building such a relief highway for Merrick Road and hoped to have the pipeline "made a part of the city system of roads, which will mean its improvement within a short time." The possibility became even stronger the next year when the aqueduct system was almost completely shut down since New York City had begun to receive water from its Catskill watershed.

The use of automobiles in Nassau County had developed slowly. Garden City boasted of a central fireproof garage for eighty cars in 1907, but most farmers still relied on horse-drawn vehicles. Automobiles had created a real safety problem and a great public furor arose over the injuries and deaths

The stream of traffic on Sunrise Highway in Freeport passes Nassau's new skyscraper in late 1920s.

resulting from reckless driving. In 1908, the Board of Supervisors passed a resolution urging magistrates to impose maximum penalties upon traffic offenders.

The rapid improvement and lower prices of automobiles after World War I, combined with the spectacular population growth from 126,120 residents in 1920 to 303,053 in 1930, caused a massive increase in motor vehicles. Better traffic enforcement helped alleviate the problem, but as the number of registered vehicles rose from 8,766 in 1916 to approximately 40,000 in 1922, and over 112,000 by 1930, adequate roads became a necessity. The almost 80,000 licensed drivers in 1930 found an automobile increasingly

a necessity to travel to local employment, stores and recreation areas.

The virtual lack of paved roads in the county, outside of a few village streets and a few main county arteries, was recognized as a pressing governmental problem. Even Merrick Road, Jericho Turnpike, Bethpage Turnpike and other main arteries were narrow two-lane roads with poor macadam surfaces in need of much repair. Road construction, however, depended on local revenues and the sums needed for really good roads were enormous. The financing of road construction became the essential core of the problem. A continuous controversy raged in the county over the question of obtaining large funds through long-term bond issues to construct complete roadways, or continuing to perform small amounts of road work within current available revenues. The solution was further complicated by the various jurisdictions of the different levels of local government and the unwillingness of each to accept the tax burden.

William K. Vanderbilt II had shown that a fine road could be constructed when he built the Long Island Motor Parkway between 1908 and 1914. It was the finest road of the time, made of reinforced concrete with a bituminous top, and ran from Nassau's western border to Ronkonkoma in Suffolk County—a forty-eight-mile stretch of private roadway twenty feet wide. In the 1920s, more than 150,000 cars used the parkway, but the daily one-dollar tickets collected at its twelve toll lodges were never sufficient to pay expenses. It was apparent that roads would have to be provided by government.

By now, long lines of traffic were an accustomed sight along the south shore, particularly on weekends during the summer, such as August 20, 1922, when visiting relatives from the city jammed the roads and 1,687 cars passed westbound on Merrick Road in Rockville Centre between 5 and 6 P.M. Residents viewed the increasing traffic with wonder and Alonzo Gibbs, then a young boy in Valley Stream, recalled, "We used to sit in an open touring car on Sunday nights eating ice cream cones and watching the traffic flow by. It was all new, all entertaining."

The critical nature of the problem transgressed local boundaries, and legislators obtained state action. The New York State legislature created the Long Island State Park Commission in 1924 and it was given authority to acquire, improve and operate parkways in addition to parks. In cooperation with the county governments on Long Island, the state government also began a major roadway construction program beginning with the Sunrise Highway improvement. Construction was scheduled in 1926

and in June of 1927, the $1,398,757 paving contract was awarded, with the state contributing 65 per cent and the counties 35 per cent of the project's cost. In addition, other major roads, including Jericho Turnpike, Hempstead Turnpike, North Hempstead Turnpike and Merrick Road, were widened and paved with concrete.

The Long Island State Park Commission, guided by Robert Moses, began to develop far-reaching plans for a network of parkways on the island. Its plans for a through parkway along the north shore ran into a hornet's nest of opposition. Residents contended it would be an "outlet to hordes of motorists" descending on Nassau. The large-estate owners who were most affected attempted to persuade the commission to use the old Motor Parkway route rather than a new right of way, but were unsuccessful. Their planning expert, Charles Downing Lay, criticized the plans and disputed the need for such wide highways along the north shore. He urged the county Board of Supervisors to study the problem and formulate countywide park and road plans if the unique character of Nassau was to be preserved. The commission eventually modified its route plan and Moses secured the cooperation of the wealthy landowners, who in return donated over 60 per cent of the land required for the right of way for the Northern State Parkway.

Along the south shore, the parkway system grew rapidly and the Southern State Parkway was under construction several miles north of Sunrise Highway. It was a major roadway restricted to pleasure traffic. The right of way, 160 feet wide through mostly wooded areas, was a scenic route to the area's new state parks at Valley Stream, Hempstead, Jones Beach and Belmont Lake. The parkway also provided quicker access to the burgeoning south shore villages. By the late 1920s, the county was also undertaking major projects including the improvement of cross-island roads such as Long Beach Road, Nassau Road, North Village Avenue and Middle Neck Road. After 1929, highway construction was greatly increased, since the

First electric train is welcomed to East Rock-away station, 1910.

county began to receive large refunds from the state as the county's share of the gasoline tax.

Despite the increase of vehicular traffic, the most important transportation means contributing to Nassau's growth was still the Long Island Rail Road. The fast access it provided to New York City and Brooklyn enabled suburban living for thousands of city workers. George Le Boutillier, vice-president of the railroad, was not excessively boasting in 1925 when he claimed the "fast, clean, adequate electric passenger train service on the LIRR for more than a generation . . . is primarily responsible for the marvelous growth, residentially, industrially and otherwise, that Long Island has enjoyed for many years past and continues to enjoy at the present time."

Electrification of the railroad's lines was a major factor in providing better service. Ralph Peters served as president of the Long Island from 1905 until his death in 1923. During this period he actively pushed electrification and obtained the investment of over $50 million in capital improvements. In

The Long Island State Park Commission preserved the rural atmosphere in constructing its parkways such as Northern State.

September of 1910, Pennsylvania Station was opened and through traffic to New York began a new era for commuters. This was a major stimulus to commutation and a new passenger station at Jamaica was required for the increased traffic. By 1918 the central line was electrified to Hempstead and the Long Island Rail Road was soon the most electrified trunk line in the nation. The entire Montauk division along the south shore to Babylon was included by 1925, allowing more elastic schedules, more trains and easier handling of increased numbers of passengers.

After through service began, commutation jumped dramatically. Along the north shore, Great Neck and Port Washington increased from 132 and 128 commuters in 1911 to 626 and 857 in 1923. In the next decade the population expansion jumped commutation at these stations to 1,306 and 1,074 people. Similar increases occurred on the south shore line in Freeport and Rockville Centre, which had 475 and 589 commuters in 1911 and by 1923 some 2,211 and 1,751. Many villages leaped ahead in the 1920s, such as Rockville Centre, which by 1929 had over 3,000 commuters, and Floral Park, where eighty trains carried 2,582 people daily to the city. By 1930 there were over 30,000 commuters using the railroad daily from Nassau County to city destinations.

Although service was constantly improving, commuters were never quite satisfied. In 1903 a permanent Commuters Association was formed by twenty-five residents of Freeport for their "mutual protection and to procure better train facilities." Since there was little increase in fares even during the rising costs of the 1920s, the cost of commutation was not then a major problem or complaint but delays and schedules were always a concern. A typical fare was $11 for a sixty-trip monthly ticket from Hempstead. Residents realized the importance of the railroad and Port Washington staged one of its largest celebrations on June 23, 1923, to commemorate the twenty-fifth anniversary of train service there. Over ten thousand people watched hundreds of marchers, bands and firemen parade to honor the reliable daily transporter of the family wage earners. It was unavoidable that with the great number of people dependent upon the line for daily transportation, the irregularities of train schedules became a distinct part of local folklore. But despite all the complaints and jokes about delays and changing trains at Jamaica, the railroad occupied a major and rather well-loved role in the life of Nassau County. Christopher Morley indicated this affection when he wrote, "Good old Oyster Bay Branch, I'm the only one who never grumbles about it. Woodsworth on Windermere (or Whitman on Timber Creek) had no better pleasures than I when I see the 9:30 blow for the bend of Harbor Hill and clank into the station at Salamis [Roslyn]."

Intracounty transportation developments had also kept pace with other changes. Throughout 1900, several groups of local and outside businessmen attempted to organize electric street railway lines and obtain approval from all the local governments concerned in the county. Finally after over a year of bitter rivalry, the county Board of Supervisors gave approval to the Mineola, Hempstead and Freeport Traction Company to lay track.

Construction started that summer, though not without some local difficulties. August Belmont, Jr., and H. Van Rensselaer Kennedy blocked work in front of their properties in Hempstead, claiming the trolley would be a "public nuisance." Belmont, who usually was a leader in community improvements, was chided for this stand by the local newspaper, which stated in shocked terms: "to believe that he is personally identified with a plot to block the trolley seems almost incredible . . . the trolley is a necessity and ought to be built."

The company overcame the opposition and track construction continued, particularly after the line was purchased by Cleveland interests, who supplied a new infusion of funds. On May 16, the streamlined olive-brown trolley, with gold striping and dazzling red plush seats, made its first run from Hempstead to Freeport. It was a great initial success and seemed to be "increasing trade and giving indication of activity." Within five years the renamed New York and Long Island Traction Company had completed an interurban network through fourteen towns and villages with a main line of twenty-four miles and several seven-mile branches into Queens. A controlling interest in the line had been obtained by the Long Island Rail Road in 1903, and it planned future development so as not to conflict with the railroad lines. In 1907 the last north-south segment was completed, linking Old Country Road and Jericho Turnpike.

On the north shore, local leaders organized the Mineola, Roslyn and Port Washington Traction Company in 1902. Through careful planning and outside funding, they avoided opposition and received a complete franchise in 1903. Additional funds required several reorganizations, and finally in 1907, the New York and North Shore Traction Company began work on a line between Roslyn and Mineola. Car barns were located on Northern Boulevard outside Roslyn and service to Port Washington began February 1, 1908. By 1910 the line had been extended through Port Washington to Flushing and

The first trolley car arrives at Freeport.

Trolley car on Main Street in Hempstead.

easterly from Mineola to Hicksville. Since this line traversed rather rugged terrain, it suffered badly in poor weather and had to fight a constant battle to operate during winter storms. From 1913 to 1920, its business gradually dropped on the Nassau section of the line. Poor finances and power troubles finally spelled the end of the line in May of 1920.

The New York and Long Island was at the height of its prosperity from 1913–17. Great activity in Hempstead due to Camp Mills stimulated receipts with revenues of $500,000, but income took a nose dive after the war. Rising labor costs and a continual succession of mechanical and power troubles, climaxed by disastrous fires at both the Hempstead and Rockville Centre car barns,

put the line into receivership in 1923. It limped along until Easter Sunday, April 4, 1926, when the last trolley clacked down the line through Nassau. Only a few residents mourned the demise of the ten-cent ride from Freeport to Mineola on the clattering trolleys, but they were fun to ride!

Trolleys were unable to solve their technical problems and had to compete with a new means of intracounty transportation that had developed after World War I. During the war, some bus service had operated on an informal basis in Hempstead and Garden City to transport servicemen. There were attempts to continue this after the war but higher operating costs and legal action by the county's traction companies blocked initial efforts. In 1923, Richard Semke received a franchise for a bus line between Rockville Centre and Hempstead for a twenty-cent fare and began successful operations. In the previous year, Bee Line, Inc., had been established with two buses to provide service to Queens County. The Hempstead Bus Company began a route in 1925 and soon had six buses running between Mineola and Freeport.

The bus lines expanded rapidly during the boom years of the 1920s. By 1930 Bee Line had a large new garage in Rockville Centre and its seventy-passenger buses provided twenty-four-hour-a-day service from Jamaica to Hempstead and Freeport. The Hempstead Bus Company was then operating twenty-three buses, and the Semke Line, Schenck Transportation Company and five other small operators covered various routes throughout the county. These bus lines provided adequate internal transportation needed by the county's population at that time. Trolley development in the early 1900s, followed by the bus lines, provided fairly rapid means of travel from one community to another and greatly aided transportation of workers and shoppers in the developing county.

The close relationship between improved transportation and community expansion was recognized by local residents soon after the turn of the century as the trolley companies combated to lay lines across the county and the railroad tunnels under the East River were a promise of through traffic to Manhattan. The *South Side Observer* rhapsodized, "The future for Long Island real estate and Nassau County in particular looks very bright." Dependent upon commuter traffic, the Long Island Rail Road played a major role in promoting local real estate and development on the island. Although its exhibit in the 1903 Sportsmen's Show at Madison Square Garden was a diorama of a Great South Bay scene complete with hunter's shack and boat, the message was simple and direct—come to live on Long Island and enjoy its recreational pleasures all year round! It spread the message in leaflets, maps, booklets, posters and every way then conceived by promoters, proclaiming, "Long Island is unique; its beauty grows upon one . . . and every month spent in the land of the Sunrise Trails is new to the gaze in the changing hues of the foliage and the altering light of the skies."

Promotion concentrated first on the older-established villages along the rail lines, and they were imbued with individual characteristics. Freeport was the ideal home for the New York businessman—substantial character, conservative; while Garden City was recognized as taking care in admitting new residents, and its families typified the high-est standards of American citizenry. The rail-road even recognized that many workmen desired homes in a rural setting and promoted development in New Hyde Park since "many could find employment in local industries and villages. There has always been plenty of work for gardeners, mechanics, masons, carpenters and the like."

Elephants were used during Long Beach construction in 1914, which included a long boardwalk along the ocean beach.

Overriding all the appeals was the continual emphasis on the easy accessibility to the waterfront and the long beaches, "as smooth as ivory and almost as white. No quicksands, here, but good, honest, hearty noisy breakers pounding on beaches hard as adamant! Nowhere on the Atlantic Coast are there greater reaches of white sand." The attraction of the sea was a great magnet. To a young Whittaker Chambers growing up as a boy in Lynbrook, life was engulfed by "the tremendous presence at its edge of the ocean, with its separating miles of salt marsh. Inland, too, the sea was always around us. Sometimes as fog . . . sometimes it came as sound—the terrible sound of the surf pouring without pause on the beaches seven miles away. I used to hear it while I tried to fall asleep." To a grown-up Christopher Morley it had the ringing appeal of nature at its best and thoughts "of old Walt and his lonely ecstasies on Long Island beaches, shouting Homer and Shakespeare to the surf and the gulls. I think of the woody prom-

ontories of Lloyd Neck, of canals and shell-fish smells." The sea had its effect on all who came out and was without question one of the special appealing elements of life in Nassau County.

In response to the promotion, people came in ever increasing numbers, filling the vacant areas in older communities, and causing new villages to rise on former farm fields. In 1907 the Long Beach Improvement Company received clear title to that resort area and began development of a year-round community and vacation resort. William Reynolds directed the dredging of tremendous quantities of sand to fill in its meadows and swampy areas, even using elephants in the herculean task. The grand Nassau Hotel was erected and soon a fifty-foot-wide boardwalk was filled with promenaders on sunny days.

In 1912 Malverne was a sparsely settled farming area when realtor Alfred H. Wagg organized the Amsterdam Development and Sales Company and purchased eight farms,

then under cultivation, for real estate development. By 1920 Malverne was the smallest incorporated village in New York State with over one hundred dwellings, a school and churches grouped around the railroad line. New communities clustered along the railroad tracks, receiving their sustaining infusion of people from its rushing commuter trains. New stations were established, such as Nassau Boulevard, just west of Garden City. In 1906 it was the center of a one-square-mile tract of empty plains lands sold for $1,500,000 by the Garden City Company to a private group that developed the Garden City Estates community there. Its wide streets, extensive parking, attractive building lots and open park areas converged on the central railroad station.

Along the north shore, the Great Neck peninsula received the heaviest influx of new residents and was aggressively developed by realtors and city businessmen such as New York City mayor W. R. Grace, who owned considerable property in the area. Exclusive communities such as Kensington were created almost overnight. Incorporated in 1917, it was developed by Charles E. Finlay, who planned two hundred individual parcels of land with complete rural privacy on a 135-acre site. The great importance of the railroad to new communities was also clearly evident in William R. Gibson's development near Valley Stream. In three years after 1925, he built 725 houses on 700 acres. As the community matured, the need for a railroad station became so urgent, Gibson built a new station in 1929 at a cost of $54,000 and turned it over to the railroad.

Small-Town Society

The great infusion of population following this promotion not only created entire villages of new residents but drastically changed the composition of older villages. A Port Washington resident observing this in 1910 commented, "Our village is gradually being converted from a quaint old fisheries town into a purely high class residential section. Our oystermen of the past have gone into business of some other kind or are working as craftsmen. Our population is largely made up of New York businessmen." John Radigan noticed this change in 1927 when he was in the crowd watching Roslyn's schoolhouse burn down. The town had grown so, that very few of the faces in the crowd were familiar to him. Only thirty years before, however, when he followed the clang of the fire engine to the fire of the schoolhouse in 1897, he knew every child and grownup.

The county's population had increased slowly from 1900 to 1920 with the major increase occurring in the Town of Hempstead, which had 70,790 out of 126,120 county residents. In the next ten years, both Hempstead and North Hempstead doubled their population to 192,552 and 62,202 respectively. Oyster Bay Town had a much less vigorous growth to only 48,299 residents. Within a short period of thirty years, the county's population grew from 55,448 to 303,053 residents.

Despite this great increase, the population still retained a great deal of homogeneity, and undoubtedly this was a major factor in ameliorating any problems in the relocation of so many people. Native white residents comprised 74.1 per cent of the population in 1910 and rose slightly to 76.3 per cent in 1930. Black residents decreased slightly in the same period, from 2.8 per cent to 2.6 per cent, which was a little lower than the statewide percentage of 3.5 per cent in 1930. Foreign-born residents, who constituted less than a quarter of the population throughout the period, did evidence some change in place of origin. In 1910, English, Scottish, Welsh and Irish immigrants made up the largest percentage, followed closely by German natives. Italian and Russian groups were about equal, with Scandinavian natives the least populous. By 1930, German foreign-born residents now led, trailed by those of Italian origin, and Irish, English and Polish nationals of similar numbers.

The most visible impact this strong infusion of immigrant groups had was upon the religious activity of the county. Increasing numbers of Irishmen, Italians, Germans and Poles had caused continual expansion of the Roman Catholic Church, which doubled in parishes to thirty-seven in 1930. Nassau County was part of the Brooklyn Diocese, which was led by Bishop Charles E. McDonnell from 1892 to 1921. St. Hedwig's Roman Catholic Church in Floral Park was a typical immigrant parish of the period, with about 75 per cent of the parishioners of Polish origin. Organized in 1905, it constructed a church school the next year, and in 1922 built a new twelve-room school.

The Very Reverend Lawrence Fuchs, pastor of St. Ignatius Church in Hicksville from 1872 to 1923, was one of the most active and widely beloved Catholic priests. The entire community closed in mourning the day of his funeral. Regina Teresa Sherwood of Glen Cove was a prominent Catholic lay figure extremely active in St. Patrick's parish and school activities. She was also a supporter of Catholic Charities and was created a Papal Marchioness in 1919. The Catholic Church strongly emphasized the development of its own parochial school system and was also developing a broad program of social work under Bishop Thomas E. Molloy in the late 1920s for the county's 45,000 Catholic residents. These new residents and the church leadership actively entered community life.

The Lutheran Church also underwent tremendous expansion with the increase of people of German and Scandinavian descent. There had been a Lutheran church in Hicksville, which was settled by German immigrants in the mid-1800s, but after 1897 additional congregations were established throughout the county in almost every major village. Freeport had the largest Lutheran congregation of the twenty-two in the county in 1928, with six hundred members

St. Mary's Roman Catholic Church in Manhasset.

Temple of the Nassau Hebrew congregation built in 1914 in Rockville Centre.

and a large building valued at $186,000. Many of the Lutheran churches began as missions, such as Port Washington's, which met in a converted barracks moved from Camp Mills. There were two principal Lutheran churches. The Missouri Synod included most parishes along the north shore and in the center of the county, while the

United Lutheran Church was larger and covered more populous areas on the south shore.

Another major change that reflected new elements in the population was the establishment of Jewish temples. In 1900 only one Jewish congregation existed in the county, Tifereth Israel in Glen Cove, which had been organized the year before. Other congregations were established in Rockville Centre, Long Beach, Lynbrook, Freeport, Hicksville and Great Neck by 1930. Temple Israel in Freeport was the largest group, with about 150 members.

Methodism continued to be the largest Protestant church but was now trailed closely by the Episcopal Church. The Freeport Methodist Church led Methodist congregations with 1,360 members and an annual operating budget of $85,000. By 1930 there were thirty-one Episcopal churches in the county, matching the Methodist total which included five black Methodist congregations. Presbyterian congregations had doubled between 1900 and 1930 to eighteen churches, as did Baptist churches, which numbered eleven. In the 1920s new religious thinking led to the formation of seven Christian Science centers and thirteen Congregational churches. The older Friends Meetings and Reformed Dutch churches had not grown, and remained at the same level as they were in 1900. Many of the Protestant churches established separate missions for blacks and by 1930 there were twelve black churches in the county—three in Hempstead, two in Freeport and Glen Cove, and one each in North Bellmore, Oyster Bay, Port Washington, Rockville Centre and Westbury.

Although churches were expanding rapidly, the great influx of people had created demands beyond their control. The Right Reverend Ernest M. Stires, Episcopal Bishop of Long Island, in his annual address in 1926, stated the problem: "The incoming tides of population are developing villages into towns, and towns into cities within a few weeks and months. Not only is the church failing to keep pace with this tremendous development but we are unable to claim that we are even attempting to deal with it in an intelligent and statesmanlike fashion." It was difficult for the denominations to plan locations of future churches, and there was the constant problem of competitive Protestant fund raising in new communities where the residents were generally burdened with high home mortgages.

The increasing materialism of the times also reduced parishioners. Many Protestant churches met the problem by extending their activities to provide recreational and fellowship pursuits for members so that their life could revolve more fully around the church. Larger churches such as St. George's Episcopal Church in Hempstead constructed gymnasiums. St. George's included a swimming pool, basketball court and other equipment. The church hummed with social activities, and "the thunder from the bowling alleys,

St. George's Episcopal Church in Hempstead.

the whirl of the Indian clubs and the click of the pool balls were most alluring and cast their spell over the entire village." By the end of the twenties a great deal of the fervor to make the church an active social recreation center had diminished and the same commentator was "happy to see that we are coming back to it [religion]."

Church activities, to a considerable extent, centered around the special Sunday school programs which provided religious instruction for both young and old. They were enormously popular and the annual Sunday school parades and picnics attracted thousands of participants and were eagerly awaited community events. Despite the trend toward church encouragement of recreational and social activities, strong elements of puritanism still existed. Individual churches often brought pressure on political leaders concerning ethical issues. The Freeport Presbyterian Church Session passed resolutions urging the banning of prize fights in the county in 1910 and several years later passed a resolution against motion pictures on the Sabbath.

Many churches expressed concern about keeping the Sabbath for religious activities and frowned on business openings and even baseball games. In 1917 the churches of the county were also successful in establishing a temperance zone around Camp Mills. Despite this role and the principal part it played in many residents' lives, religion no longer held the central role and influence it possessed in the late nineteenth century. By 1930, the extensive growth of other social and welfare activities, clubs and organizations had split the loyalties and interests of many individuals, and the church now had to compete actively for the participation of villagers.

Throughout the early 1900s, the educational system of the county continued to expand in size and importance. By 1930 the school district had become the central institution of local community life. School systems were the largest community institutions, required the largest share of public

funds and received the greatest amount of continual community attention and participation. The county's fifty thousand pupils in 1930 gave almost every family and resident a direct interest in school affairs. As an organization generally cutting across political, economic and religious affiliations, local schools provided a common meeting ground of interest to all segments of the local village.

In 1915 the sixty-three independent school districts in the county had a total of 14,636 students. The rapid growth after World War I up to 1930 was reflected in a corresponding 300 per cent increase in school population. Providing the necessary physical facilities for these pupils was the major problem and focus of action in education. There was also an acceleration of the development of high schools, which began before the turn of the century, and several joint high school facilities were developed.

A major new factor in Nassau's local educational system was the creation of an extensive school system by the Roman Catholic Church in the county. Fostered by their desire for a religiously oriented education,

St. Agnes parochial school in Rockville Centre.

Construction of Westbury High School in 1935.

Catholic parishes rapidly constructed grade schools to provide religious educational facilities for their growing congregations. By 1930 there were nineteen parochial grade schools with 6,300 students and three high schools in Rockville Centre, Great Neck and Oyster Bay for 364 students. The schools were completely supported by church and private funds with teachers drawn from the ranks of various religious orders. These schools provided a significant number of new classrooms and relieved the pressure created by the increasing school-age population on the public school systems.

There were still twenty-eight school districts with schools of four or less rooms, including seven one-room schools, in the rural areas of the Town of Oyster Bay in 1915. The rapid population influx of the twenties soon changed that, and by 1922 the *Daily Review* observed that "In all the villages of this county there was a large registration of school children and not a few of the villages have a serious problem in finding seats for all of those who seek to enter."

Mineola was a typical community facing such problems and had begun third grades on a part-time basis as early as 1920. By 1923, every grade level was on such a limited schedule despite several school building additions. Continued overcrowding caused the school board to purchase four portable classrooms in 1925. Other districts either reduced the length of classes or, in some cases, extended the hours of teachers so that more children could be accommodated.

The only real answer to the problem was the construction of new facilities. Some districts, affected by earlier growth, had built feverishly before the war, such as Freeport, which constructed three grammar schools between 1907 and 1915. Everywhere the construction programs met some resistance due to the increased tax costs. Since each school district was an independent governmental body, its residents had to approve the expenditures of funds for new construction. Community controversies over new school buildings were a continual, divisive element in local villages.

The new Glen Cove High School in 1939.

In 1922 when Rockville Centre was considering a new high school, a large audience attended the school board meeting held to explain the project. During the ensuing public discussion, tempers flared and "at least one person fainted. The local police were called to keep the meeting from getting out of hand." Despite this uproar, the measure carried by a vote of 422 to 228. And so it was in many other communities—despite battles over the needs and merits of new buildings, a steady stream of construction went ahead, providing fine new school buildings all over the county.

As the local school systems became larger, newer organizational techniques were developed to provide adequate administration. An important change was the increasing number of districts which had independent school superintendents. State law provided the basic regulations governing education, with the county school superintendent exercising administrative authority. Once a district exceeded 4,500 residents, a school board could appoint its own superintendent

and independently administer its system. Other districts came under the control of one of the two supervisory districts in the county. In 1930 the First Supervisory District, under Superintendent Ambrose J. Fry, covered thirty-four districts in the towns of Oyster Bay and North Hempstead. Roslyn, Port Washington, Great Neck, Glen Cove, Hicksville, Westbury, Mineola and Oyster Bay were individual superintendency districts and, with three of the other districts, provided high schools for the whole area. Sixteen of the districts were still common school districts while the remainder were union free districts.

Wellington C. Mepham, a prominent leader in local education, was superintendent of the Second Supervisory District, which covered the Town of Hempstead's thirty-one large school districts. This area included independent superintendencies in Hempstead, Freeport, Baldwin, Oceanside, Malverne, Woodmere, Lawrence, Lynbrook, Rockville Centre and Long Beach. It also included five common school districts. The school

Sewanhaka Central High School.

centage to over 97 per cent of the children under fifteen years by 1930. However, there was still a large fall-off in the upper age brackets and only 59 per cent of the sixteen- and seventeen-year-olds continued to attend school in the county. Because of the inconvenience of traveling out of their districts to nearby high schools and the lure of full-time jobs, many eighth-grade graduates did not continue on to high school.

Although many districts did provide high school facilities, the problems connected with their construction and financing by individual districts led to persistent proposals for more efficient school organization in the county. As early as 1915, the New York State legislature considered proposals to create townwide school boards and abolish local boards. However, public opposition was reflected in newspaper headlines that screamed LEAVE SCHOOLS ALONE and no action was taken. In 1918 an extensive survey of the schools in Nassau County was completed by the State Education Department. The report examined thoroughly the cost of education and the great differences in costs between districts with little regard to their ability to pay. The report indicated the high costs of administration and building upkeep by individual districts. It concluded with a strong recommendation for the establishment of a single countywide school district. The proposal met a solid wall of indifference, however, and there was no public support evidenced for it.

districts ranged in size from Wheatley, which actually had no school but contracted out its pupils to nearby districts; to Jericho and Island Trees, which had one-room schools; to Lawrence, the county's largest district, with five schools. Lawrence's teaching staff of 143 instructed 3,700 students with a district budget in 1929 totaling $585,051.

In addition to the area's population increase, school growth was stimulated by much better student attendance. Although the statistics are not highly reliable, due to poor teachers' records and inadequate census reports, there was a steady improvement in the attendance of school-age children. In 1900 probably not more than 80 per cent of the eligible children attended school. Gradual improvement and the expansion of high school programs had increased the per-

Local educators were not entirely unaware of certain advantages from consolidation and developed the concept of centralized high school districts in the late 1920s. Through this technique, districts could still retain local control over elementary grade schools and jointly establish a better high school than each could provide individually. By 1930, Valley Stream Central District and Sewanhaka High School, a district composed of Bellerose, Floral Park, Elmont, Franklin Square and New Hyde Park, were in existence. The central high school districts received support since they could employ specialists in all subjects and provide more comprehensive courses for students.

Districts also realized that if school district lines could be redrawn, many inconveniences would be relieved. The original drafting of districts was done by state law in the early 1800s, and the original geographical considerations setting boundaries had now been outmoded by the growth of villages. In most cases, village lines didn't correspond with school districts. The Malverne School District was a typical example, covering parts of three villages. The districts did not possess the authority to change their boundary lines and the complications of relocations between districts, and continually changing residential and business development, made agreement on changes difficult. Legislation was therefore impossible to secure and the resulting confusion could not be cleared.

Financing was a continual problem, particularly due to the upward-spiraling costs of education. State aid was very nominal, and in 1918 provided about 5 per cent of the local education costs. It was based on grants of $125 for the first teacher, $100 for each additional teacher, $20 for each high school student and a quota amount based on pupil attendance. Countywide educational costs were over $900,000 that year, with an average cost of $51.27 per pupil. Real estate tax rates per hundred dollars of assessed valuation varied greatly from district to district, from $.18 in Jerusalem (District No. 5) to $2 in Hicksville (District No. 17), with the countywide average $.715 per $100 of assessed valuation.

By 1920 the average tax rate had climbed to $1.24, and per pupil costs to $86.51. That year, $2,299,633 in taxes were levied for school purposes and the total multiplied in the next ten years to $18,705,283. The cost per pupil skyrocketed to $295.38 by 1930, and the average tax rate now slightly exceeded $2 per $100 of assessed valuation. The great increase in total assessed valuation, due to commercial and residential expansion, made possible much higher per pupil expenditures without a corresponding increase in the tax rate percentage. Despite this factor, school debts due to new construction had increased tenfold to over $34 million. The costs of education greatly exceeded the total of all other governmental services in the county, and despite surges of great interest at times of building propositions, there was a remarkable inconsistency of interest by the public in view of the amounts of tax funds involved. School district elections usually drew only a small number of eligible voters—indicative of the degree of apathy by residents who were basically satisfied with school services.

The professionalization of teaching staffs, which had developed by the turn of the century, continued in the early 1900s. Although Dr. James Cooley, county school commissioner in 1908, complained about low salaries and the competition of New York City, which gave teachers "permanent positions at comfortable and annually increasing salaries," there was continual improvement in teaching staffs. By World War I, salaries averaged $760 for elementary teachers and $935 for high school teachers, with a typical increment being $50 a year. There were almost two thousand teachers in the county's schools in 1930. Annual replacements and additional positions due to expansion required continual recruitment of teachers. Although the financial problem of obtaining teacher staffs was no longer as pressing as it once was, employment of sufficient numbers of well-trained and educated teachers was still a problem. Professional leadership was very high in the county, particularly among the new young school superintendents. Educators Truesdale P. Calkins in Hempstead, John W. Dodd in Freeport, Paul D. Schreiber in Port Washington and Williams S. Covert in Rockville Centre provided strong professional guidance and imaginative administration of burgeoning school programs.

The development of junior and senior high schools greatly broadened school curriculum. Home economics, vocational training and a greatly expanded science curriculum were introduced in the schools. Every

Hempstead school orchestra practicing in early 1920s.

district offered musical instruction and many were developing good internal library facilities. Commercial branches were added to most high schools and provided typewriting, stenography and business instruction. Attention was being given to student health —all schools had nurse service and most were providing physical education programs. School usage was also expanded, and as early as 1915, Freeport began to hold summer school sessions for special work.

By 1930 a decade of school expansion had slowed down and even Mineola's schools were back on a full-time schedule. Despite community disputes over "wasteful and extravagant" schools, local realtors throughout the county applauded the virtues of the local school systems and newcomers were always appraised of the good schools that existed in the county. These individual school districts, despite their problems, were well staffed and provided their students with very adequate training. One satisfied student with a more developed critical sense than most, Whittaker Chambers, recalled: "The rudiments of knowledge were taught

simply and thoroughly. I was given a grounding that served me well throughout life."

An interesting side development in education was the growth of parent-teacher organizations in the county. In 1918 only two schools out of thirty-four districts had such groups, but by 1926 almost every district had a group. On November 11, 1925, the Long Island District of the parent-teacher association held its first district conference in Floral Park. The parent-teacher associations took an active part in urging the improvement and expansion of school programs such as manual training and school lunches, while they also branched out into providing special activities for children such as Saturday motion pictures to discourage attendance at unsuitable movies.

Growth of public libraries was at a somewhat slower pace than public school development. The half-dozen small libraries at the turn of the century had expanded to twenty-one libraries by 1930. Lacking the professionalism of public education, the libraries were organized in a variety of ways

Roslyn girls volleyball team, 1923.

and were still searching for adequate standards and organizational methods. Many were closely related to the local school system, as in Glen Cove. Its public library was actually part of the school district, with a separate board composed of two members elected by the school board and three members elected by the public. This library, as many others, operated in a local schoolroom. Many communities had free libraries that depended upon public contributions and special fund raising for their resources. Hicksville's library was established after a citizen meeting in 1926, and the Hicksville Musical Club provided over $1,200 for the initial purchase of books.

Gradually separate independent public library buildings were erected, particularly with the aid of Carnegie funds. The newest library in 1930 was the Lynbrook Public Library, which had been built the previous year at a cost of $72,500. It is an example of the continual change in library organizations as the supporters of such facilities attempted to find the proper method and adequate means to achieve good library re-

sources. First organized in 1913, a voluntary founder's committee of twelve women nurtured the library until it received a state charter in 1924. It then became a public library with a five-thousand-volume collection under a village board of trustees and was able to obtain tax funds for its new

Lynbrook Public Library.

building, capable of holding twenty thousand volumes.

Glen Cove's and Lynbrook's libraries both possessed about fourteen thousand volumes in 1930, and libraries in Freeport, Great Neck, Hempstead, Oyster Bay, Port Washington and Rockville Centre had collections exceeding eight thousand books. Other libraries ranged down in size to Glenwood Landing with two thousand volumes. In addition to the attempts to provide adequate organizations to administer and support public libraries, there was a movement beginning to develop professional leadership. In May of 1915, the first annual Conference of Librarians of Nassau County and Queens was held at the Rockville Centre Public Library. Librarians and interested volunteers pointed out the importance of supplying books the public wanted and the need to visit schools to interest children in reading. The founding of a community library was usually taken as a sign of community maturity and people within the county were beginning to realize the educational and recreational benefits of library facilities.

Development of higher educational facilities was very slow in the county and students had to attend colleges out of the area. In 1912 the New York State legislature approved the creation of a New York State School of Agriculture to be located at Farmingdale, on the eastern edge of Nassau County. The state purchased 314 acres of land at an average price of $306 an acre,

and a Board of Trustees under President H. A. Reeves of Greenport began to plan the institution. An initial appropriation of $440,000 was provided by the legislature for buildings and equipment for the planned enrollment of eight hundred resident students and four hundred day students. The school was soon producing technically trained graduates. Its agricultural sciences curriculum included vegetable raising, animal husbandry, dairying, horticulture, agronomy, poultry raising and domestic science.

For college or professional training, local students had to go away to colleges until 1929. In 1927, Adelphi College, a women's college in Brooklyn, reconsidered its location and decided to relocate farther out on Long Island to provide for the area's needed college facilities. A million-dollar fund drive was initiated and Frederick W. Rowe, chairman of a special committee, picked a sixty-five-acre site in Garden City for the new campus. McKim, Mead and White was engaged to design the initial three buildings for a planned student body of one thousand. The cornerstone of the first building was laid on October 8, 1928. Construction proceeded rapidly and the college opened its new campus the next September with an enrollment of 625 students. Adelphi's major emphasis, under President Frank D. Blodgett, was the preparation of students for the teaching profession.

Another addition to the county's educa-

Adelphi College's new Garden City campus.

Hofstra College campus after first quadrangles of new buildings.

tional resources took place in 1935 when New York University created Nassau College-Hofstra Memorial-New York University as a branch on the former William Hofstra estate on the eastern edge of Hempstead. In 1937, the Board of Trustees, after mutual agreement with New York University, separated and established an independent Hofstra College. Under the dedicated leadership of its first president, Truesdale Peck Calkins, the college grew to some one thousand students by the beginning of World War II.

A Commuter Economy

Changes of the early 1900s evident in the county's economic base continued with increased acceleration in the intensified growth of the 1920s. Agriculture was particularly affected by the population influx and changing food demands of the metropolitan markets. Ready buyers existed for farm land and the farm acreage of 59,353 acres in 1920 drastically decreased in the next ten years to 23,477 acres.

In 1915 over sixty farmers met and organized the Nassau County Farm Bureau to exchange information and work toward modern farming methods. The bureau's first president was E. V. Titus of Glen Cove, and membership quickly built up to over two hundred. A solid core of old-time individual owners still remained on the 296 owner-operated farms, but rental operators and tenant farmers dropped in half to 571 and farm size also decreased to an average of 40.5 acres. The extensive sales of farm lands for real estate development even caused potato acreage to drop to 8,107 acres and a production of 805,207 bushels.

Potato production had become the major product of local farming. From over eight thousand acres producing 1,168,000 bushels in 1910, potatoes became the dominant crop with a harvest of 1,825,650 bushels in 1920. In 1922 the market for potatoes dropped drastically and local farmers were unable to obtain sufficient prices to break even. Pro-duction costs of $3 a barrel were not being met by the market offers of $2 a barrel and farm activity was sharply curtailed.

Market gardening to supply the ever increasing vegetable needs of New York City markets required almost one fifth of available farm acreage, and corn production was still a major factor. Dairy production had dropped to 619,585 gallons of milk sold in 1910 and remained at this plateau throughout the period. There was little crop rotation practiced and large quantities of fertilizers were used. Very intensive cultivation of the decreased acreage obtained two to three crops per season of some vegetables so that total produce increased. The total value of farm crops was $6,355,062 in 1920.

Farms in Franklin Square and Valley Stream specialized in vegetable crops while the less valuable land on the plains from Hempstead to Hicksville was used for potatoes, corn and cabbage, the next-ranking products. Despite a drastic decrease in farm

Digging up the famous Long Island potatoes. In 1919, the peak year of potato pro- *duction, over 2 million bushels were harvested.*

income to $3,163,308 in 1930, farm owners still retained considerable capital value in their properties since increasing land prices maintained the average farm value of over $60,000 equal to that of 1920, although farm size had diminished.

After World War I, mechanization began to appear on local farms and early Fordson tractors replaced horses. This trend continued, although in 1930, farmers were still using over three thousand horses in the county for work purposes and also retained over two thousand head of cattle and as many pigs. Most farmers then trucked their own crops into the various city markets.

Horticultural production continued to be an important aspect of local farming. There were thirty-five nurseries in the county, with a product value of $690,815, and the eighty-six greenhouses produced flowers and plants which sold for $994,238. Although of considerably less importance to the county's economy due to the expansion of other as-

Nassau County farmers such as the Rushmore family trucked their produce into city markets.

pects, agriculture, with its 5,977 workers, still provided major employment and a significant economic resource for the county.

The very basic change in the position of agriculture during these years can be observed in the transformation of the annual

Mineola fair harness horse races.

Mineola fair. After the creation of the county, the Queens-Nassau Agricultural Society continued operations and further development of the fairgrounds at Mineola. In 1910 a new grandstand was constructed, and through the 1920s many buildings were added and old ones modernized and expanded. The usual agricultural exhibits continued but interest focused equally on other attractions such as trotting races, a baby show, a carnival midway and the new education and motorcar halls. The fair now was principally a show with auto races, live entertainments and special displays. By 1926 it was evident that animal and poultry exhibits were rapidly disappearing and fair managers felt the "interest of the public seems to be deepening in the attractions and entertainment rather than in the agricultural exhibits."

Life along the waterfront had also been altered drastically in some areas. The small groups of salt-bleached houses perched on marsh-lined creeks at the turn of the century were now crowded by spreading housing developments. All along the south shore, marshland was being filled in, canals and drainage ditches dug and swamps drained to provide subdivision land. The old oyster industry had declined greatly and there seemed to be no answer to its ills. Congressman Frederick Hicks attempted unsuccessfully to have the Federal Bureau of Fisheries conduct an investigation in 1916 to determine how the oyster industry could be rehabilitated.

Excessive use of dredges had stripped the once plentiful beds. Increased water pollution and disruption of the fresh-water flow down the creeks to the bay completely destroyed the oyster industry on the south shore. Oystering gradually died out as the older baymen passed away, and by 1930 only fifteen boats and several hundred men still went out to the beds regularly in Oyster Bay and along the north shore. Total production was less than ten thousand barrels. Clamming and commercial fishing still provided considerable employment along the south shore to supply local markets and the city with seasonal fresh fish.

Although some waterfront lands were developed, the greatest portion of the southern bay and marsh area remained untouched. With the development of Jones Beach on the barrier reef, and the continued expansion of waterfront recreation, pleasure boating was becoming a major activity. Early in the century, the departing boats from Freeport Creek formed a long white parade, with the small boats and sloops sporting one or two sails. There, in Baldwin Harbor and East Rockaway, the creeks were lined with the large wooden-reel net dryers of the fishermen and weathered gray oyster houses. Gradually this gave way to docking space for the new pleasure boats. The first powerboats appeared and the mysterious mechanics of operating naphtha launches became a part of waterfront lore. Regular gasoline engines soon were installed in craft and there was even a problem of speedsters disturbing the tranquil bay waters. By the end of the 1920s, the old waterfront of the bayman was under change. Party boats serving groups of fishing enthusiasts and pleasure boats were replacing commercial boats as a new phase of activity took over the south shore waters.

The dramatic shift away from agriculture and fishing as important parts of the county's economic base was evident in the increasing dependence upon employment outside the county. Commuters were part of the new industrial twentieth century and depended on a wide range of industrial and commercial occupations for a livelihood. They were highly skilled technical workers, professional and management personnel, in the growing corporate mercantile, finance and insurance business in New York City. By 1930 over 120,000 Nassau residents were employed in industry, including 28,861 women. Almost all were commuters to jobs in Brooklyn or New York City, since local industry within the county had expanded very slightly.

Doubleday, Page & Company provided one of the few major local businesses after

A power dredge at work harvesting oysters.

Fish net drying reels along the Baldwin waterfront.

By the late 1930s elaborate powerboats were popular along the south shore.

The Doubleday, Page headquarters at Garden City were surrounded by well-tended gardens. Theodore Roosevelt dedicated the plant in 1910.

its move in 1910 to a suburban location in Garden City. Attracted by the lower cost of land on Long Island compared to other areas adjacent to New York and the promise of good train service, "perhaps the best in the country," the company established a new plant capable of producing 6,500 books a day. Garden City was chosen since it was a developed community with water and gas and was easily reached by trolley from other villages where employees could live. Doubleday, Page & Company was proud of its location and pointed out the advantage to employees that when the home is nearby they "increase their living day perhaps 20 per cent and working conditions and comforts probably 20 per cent more."

The press soon became the largest manufacturer in the county with over seven hundred employees and made every effort to make its plant a community asset. Extensive gardens, featuring all types of plants, in-

cluding peonies, roses, irises and 130 species of evergreen, set off sparkling pools around the 750-foot-long main building. By 1930, the plant was able to produce 40,000 books and 150,000 magazines a day to be shipped from its own railroad station behind the plant.

There were few examples of ideal suburban industry elsewhere in the county. In 1915 only 3,282 employees worked locally, with the major portion at Doubleday and the extensive sand mining pits in Port Washington which provided jobs for over four hundred men. The only other major corporation was a leather and canvas belting firm occupying the former plant of the Duryea Starch Company in Glen Cove. Smaller industrial concerns were located throughout the county producing boats, house trim and sash, blinds and doors, and children's dresses. Local manufacturers paid out $3,567,496 in wages in 1920.

Despite all the population growth after World War I, there were still less than four thousand local industrial wage earners in 1930. Wages had risen to $5,561,316, but in view of higher salaries, relatively this was not a meaningful increase. Glen Cove continued to be the county's major industrial center with a large photoengraving plant employing two hundred persons, and in 1929 the Columbia Ribbon and Carbon Company opened a factory there with ninety-three employees. Freeport also had various small manufactories, including the Columbian Brass Foundry, which was founded in 1905 and had become a principal national supplier of boat propellers. In nearby Baldwin, the United States government had opened an ordnance plant and engaged two hundred men to make parachutes. The infant aviation industry was concentrated around Garden City with the Curtiss Engineering Corporation providing steady employment. Other aircraft companies were just beginning to develop near Farmingdale. Two organ works were located in south shore villages. The Midmer Losh organ factory in Merrick built some of the biggest instruments in the world and the organ pipes produced by the G. W. Badger Company in Rockville Centre ranged from one-half inch to thirty-four feet. The older brickmaking works at Bethpage and the sand mining industry in Port Washington continued to be major local employers supplying construction materials for New York City's growth. Industrial development continued on a very limited scale up to World War II. Other than the establishment of Doubleday, Page & Company, local industry was of no more importance to the county's economic life in 1930 than it had been thirty years before when the county was essentially a rural area.

The growth and significance of retail and wholesale business between 1910 and 1930 was a completely different situation. A tremendous commercial expansion occurred to keep pace with the increased demands for consumer goods by the county's new residents and provided a major new element

An example of the gigantic organ tubes produced by Midmer Losh factory adjacent to the railroad in Merrick.

of economic vitality and support. Out of 16,857 retail and wholesale employees, some 9,844 people manned the county's 4,569 retail stores by 1930, enriching the local economy with an annual payroll in excess of $16 million. Clothing stores, some 325 of them, were now required to supply county residents with almost $8 million worth of knickers, double-breasted suits and Panama hats. Hempstead and Freeport were the principal centers of this great commercial expansion and both had blocks of concentrated shopping area with several hundred stores. Hempstead was the county's undisputed shopping center with sales exceeding $20 million, and in 1927 the county's first department store, the Franklin Shops, opened a six-story building there. Its first floor, mezzanine and basement provided extensive selling areas, and the store even had its own large parking field.

Intersection of Fulton and Franklin streets in Hempstead with New York Telephone Company building on right in late 1930s.

The total net retail sales in 1930 had soared to $166,656,000, with food stores accounting for one third of the total. Building expansion was apparent in the 71 lumber and building materials suppliers, 82 heating and plumbing concerns and 123 hardware stores, which had total sales of $18,458,000. Some 78 coal and ice yards, 356 filling stations and 52 farmers' supply houses provided needed services and products totaling $16,093,000. Fourteen rural general stores with sales exceeding $400,000 were scattered throughout the county. Despite all of this commercial growth, the needs of local residents were not fully met and large numbers of people still shopped in Jamaica and Brooklyn. Department stores in the city had larger selections of goods and catered to suburban shoppers by providing local delivery service. The expansion of retail business provided local employment, stimulated land

values and increased all the indirect services and trades required to support local businesses.

The small banking system of the county in 1900 expanded along with the population and business growth. In 1914 there were six national banks, fifteen state banks, one trust company and three cooperative savings and loan associations in Nassau County. In the great expansion after World War I, banks were organized by local investors in almost every community following the established trend of local ownership and leadership. By 1924 there were forty-eight banks in the county with total resources of $72 million and some 110,000 depositors. There was no part of the county without local banking facilities, and some of the new banks had attained resources of over a million dollars in less than five years.

Stimulated by the need for home building

loans, there was a great interest in the establishment of savings and loan associations. Between 1914 and 1923, eleven associations were formed in the growing villages along the south shore. Most of them had modest assets except for the Baldwin Savings and Loan, which had $250,000 in resources.

Financial institutions grew spectacularly, especially in the central business communities such as Freeport. In the four years before 1923, the Freeport Bank's assets rose from $1,223,880 to $2,725,819, and the Citizens National Bank opened and grew to an institution with $1,800,000 in assets. From 1925 to 1929 the national prosperity was reflected in rapidly climbing local bank deposits, which gained over $50 million in that brief span of time. The Nassau County Trust Company in Mineola and the Roslyn Savings Bank, both older institutions, each gained over $2 million in deposits. During this period sixteen new banks were organized to provide some sixty-seven banking institutions with capital resources in excess of $150 million for the county.

Banking was very profitable during this time and dividend rates ranged as high as 15 per cent for bank investors. By this time local resources were even capable of supplying fairly large amounts of required capital for local projects. The Bank of Rockville Centre purchased a $500,000 bond issue for South Side High School in 1922. Despite these resources, the credit needs of the area still required a considerable use of city banking facilities. Many wealthy local individuals were also sources of private loans and mortgages to residents.

Bankers also began to see the usefulness of mutual action, and in 1924, the Nassau County Bankers Association held several dinner meetings. Although initially it was mainly a means toward a social meeting ground for bankers, it did begin to exercise some professional aims. It raised reward money against holdups, and in 1925 led to organization of the Nassau County chapter of the American Institute of Banking.

With the growth of villages and main street businesses, many local newspapers were established, some covering a group of neighboring communities. Their circulations were low but they actively disseminated local news and advertising. Operation of a weekly newspaper was regarded as "a leisurely task, fairly profitable and eminently respectable," so there was never a lack of local entrepreneurs to carry on. By 1910 there were twenty-nine weeklies in the county, Hempstead alone having four papers and eight other large villages having two or three papers.

The *South Side Observer,* published in Rockville Centre, was among the most widely read since its editor George Wallace, a former assemblyman, was a practicing lawyer with wide-ranging and controversial political and civic ideas. It had an attractive style, having changed from the traditional front page featuring fiction to a modern layout with news stories. Wallace provided fairly good coverage of the whole south shore and reports of county happenings. During the early 1900s, Wallace had a persistent feud with both the county government's administration and with other local newspapers. All of the county's weeklies were highly flavored with the personal journalistic beliefs of their editors and publishers, but none were quite so imperious as the *Observer,* which commented after a clergyman's letter, "This is the kind of encouragement the *Observer* is getting from honest people all over the county."

There were thirty-four weeklies in 1914 and *The Nassau Post* was among the newcomers that year. James E. Stiles, the paper's young editor and publisher, provided an attractive layout with headlines and pictures. Stiles was a highly ambitious man, and by 1918 purchased the *South Side Observer* and combined it with *The Post* into Nassau's largest weekly, with a circulation of 3,500. He rapidly moved ahead with other consolidations and in 1920 absorbed the old Hempstead *Inquirer* and *Nassau County Review* at a cost of $37,000. He constructed a large building in Rockville

Business district of Mineola before World War I.

Centre and on March 7, 1921, issued Nassau County's first daily newspaper.

The Daily Review was an eight-page, six-day-a-week paper with the aim and "desire of management to make it a means of developing the best that is in Nassau County." The first years were difficult ones and Stiles was in constant financial straits. By 1924 the newspaper was changed to *The Nassau Daily Review*. The real estate boom provided a great boost and by 1927 it had a circulation of over ten thousand and printed regular twenty-four-page issues. Stiles constantly promoted community betterment and was a progressive newspaperman, establish-

Nassau Daily Review *publisher James E. Stiles congratulated Robert Moses at dinner with J. Russel Sprague and Governor Herbert Lehman.*

ing separate sports and society sections. The newspaper's growth was slow, however, and reached a circulation of sixteen thousand along the south shore by 1930. Stiles aimed the newspaper to serve "the people of the South Shore of Long Island . . . a group of more than 18 villages," but he also felt a strong sense of county consciousness and attempted to foster development of such a feeling "by welding the friendships and interests of the rival villages on matters which are vital to the entire section."

The main news media for local residents were New York City newspapers that commuters brought home or were purchased at local newsstands and through home delivery boys. The Brooklyn *Eagle,* Brooklyn *Times,* New York *Journal* and the New York *Daily News* all had high circulations in the county. Even along the south shore, they were circulated at a rate of one and a half copies per family, as in Lynbrook, which had city newspaper sales of over 5,000 copies for 2,750 resident families. Although the local newspapers provided news of village social events, major news dissemination was still provided by the great number of city newspapers, which, to varying degrees, also provided coverage of local events on Long Island.

An important portion of newspaper advertising revenue came from real estate dealers and builders in the great boom of the twenties. The expansion of housing was due both to active real estate promotion and to the great demand by city residents for new and better housing. Real estate sales are indicated by the increase in the county clerk's fees (principally for filing mortgages) from $4,920 in 1899 and $33,290 in 1919 to over $200,000 in most years of the 1920s. By the early 1930s, over 40 per cent of the acreage was developed in the Town of Hempstead, 26 per cent in the Town of North Hempstead and 6 per cent in the Town of Oyster Bay.

Although all the favorable aspects of suburban life were factors in attracting new residents, a new generation of real estate

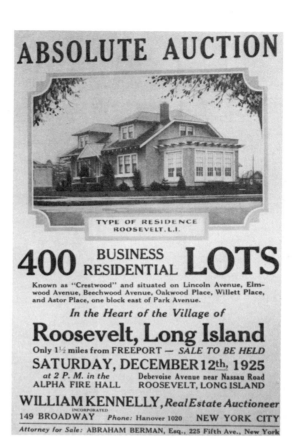

promoters and developers actively stimulated local growth. They ranged from conservative organizations such as the Garden City Company, which advertised the merits of the community's "beautiful trees, spacious parks, wide avenues, distinctive homes," to speculative fly-by-nighters. Many places, such as Biltmore Shores in Massapequa, were mainly a gleam in the eye of the promoters, and despite lavish brochures and folders the "paved streets, fine homes, a vast park, modern shops, churches, schools, golf, tennis, yachting and riding clubs, and splendid fire department and complete administrative system" existed mainly in the imagination of the developers.

Almost all the promoters used basically the same appeal of the great new life a city person could enjoy in the country with sports and recreation in winter and summer. The appeal to parents for a better atmosphere for growing children was strong, and people were motivated to become suburbanites, "to seek more congenial social surroundings, a cleaner moral atmosphere, not only for themselves but principally for the sake of their children."

An important factor in real estate activity on Long Island had become the appeal of speculative profits in real estate as an investment. In the mid-1920s large auctions of land tracts were openly promoted as investment speculations. The great rise in land values which boosted one two-hundred-foot strip of land in Baldwin from $6,500 to $18,000 in three months was cited as evidence of the great profits to be made. Realtors promoted every possibility, such as the electrification of the Long Island Rail Road, which auctioneer Stephen Pettit proclaimed meant "that big profits will be made in South Shore real estate during the coming summers." Sales of blocks of three hundred to four hundred lots were promoted with voluminously illustrated folders and multicolored maps. They included land from the south shore to north shore, with all price ranges and values. The great diversity of areas, building lots and sizes provided

something for almost any home seeker, even a Love Nest Colony in southwest Freeport for newlyweds.

Although land prices had risen greatly from the $124 per acre average in 1900 to $629 in 1910, prices in the twenties still enabled economical housing development. Building lots of twenty-foot frontage ranged from $250 upward, although an average price in 1925 at the height of the boom was between $1,000 to $1,800 for a minimum building lot of sixty-foot width.

The Biltmore Shores development in Massapequa required two twenty-foot lots for building at a minimum cost of $1,880. Terms were 25 per cent down and 2 per cent monthly with 6 per cent interest. This project illustrated some of the pitfalls developers faced. The land, covering over five hundred acres, had first been obtained by prominent local attorney George Morton Levy at an option price of $550 an acre. He brought in motion picture magnate William Fox and two others to obtain financing on the basis of equal shares of profits. Soon after, Edward West Browning offered Levy $2,000 per acre, half of it in cash. Fox refused the deal and Levy loyally stuck with him. Before they could develop the property, the Depression struck, and they had to dispose of the land with hardly any profit.

There were many local realtors who were instrumental in the expansion of their villages. John J. Randall, who moved to Freeport in the late 1880s, was a principal developer of several sections of that village. William H. Runcie, also of Freeport, was another leading developer and builder who interested large city financial institutions in local mortgages. By 1925 he had a staff of over thirty-five salesmen and was building homes in Bellmore, Freeport and Wantagh, where he had completed one hundred out of four hundred planned dwellings. A three-room bungalow could then be purchased for $3,500, while the more popular five rooms sold for $6,500. From that price level, housing ranged upward to large country homes of twelve rooms, two-car garages and two baths near railroad stations for $35,000.

All of the residential building in the county created a great construction work forced with almost sixteen thousand employees in 1930. There were 198 construction companies with an annual payroll of $5,873,-000 consisting mostly of local employees. In 1923 over 5,000 dwellings and 400 stores were constructed in the county, with 1,383 buildings in Valley Stream alone. Two years later a peak was reached when in the Village of Hempstead alone, $3,360,659 of new structures was erected, including the Rivoli Theatre, Bohack Building and several churches. The construction work was not limited to single-family dwellings. Larger structures began to play an increasing role in building. As early as 1922, a three-story apartment house was constructed in Garden City, and by 1929 there were three apartment houses in Rockville Centre valued at over $225,000. Freeport by then had a major county landmark on Sunrise Highway—a six-story office and bank costing over $250,000.

Real estate activities had become such a large industry that in 1924 the Long Island Real Estate Board hired a paid secretary. Organized in 1910, it had grown very slowly but greatly expanded activities in the 1920s

and by 1930 had over 1,100 members with five chapters in Nassau County. It promoted higher standards within the real estate business and urged necessary public developments to maintain the area's growth. In 1925 the Board assisted the Sunrise Highway project by acquiring some of the needed lands and also supported the idea of an Ocean Boulevard on the barrier beaches.

The combined work force of 4,678 real estate employees and 15,905 construction workers provided the greatest single source of local employment in the county by 1930. The necessary support services of building material suppliers, utilities etc. were a major stimulation to Nassau County's economy. The commuter obtained his livelihood from industrial sources outside the county but his demand for housing and consumption of consumer goods had, in only a period of thirty years, changed the economic base of the county.

When the Depression struck in the 1930s, the county's growth came to a sharp stop. The deepening clerical and manufacturing unemployment had disastrous effects on county residents. The Depression's crippling effect on employment severely restricted the residential construction growth in the

An early pre-World War II apartment house in Rockville Centre.

Typical English Tudor-style house built in Strathmore at Manhasset development which was popular throughout the county in 1920s and 1930s.

county. During the 1920s the value of new building permits had exceeded $300,000 a month in villages such as Rockville Centre and Freeport. New building values dropped to less than $200,000 for the entire year of 1934 in these same communities. In addition to the decline of construction, many home-owners were unable to continue their mortgage payments and foreclosures increased. A great deal of real estate was abandoned by people and lost for failure to pay taxes.

Although banks experienced severe difficulty in most of the country, the county's banking institutions were able to overcome the crisis. After the Long Beach Trust Company and the Bank of North Hempstead at Port Washington closed in 1931, over two hundred bankers from the sixty financial institutions in the county met at the Garden City Hotel on January 7, 1932, and created the Nassau County Clearing House. The immediate necessity was to plan a smooth closing of the First National Bank of Rockville Centre, which was in severe trouble and was not able to stand a sudden run on its deposits. Stimulated by Surrogate Leone D. Howell, the bankers in an all-night session organized a cooperative association under chairman William F. Ploch. They acquired the bank building by mutual assessment and arranged for the Bank of Rockville Centre to take over its liabilities. After the national bank holiday in March of 1933, several other small banks in the county were closed but there was no major financial panic. The cooperative action of the bankers provided a stable financial climate for county businesses and residents.

Although construction was greatly restricted, it did continue at a slow pace.

Road congestion had increased so greatly that grade crossing eliminations were begun *to provide elevated tracks at Lynbrook by 1940.*

Single-family houses costing between $3,000 and $5,000 were the most common and popular units. The general business improvement and initiation of war industries in the county stimulated the building of several thousand housing units annually in the late 1930s. Increased natural growth and the influx of new residents provided a total population of 406,748 in 1940.

Improved electric railroad service direct to Manhattan and the widespread use of automobiles provided increased access to Nassau County in the 1920s. City residents were in need of residential housing, and real estate developers quickly met the demand with extensive housing developments. Although the new growth was homogeneous in character with the county's existing population, the great numbers of newcomers created new demands on local educational systems and many additional social organizations. Mainly industrial and business workers, the new residents shifted the county's economic base to a dependence upon New York City. Local retail sales and services were growing as a major source of local employment, and the expanded residential con-

struction industry provided a strong economic stimulus.

These basic changes in the county and the reactions which they caused in the area's physical appearance, governments, schools and social institutions were part of the painful process of creating a suburban county. Many of the area's more thoughtful residents were aware of these pressures. Christopher Morley, author and resident of Roslyn, believed it "... one of the loveliest places in America, but I never write about it by its name because I don't want a lot of people coming here to 'sitt down upon itt.' I get worried sometimes when I see a great tide of real estate development, country clubs, seven-passenger sedans and picnickers who leave Sunday papers and olive bottles behind them." Morley, like most other new commuters, quickly became enamored with the wonderful rural aspects of suburban life in Nassau County. However, the question was already being posed whether uncontrolled suburban development would in the end destroy the very attributes that had attracted people to the Sunrise Homeland.

Overflow crowd filled steps outside Hempstead Town Hall during May 27, 1947, hearing on building code revision to make Levittown possible.

Veterans crowded the Levitt office on August 18, 1949, to buy houses.

CHAPTER VI
SUBURBIA TRIUMPHANT

Population Explosion

Prospects for Nassau County's quick recovery after World War II were suddenly enhanced on May 7, 1947, when a *Newsday* headline proclaimed, 2,000 $60 RENTALS, DUE IN L.I. PROJECT. The article detailed the revolutionary mass subdivision planned by the construction firm of Levitt & Sons to be built toward the eastern end of the flat Hempstead Plains land south of Hicksville. The homes were intended for returning war veterans, who were clamoring throughout the United States for adequate housing. An overwhelming response followed the announcement of the project. Long lines formed and by the end of the month, veterans had filed over 6,500 applications for the initial housing units.

Abraham Levitt and his two sons had prior experience with several small residential developments in Nassau County and were prepared to construct housing on a mass production basis. Aspects of their new building technology, including the lack of basements in the houses, required a change in the existing Town of Hempstead building code. At the public hearing to consider the revisions on May 27, over eight hundred veterans crowded the town hall to hear various construction experts testify about the merits and demerits of the code changes. One veteran shouted his feelings from the crowd: "No cellar beats one room in an attic where you freeze to death." The town board heard his message and approved the change.

An unequaled episode in the development of American communities began to unfold.

More land was acquired to build four thousand additional units, and in the next year Levitt continued land purchases as rapidly as expansion could be planned. By October the first two hundred families moved into Levittown—America's first great postwar community was alive and growing on former potato fields. It was a development like none ever seen before and which will probably never happen again. The leading magazines of the country, including *Time, Reader's Digest* and *Harper's Magazine,* carried stories of amazement about the evolution of an entire community within a few short years.

The initial practice of renting homes soon led to their outright sale as federal loan guarantee programs enabled veterans to purchase houses with very little down payment. Levitt announced the sale of 350 units would begin on March 7, 1949, a Monday morning, at a cost of $7,990 with a $90 down payment and $58-a-month payments. Veterans with their families began to form an orderly line the preceding Friday night. By Sunday such an enormous crowd had gathered that the Levitts came down and began to hand out application cards—they immediately filled the first 350 units. Police finally had to explain the situation and dissolve the long line of disappointed home seekers.

Construction continued to expand across the easily developed farm land for four years and finally on November 22, 1951, the enormous project came to an end. Appropriately on that day ex-Marine Ernest

Southard and his expectant wife, former apartment dwellers from Queens County, took title to the last home on Trudy Lane South—the 17,447th built by Levitt & Sons. This massive development, which changed a major portion of the center of Nassau County and began an unprecedented period of growth, was a surprise even for the energetic thirty-seven-year-old William J. Levitt, who commented, "After we saw originally what response we got to our plans, we had an idea of what we were in store for. But of course, there was an element of astonishment . . . as Levittown grew and grew and grew."

The pent-up housing demand which fueled this growth originated in the serious slowdown of metropolitan-area housing construction caused by World War II. Nassau County's growth of the 1920s and 1930s was sharply curtailed, and as *Nassau Daily Review Star* editor Arthur Hodges observed, "World War II had a more desolating effect on Rockville Centre than the depression, as far as outward appearances were concerned . . . when America entered the war it proved a great setback to local business." Housing became increasingly scarce as construction was brought to a virtual standstill. Government restrictions and manpower and building material shortages had curtailed the revival of residential building that occurred in the late 1930s. Electric meter installations for new housing units dropped from an average of five thousand a year to less than one thousand during the war years. The housing vacancy rate dipped as low as 3 per cent in 1946. There were virtually no residential units available in the county. Housing required for newly married couples and the infusion into the county of defense plant workers caused the conversion of many one-family houses into two-family or multiple-dwelling units. This moderate growth and considerable doubling up of married children with parents enabled the county's population to exist through the war years' scarcity of housing.

Here, as elsewhere in the country, a major change resulted from the large number of men who joined the armed forces. The United States had initiated military preparations in 1940, and the Selective Service system registration began on October 16. Local draft boards, composed of leading citizens, were established in fifteen places throughout the county. Each board included an area with a population of from twenty-seven to thirty thousand. By the end of 1940, they had efficiently registered over sixty thousand men between the ages of twenty-one and thirty-five.

The first call for inductees to report between November 25 and 30 included a quota of 134 men from Nassau County. Originally there was a high rejection rate because of the strict medical examination, but as the need for men became more urgent, the restrictions were lowered and large numbers began to enter the service. By June of 1941, over three thousand Nassau men were in the service, about two thirds of them from the Selective Service system and one third from the call-up of National Guard or reserve units. Subsequent monthly quotas were met, but as the war continued, older men, professionals and even public officials were called to duty. The area's State Appeal Board, consisting of a respected panel of labor, medical, business, farming and legal representatives coordinated by Ferdinand Haber, decided on some seven thousand hardship and other appeals. As late as July of 1945, local boards such as that at Hicksville, which supplied thirty-two men that month, were still meeting their quota of inductees.

The 102nd Anti-tank Battalion of the 14th Infantry, housed in the Hempstead Armory and commanded by Lieutenant Colonel R. L. Vandewater, was the first local National Guard unit called to duty, in January of 1941. By the end of the war over sixty thousand Nassau men and women had entered the Navy, Army, Air Force and Marine Corps. Local women served as WACs and WAVEs and men were in every unit of the services from the Seabees to submarines.

Draftees arriving at Mineola for Mitchel Field.

Mitchel Field was a bustling military center with troops embarking for overseas and wounded veterans returning to the States.

Residents observed some military units at Mitchel Air Force Base but their major contact with servicemen was the tissue-thin V-mail letters bringing news from the war theaters. Local newspapers daily reported the news and exploits of local service personnel—their inductions, graduations from training camps, promotions, assignments overseas, valor in winning medals, and tragic deaths.

The men of Nassau County's villages had gone off to wage war against the Axis with a determined spirit. As the war drew to a close in 1945, residents must have felt a warm pride when they read of the fine performance of local men. Two Air Force lieutenants, Alfred Sertl and Leonard Welton, Jr., who received Air Medals for flying their B-17 Flying Fortresses during the waning days of the air war over Germany, exemplified this heroism—and they were only twenty-one and twenty-two years old. The distant battlefields were stilled after the surrender of Japan, and the local veterans began to stream back home. Many who had served in the Navy were discharged from the service at a special U.S. naval personnel separation center at Lido Beach. By November the center had discharged over 33,000 veterans and was processing 1,000 to 2,000 men a day into civilian life after two days of separation activities.

Even before the war had begun, preparations were initiated for necessary home-front activities. In October of 1940 County Executive J. Russel Sprague appointed a Nassau County Defense Council, which was replaced in 1942 by a War Council of twenty-five area representatives. The council coordinated the civil defense and home-front activities during the war. Civil defense became a major priority, particularly due to Nassau County's location on the Atlantic Ocean and the fear of possible German submarine or naval assault. The many vital war plants in the county added to concerns of a sneak attack. Civilian protection units were organized in localities with some 54 units of 27,000 trained volunteers providing a strong sense of community security to local residents.

During the summer of 1942, there was an increase in activity by German submarines off the New York port area, and a blackout

Bonds purchased by residents of Port Washington provided this ship for the war effort.

system was established on Long Island. Window shades were drawn nightly and no street lights were allowed. During the war there were actually seventeen blackout alerts and five daytime alerts, including an alert on Christmas Day, 1943, bringing the impact of wartime reality to the county. The civil defense units included air raid wardens and block captains who enforced the blackout regulations. Special hospital station and casualty teams were also trained. Airplane spotter stations were manned around the clock to detect any possible German aircraft raids, including a special tower on the top of the six-story First National Bank and Trust Company in Freeport.

Local residents eagerly assumed wartime projects and vigorously participated in the raising of war loans. Popular surrogate Leone D. Howell planned and administered an energetic organization of volunteers who put the county over the top in every war loan drive. In just the initial month of the first drive in May of 1941, over $400,000 of defense bonds were purchased by local residents in post offices and banks. The Series "E" Bond then paid 2.9 per cent interest a year and many were sold by local industry and businesses through regular payroll deduction plans. Local loan committees left no possible sales source untapped, including regular drives in schools. A program of selling war bonds and stamps at Belmont Park Racetrack resulted in purchases of almost $5 million of bonds there in 1944. In the eight war bond drives in Rockville Centre over $20 million was raised, with the first drive goal of $1 million being increased in each succeeding effort. Communities vied with each other to top their goals and a total of $373 million of war bonds and $143 million of "E" bonds was sold to Nassau residents during the course of the war.

Residents participated in a host of special activities to assist the war effort. The large number of servicemen stationed at Mitchel Field were provided by the United Service Organizations with an $80,000 USO club on Nichols Court in Hempstead, and local groups provided entertainment and special activities for the servicemen. Red Cross volunteers turned out surgical dressings and other special needs for the war effort.

The war effort caused a host of new problems for civilians and rationing of critical supplies became a major concern. Augustus B. Weller, a Merrick banker, became administrator of the local rationing of gasoline, food and fuel. The supplies of meat, coffee, sugar and canned milk for babies became very tight and residents carefully husbanded their OPA rationing stamps. Victory or defense gardens became a regular activity, with local residents raising beans, tomatoes and other vegetables to relieve food shortages and combat rising prices. In 1945 almost five thousand students planted home victory gardens on over two hundred acres of land throughout the county to ease food shortages. Unfortunately, as one resident observed, "You couldn't raise a beefsteak on a bush."

Despite the urgent demands on fuel supplies, sufficient gasoline was made available by a judicious rationing system, and carpooling provided transportation for defense workers to the wartime factories. Fuel oil shortages were severe and many individuals converted back to coal for home heating systems, but shortages also developed in its supply. Local salvage committees collected waste paper, scrap metal and even milkweed pods for the war effort.

The evolution of the aircraft industry before the war had created a major industrial resource which mushroomed after Pearl Harbor and provided aircraft that were instrumental in American victories on both fronts. The tremendous increase in production at the Grumman and Republic plants required special classes for mechanics, sheet metal workers, draftsmen and riveters in Nassau communities to provide trained production-line personnel. Propellers for naval warships were produced at the Columbian Brass Factory in Freeport; the Baldwin Naval Ordnance plant produced naval weapons; and flares were manufac-

Women worked alongside men on the production lines of aircraft and military factories in the county. "Rosie the Riveter" was essential to the war effort.

tured at the Aerial Products Company in Merrick. The Sperry Gyroscope Company provided the necessary guidance instruments for Navy and Air Force weaponry systems. There was an enormous shortage of factory workers and many employees were recruited from outside the county.

In addition to the special defense efforts, the county government had to provide increased public services due to the great expansion of the aviation plants in the county and the steadily increasing population. After war was declared, the administration realized that property tax collections might be highly uncertain and that the heavy indebtedness of the Depression years had to be refinanced. County Executive J. Russel

Sprague immediately established a policy of minimal governmental services during the war. Vacancies were not filled in county offices and no new public construction programs were started except those essential for access roads, drainage and traffic control required by wartime industries. Considerable planning for needed highway, sewerage and water supply systems was done in anticipation of needs after the war.

The county government also arranged a long-term debt equalization program to spread the maturities of its $53-million indebtedness. These stringent economies enabled the debt to be reduced to less than $40 million by the end of 1945. Enormous manpower demands during the war had created employment opportunities for almost all residents. There was a tremendous saving in county welfare expenditures, which dropped by the end of war to a little over $2 million a year, with a case load of less than one thousand residents.

Officials also protected county interests by opposing efforts of New York City to sink thirty wells along its watershed property in Nassau County in 1940. After two years of contention, the State Water Power and Control Commission ruled the city should develop upstate sources and the ground water resources should be reserved for the people of Nassau. The county emerged from the war with a strong financial base and a host of plans that were ready to prepare the county physically for a new period of growth which it was hoped would rival that of the post-World War I years.

As soon as the war concluded, the pent-up demand for housing affected every area of Nassau County. The amazing development of the six square miles encompassed by Levittown was an indication of the tremendous need and desire of urban residents for suburban housing. Although rental housing was initially planned, new federal regulations after 1948 made financing difficult and homes were then constructed for sale. Eventually all of the previously built rental units were also sold, so that by the end of the

1950s, only a few rental units remained in the community. The Levitt organization had no need to establish a marketing program for the homes since they were sold as fast as they could be constructed.

The development of special construction techniques was one of the major contributions of Levittown to the growth of suburbia nationally. The original Levitt house was a Cape Cod with 720 square feet of first-floor space. Later ranch-style homes provided somewhat larger space. The major technical innovation was the lack of a basement and the setting of the house on a concrete slab which contained radiant heating coils. Each house included a kitchen, two bedrooms, a bath, a living room, sufficient closets and a stairway to an unfinished attic. The ranch houses, which were constructed after 1949, also had an attractive brick fireplace which opened into both the kitchen and living area. Kitchens were in front of the house and a sixteen-foot insulated glass window wall in the living room of the ranches faced the rear yards of the properties.

The houses were constructed on a mass-production basis by non-union contractors. Each subcontractor completed an individual part of the house construction, including such simple functions as installing doors. Levitt aggressively planned the maximum housing for the minimal amount of money and convinced manufacturers to sell directly to him so that all of the appliances, which were supplied with the house, were obtained at the lowest possible cost. The Cape Cod models sold for $6,990 but prices were raised later to $7,990 for the ranch models. The ranch cost eventually increased to $9,000 for the last units built in 1951.

In addition to his emphasis on economy, Levitt also attempted to plan an attractive environment for the community. Homes were built in several style variations and located differently on plots to avoid a dull row pattern. Random street layouts were used with four-way intersections avoided wherever possible. The curvilineal streets and homes were well landscaped under the

Cape Cod–style Levitt house.

Ranch-style Levitt house.

personal supervision of the family patriarch, Abraham Levitt, who was responsible for the planting of fruit trees and shade trees throughout the area. The combination of a well-planned road network and horticultural plantings resulted in a varied and pleasing community appearance which increased as the trees and greenery matured. Several decades later many of the small maples planted alongside the roads had grown into thirty- to forty-foot-high trees. Onetime flat potato fields had been transferred into a sylvan suburban setting.

Mass-produced housing caused great concern and many commentators predicted the low-cost homes would rapidly deteriorate and become slum housing. Quite the con-

Unoccupied farm fields of central Nassau, 1946.

trary occurred as residents found that the structures were easily renovated and expanded. So much do-it-yourself home modernization ensued in the next few decades that a Levitt home in its original condition was a curiosity. A wide diversity existed by 1970 in what were once blocks of similar houses. Levitt homes appreciated enormously in value but despite the rise in average resale price to over $25,000 for an improved model in 1970, it still represented one of the best housing bargains in Nassau County.

Initially almost every resident of Levittown was an ex-GI. New governmental home loan programs after World War II, including the GI Bill and FHA mortgage insurance programs, provided an entirely new financial resource for housing construction, enabling veterans and others to purchase homes with small down payments. City financial institutions, such as the Dime Savings Bank of Brooklyn, played a major role in the support of housing on Long Island by providing builders with ready mortgage financing for the former veterans. Construction of Levittown was only the start of a dramatic change across the entire eastern end of the Hempstead Plains. Complete new communities started from scratch—new houses, new roads, new schools, new houses of worship, new stores, new everything. To the west of Levittown, Uniondale and East Meadow spread across former farm fields. The older communities of Hicksville and Farmingdale expanded as their surrounding farm homesteads

The same area after construction of Levittown.

disappeared into housing developments and the open lands of Island Trees, Plainview and Bethpage were rapidly subdivided.

The growth of the Town of Hempstead reached its peak at the turn of the decade in 1950, adding over 40,000 new residents. A record-breaking 55,000 new residents moved in during 1951—an addition of more people into this one township of the county in one year than its entire population only fifty years before. The Town of Oyster Bay received its largest growth in the years 1953 through 1956, and over 30,000 new residents annually filled the housing developments in the center of the county and along the south shore in Seaford and the Massapequas.

The expansion also changed established communities along the commuter railroad lines, and the older villages such as Freeport, Rockville Centre, Hempstead, Valley Stream, Long Beach and the Five Towns area were intensively developed. By the early 1960s, there were few empty building lots left in these older communities. Older homes that were unsalable during the Depression were now quite desirable. The western unincorporated portion of the Town of Hempstead was also completely subdivided during this period, with New Hyde Park, Elmont, Franklin Square and West Hempstead growing out across empty farm fields. Even the Village of Floral Park, which had almost thirteen thousand residents in 1940, increased over 25 per cent.

The county's total population, increased

by the natural rise, the influx of war workers and the beginning of suburban inflow in the late 1940s, had climbed to 672,765 residents in 1950. During the next decade its population doubled to 1,300,171 residents, establishing one of the fastest growth rates in the United States. The Town of Oyster Bay increased 282 per cent during this period, from 82,060 residents to 313,872. The Town of Hempstead lived up to its boast of being the fastest-growing community in the United States and almost doubled from 448,092 to 767,211 people.

The Town of North Hempstead experienced a slower, more gradual growth from 142,613 to 219,088 residents. The larger building plot requirements in the incorporated villages on the north shore necks limited development. A large unincorporated area spreading from Mineola and north New Hyde Park to Herricks increased over by 40,000 residents from 1950 to 1960, while Westbury increased by 7,500 in the same period.

The great expansion came to an abrupt end by 1960, and during the next decade natural increase and some minor new areas created a slow population rise. The enormous population provided a natural increase that accounted for 84.5 per cent of

In the 1970s many marsh areas along the south shore were filled in, bulkheaded and covered with new homes.

the new growth to 1,428,321 residents in the county by 1970. The growth had slowed down tremendously in Hempstead and in North Hempstead to less than 8 per cent, but Oyster Bay still registered a 14.9 per cent increase. New births had surpassed deaths by over sixteen thousand people in 1960 but the falling birth rate caused this to drop to less than a five thousand addition by 1970.

A good deal of the expansion after 1960 was due to the extensive development of marshland along the south shore. Bellmore and Freeport both experienced an increase of over five thousand residents, as did Oceanside and Massapequa. Merrick's population rose by seven thousand residents, a good portion living on former marshlands which were filled in for housing development. In just one year, 1961, Massapequa increased in size by 3,487 residents. As the amount of available land diminished along the south shore and in the center of the county, increasing pressure was exerted on the former estate areas in the northern sections of the Town of Oyster Bay. East Norwich, Woodbury, Jericho, Syosset, Plainview and Old Bethpage continued to be developed so that the population of the Town of Oyster Bay rose to 359,112 in 1970. The Town of Hempstead had climbed to 834,219 people and North Hempstead concluded the decade with 235,090 residents. The great population growth of Nassau County had come to an end. This tremendous expansion had transformed the county into an entirely different area in just over a twenty-year period.

It was a growth that not only transformed the existing community but even during the course of its development underwent major changes that seriously affected all the major institutions of life. Since the suburban movement was dominated by young veterans and married couples, the initial population of the county in the 1950s was very young. Over a third of the residents were below the age of fourteen in 1960. As the years passed, however, the average age began to rise. By 1970

there had been a drop of over 32 per cent in the number of children below the age of five and a decrease of 13 per cent in the number below ten. There was a corresponding tremendous increase of over 75 per cent in the teen-age and young adult age groupings and increases in those people over the age of fifty-five.

Although there was much original concern that resident turnover in suburbia would create a transient population, there was an amazing stability. In 1960 only 8 per cent of Nassau's population had resided in the community before 1939. Over 40 per cent, however, had resided in the county for five years. By 1970 over 1 million of the residents had been located in the county for over five years, while only eighty thousand were from out of New York State.

As the average age of the population increased during this period, the size of families declined from an average 3.7 members in 1960 to 3.5 in 1970. The birth rate dropped precipitously and in the early 1970s the county was approaching a zero population growth level. This societal change from a preponderance of young families with growing children to more mature families with fewer children created successive pressures on the county's educational and housing facilities that were difficult to solve.

In addition to the changing family composition, the county's population reflected the rising native-born rate. By 1970 84.3 per cent of its population were born in New York State, while 30 per cent were born of foreign parentage and 9.3 per cent were foreign-born. This still provided a strong ethnic diversity with the predominant influence now shifted to those of Italian heritage. The new heterogeneity was 21 per cent Italian, 13 per cent German and Russian, 9 per cent Polish, 8 per cent English and 7 per cent Irish. The larger population also included small numbers of diverse ethnic groups which provided pockets of new cultural influences.

Changes in non-white population of the county were not as significant as the age and ethnic differences, but did provide significant effects due to the greater concentration in individual communities. In 1960 the non-white population of 42,132 residents was principally black, although it did include 1,728 Chinese residents. The Village of Hempstead contained almost 8,000 of these residents, with Glen Cove, Freeport, Roosevelt, New Cassel, Inwood and Lakeview each having over 2,000 black residents. Rockville Centre, Long Beach, and Uniondale also contained over 1,000 non-whites.

The non-white proportion of the total population increased in percentage from 3.2 per cent in 1960 to 5.1 per cent in 1970. Communities with more than 1,000 blacks had increased in number to thirteen. Some villages, such as Inwood, Manhasset and Rockville Centre, lost more than 15 per cent of their black population while other communities greatly increased theirs. Hempstead contained over 14,000 black residents and Roosevelt grew to over 10,000. Freeport followed with 7,000 and New Cassel included 5,000 black residents. The great increase in these individual communities created a more visible black population, which began to establish its own community and organizational life.

These new population patterns reinforced the ethnic trend of the initial suburban growth after World War I. The county's population included increasingly larger percentages of Roman Catholic and Jewish residents and a lower percentage of Protestant inhabitants. Exact statistics on this change are very difficult to obtain since available data on religious affiliation is variable and inconclusive. However, there is little question that the great growth during the 1950s added considerable numbers of new Jewish and Catholic residents so that by the early 1960s between 42 to 46 per cent of the county's population were Roman Catholic. Jewish population had increased to over several hundred thousand, making up some 15 to 20 per cent of the county's population, while Protestants made up 25 to 30 per cent.

The growth of new parishes in the Roman Catholic Church was significant during this period of time. In recognition of the increasing number of suburban Catholics, a new Diocese of Rockville Centre was created in 1957, with Walter P. Kellenberg appointed as bishop. The diocese established central headquarters in Rockville Centre and initiated strong programs in Catholic charities, educational programs and communication within the church membership through the sponsoring of a newspaper, the *Long Island Catholic*. The local Roman Catholic church shared in the major changes affecting the religion worldwide and adopted English in the Mass during 1964. Folk Masses, ecumenical activities, the marriage encounter movement, increasing participation of laymen in church activities, stimulating entrance into the declining ranks of the priesthood and the struggles to expand and maintain a parochial school system were major aspects of Roman Catholic development during this period.

Lacking the central organization of the Roman Catholic faith, the Jewish population of Nassau County communities had to create complete new religious organizations. The development of the Israel Community Center, a conservative congregation in Levittown, is a typical evolution. A cavernous, grease-stained airplane hangar was rented by a few Jewish veterans in May of 1948 and redecorated by their families to hold High Holy Day services. Their president, Lou Goldberg, remarked in wonder, "Do you realize that ninety per cent of these people haven't been in a synagogue since they were Bar Mitzvah . . . we are hungry for Jewish learning and Jewish life." The congregation was later given land by Abraham Levitt and built a $35,000 building for its 450 member families. Congregation Ohav Sholom in the Merrick-Bellmore area began its existence in a local fire hall in 1961 and moved progressively from a store to another fire hall, to a veterans hall, then to a ranch house and finally into a new synagogue in 1968.

Although many new synagogues were created, the dispersion of Jewish families within largely non-Jewish communities greatly decreased their religious participation. Jewish religious leaders viewed the problems of maintaining Jewish education in the heterogeneous suburbs as a significant threat to the future of Judaism and were increasingly concerned about the rising intermarriage rate with other faiths and lack of temple participation.

During the 1950s, sixty-three new Protestant congregations were organized, with over a third of them Lutheran denominations. The increasing growth of both United Lutheran churches and Missouri Synod Lutheran churches created a total Lutheran membership of almost forty thousand members to become the predominant Protestant faith in the county by 1960. The Protestant Episcopal Church continued as a strong organization, with some thirty thousand members. Methodist and Presbyterian denominations maintained substantial membership and a great number of independent groups began to provide an enormous religious diversity including Community, Christian Science and varied special Methodist and Baptist black congregations.

The Protestant churches coordinated their activities through the Nassau Council of Churches, which had some 150 members by 1965. During the 1950s, it operated a Department of Church Planning and Research which conferred with groups wishing to start new congregations in areas of the county that were being developed. The department rendered a judgment on the proposals for such new churches and actually allocated areas to requesting churches so that the various Protestant faiths would not compete to provide facilities for the newly settled areas of the county. The council provided chaplaincies for public institutions, radio programs, a central blood bank, encouragement of ecumenical services, college ministry to local campuses and cooperative Easter dawn services. Increasingly concerned for human relations issues, the council provided support for improved social-welfare conditions. In 1950 there were some 62,000 members and

Interior of Temple Sinai, Roslyn.

The new religious diversity of the county was evident in such churches as St. Paul's Greek Orthodox Church, Cathedral Avenue, Hempstead.

149 Protestant churches, which increased by 1960 to over 165 churches with 150,000 members. Rising costs and ministerial salaries, combined with constant membership levels, caused increasing financial problems for many congregations by 1970.

The total religious community of Nassau County in 1970 included some five hundred churches and synagogues. Religion continued to provide the principal community focus for many individuals. In many of the suburban areas established during the postwar period, church membership was the major means of establishing a sense of community for new residents. The social aspect of church membership was a major function of all faiths. Despite the initial growth during the onrush of population to the county, the major religious groups shared an increasing concern over the lack of new converts and the decline of membership. Although God was not dead in the suburbs, churches were making every effort to reevaluate programs and respond to contemporary needs. Nassau's new population had provided a varied religious life for the county, with the Roman Catholic faith dominant, a wide diversity of Protestant churches and a strong Jewish minority.

One of the most significant aspects of Nassau County's growth during this period was the diversified economic range of residents. New residential development was not limited to any economic level and a wide variety of housing was available from low-priced to the very high-priced exclusive levels. The area attracted, though, energetic and rapidly rising middle-income families, and by 1960, the median income of $8,515 was the highest recorded anywhere in New York State. The economic affluence continued and by the 1970 census, the median family income was $14,632. This provided the typical family in Nassau County with the third highest average income in the entire United States. Over 40 per cent of the county's families had incomes over $15,000.

The economic consequences of this income level became especially apparent in the field of housing. The tremendous subdivision construction of one-family homes had peaked in 1958, when 7,199 units were constructed. During the growth of the 1950s, there was an enormous variety of housing available to new residents, from the low-cost Levitt homes to $30,000 or $40,000 ranch homes in more expensive subdivisions; in 1960, the median home value was $18,500.

Originally the Levitts had acquired land for construction for a little over $300 per

acre, but by the end of their development, prices rose to $3,000 an acre. Land costs zoomed through the 1950s and 1960s, so that by 1970, an average building lot of sixty feet by one hundred feet, if it could be found anywhere, cost over $12,000.

The scarcity of property and its rising costs reduced new residence construction in 1960 to 4,160 units, and the decline continued be-

Postwar development streets in Syosset were quickly lined with thick landscaping.

low 3,000 units in 1965 to only 1,019 units in 1970. The increasing scarcity of new construction and general inflation had created by then an average one-family home costing over $30,000, with prices of $50,000 to $60,000 common, while properties with larger structures and plots in excess of two thousand square feet required expenditures of over $70,000.

During the initial years of the development boom, land values were based chiefly upon chance, although locations closer to the railroad lines were more desirable. Properties with special scenic qualities also had enhanced value. As the build-up occurred in the 1960s and land became increasingly scarce and valuable, all property became more desirable, particularly areas with access

Many Nassau apartment houses were well landscaped like this one on Randall Avenue in Freeport.

to arterial highways and parkways. Housing adjacent to the major shopping center areas in the county increased in desirability, while many of the deteriorated downtown areas experienced declining values. Prime commercial land acreage grew in value from $50,000 to over $200,000 an acre, depending upon its location, by the early 1970s.

Increasing land costs influenced the expansion of multiple housing units in the county. From 1960 to 1970, while only 16,-167 single-family units were erected, some 25,583 multi-family units were added. The appeal of the two-family house had begun during World War II. The tax savings, lessened maintenance, and ability of two families to utilize one building unit greatly expanded the number of two-family houses during the war. Mounting land costs pro-

vided an additional stimulus to this trend, which particularly affected the western and southwestern sections of the county. By 1960 over 20 per cent of the units in communities such as Floral Park, Inwood, Lynbrook, Valley Stream, Long Beach and Island Park were two-family houses.

Countywide some 6.6 per cent of the housing units in 1960 were two-family dwellings. Through the 1960s, many single-family units were converted into two-family units, often without building code or zoning approval. By the early 1970s, the existence of such units had become a controversial issue in some villages. Many residents felt that the increasing number of illegal two-family homes was lessening the value of existing single-family units and posing a threat of future residential deterioration.

The acceptance of apartment housing in the county was an even greater issue. During the postwar years up to 1956 only 6,900 apartment units were constructed. In the next six years, this number doubled, and beginning in 1963, over 2,000 multiple-housing units a year were added in the county. Communities such as Great Neck, Roslyn, Mineola, Hempstead, Cedarhurst, Garden City, Freeport, Rockville Centre and Long Beach had more than 10 per cent of their available housing in multi-family units. There were also scattered apartments in Farmingdale, Floral Park and Lawrence. Generally, even in all of these communities, there were limitations on the height of apartment construction, and expansion was a frequent community issue. During a burst of building in the early 1960s, the Village of Freeport witnessed the construction of sixteen new apartment buildings in the space of less than two years. This change in the community's appearance was so dramatic that a moratorium was placed on the building of future multiple-dwelling units.

From 1960 to 1970, apartment housing units increased by 48 per cent in Nassau County. There was a subsequent decrease in owner-occupied housing units from 84.2 per cent in 1960 to only 81.8 per cent in 1970.

Apartments provided housing for 14.7 per cent of the population in 1960. Although this only increased moderately to 15 per cent by 1970, the new trend in the county toward building multiple-family units rather than one-family units was most significant. New one-family housing starts had decreased to 1,019 units in 1970, while 1,812 multi-family units were built. By 1970, many communities in Nassau County had major concentrations of apartment houses, including Long Beach with 9,562 units, Hempstead with 6,468 units and Freeport with 4,724 units.

The great increase to over 79,000 apartments, with one half in structures over ten units in 1970, had created an entirely new group of county residents. Since their construction after World War II, apartments attracted former homeowners and younger families. Over 60 per cent of these people formerly had a residence in the county and a majority intended to remain apartment dwellers. Monthly rentals in 1960 ranged up to $275 for a seven-room apartment, with a median of $95. Higher taxes, mortgage rates and maintenance costs had increased the median cost to $159, with rates as high as $260 for a one-bedroom apartment, by 1970. The drastic inflationary trend of the early 1970s caused major rent increases, and large numbers of tenants became increasingly vocal in their demands for rent control.

In the Village of Great Neck Plaza, 5,500 of the 6,000 residents lived in apartment units. Its mayor, Andrew Wurman, proposed rent controls since "throughout suburbia there are gross inequities and rent gouging going on." Apartment owners, however, fought the controls and contended that all of their costs including labor and taxes had increased and that rent controls would turn the communities with many apartment houses into slum areas.

Deterioration of central areas was a visible specter to many residents, since older villages were confronted with blighted areas alongside newly constructed housing. This decay, centering in downtown business areas and fringe housing, required massive rehabil-itation for several villages. The first urban renewal efforts on Long Island began in Rockville Centre in 1956. Despite endless processing delays and public criticism, a large blighted area adjacent to the railroad was redeveloped. An initial series of town houses was opened in 1964 and over four hundred multihousing units were eventually completed. Several other communities, including Glen Cove, Long Beach, Freeport and North Hempstead projects in Roslyn and Manhasset, obtained federal funds, which enabled rebuilding of considerable areas of deteriorated commercial and residential structures.

A special housing problem became more acute in the late 1960s due to Nassau's changing population base, with over 12 per cent of the residents over sixty years of age. Housing costs and scarcity were severely affecting this elderly group. In the mid-1960s, there were fewer than one hundred low-cost housing units for elderly citizens. Stimulated by the acute need and aided by federal funds, the town governments and local villages began to construct low-cost housing projects for the aged. By 1970, there were over 1,500 units throughout the county, the majority provided by the Town of Hempstead at scattered sites throughout the township. The Village of Freeport also developed an exemplary project for its local residents. Despite the vocal demands by senior citizens, project development was difficult for governmental officials. Many residents, such as the speaker at a public hearing for a proposed unit in Massapequa, felt "The town board is going to advertise this as [being] for senior citizens . . . But when you think of it, think of it as what is is: low-income housing." Considerable community education was required to mitigate the poor image of low-cost housing and allay fears that it would adversely affect residential values.

Although single-family housing units provided some 85 per cent of the housing for Nassau residents, the significant increase in multiple-dwelling units created an entirely new environment in many Nassau County

The rising age level of county residents led to construction of senior citizen housing and *special recreational programs such as this music session.*

communities. In the Town of North Hempstead, and along the railroad line on the south shore, extensive apartment building in some villages had created an urban atmosphere. By 1970, over 95 per cent of the residential land in Nassau County had been developed, with less than 1 per cent remaining zoned for apartment construction. Future expansion will depend, to a great extent, on whether local zoning regulations will be changed, and such changes were meeting great resistance in most communities.

By 1970, suburban subdivisions had spread across the entire south shore and the center of the county, leaving only scattered lots for future development. Most of this construction was on small building plots and development appearance varied from diversified, interesting design to standardized, unappealing grid patterns. The large, open estate areas in the central and northern portions of the county were seriously diminished, although most construction in this area required larger one- to four-acre parcels which retained the rural atmosphere.

Tremendous local diversity existed within the county, frequently within a very small geographic area. The Great Neck peninsula included small communities like the Village of Saddle Rock, with homes ranging from $70,000 to $150,000, and the apartment community of Great Neck Plaza. Although the dulling sameness of some subdivisions is evident, the overriding housing diversity in the county was a remarkable achievement of its great suburban growth.

Despite an active program to preserve recreational and park areas, much of the rural appearance of Nassau County disappeared during this growth. The changing ecological

Rising taxes and spiraling upkeep costs caused many former estates to be developed, *although some were preserved for public use, such as the Old Westbury Gardens.*

balance of the Great South Bay and its marsh areas was recognized only after a great deal of it was filled in. Development did not occur without an enormous loss of open space and natural areas. The loss was impressed on Long Island naturalist Robert Cushman Murphy by his associate Edwin Way Teale, one of the most gifted writers on natural history of our time. Teale told Murphy of his last sighting on Long Island of the plains-inhabiting sandpiper known as the upland plover. The bird was perched atop a wooden sign, and when Teale came within range he read, "A SUPERMARKET WILL BE ERECTED HERE." Exit plover, enter people.

The mass movement of over 1 million people into Nassau County after World War II was a significant portion of a much larger movement throughout the United States. The development of suburban areas around major metropolitan centers was the principal feature of American society in the postwar years. It created a new way of American life and commentators eagerly explored and examined its ramifications. As one of the principal suburban areas in the country, Nassau County was often included in such study and interpretation. The suburban phenomenon has been studied and restudied as it continues to evolve and develop. The complexities of changing age levels, economic status, maturing of communities and changing ethnic basis created a wealth of changing facts and trends which defied easy organization. Although the studies multiplied, conflicting conclusions provided no simple analysis.

Originally the scientific observers of community life, particularly sociologists, feared this new society that the "organization man" was creating. Was he building an image of his corporate ideal as a one-class and one-perspective society? In his book *The Exurbanites,* A. C. Spectorsky lamented the pressure of jobs, family isolation, extensive use of liquor and frantic leisure activities of the wealthy city commuter who had moved to the suburbs. William H. Whyte's classic *The Organization Man* expressed fears of the transient nature of the mobile junior execu-

tive, who was moving from one temporary residence to another as he clawed his way upward in the modern corporations. Whyte was skeptical of the real social value of the interminable "kaffeeklatsches" and the pressure for group participation and togetherness. He was fearful that in suburbia the families "learn how to look happy."

All of these factors were undoubtedly present in this new suburban society, but most residents were really too busy enjoying the thrill of having their own home, of being able to send their youngster off to a bright, sparkling, new grammar school and of being able to enjoy waterfront activities only a few minutes from their homes. Max Lerner, in his massive interpretation of American society *America as a Civilization,* provides a more balanced conclusion: ". . . few of the suburbanites had such fear or reflections. Instead they had a stir of excitement in them because they had a widening of horizons and an accession of experience."

Any interpretation of Nassau County's suburban growth must be a preliminary account since the course of many events will be clear only after several generations pass. Certain characteristics of this development provide a key to an understanding of suburbia and consequently Nassau County life in these years. Some of these characteristics must be explained in terms sociological or psychological rather than historical. The child-centered orientation of suburban families is one of these principal characteristics. Suburbia was attractive to many residents because it enabled children to grow up in a different and better environment than in the city.

The home itself assumed a new significance for residents accustomed to apartment living. The house, its yard, gardens and endless need for maintenance with "do it yourself" participation, established new roles for men and women in the family. *Time* magazine concluded, in 1960, that "the key figure in all suburbia, the threat that weaves between family and community—the keeper of the suburban dream—is the suburban housewife." A woman in suburbia, due to the ab-

Women provided an increasingly significant force in suburbia, and constituted the energetic membership of local civic groups such as the Birchwood at Jericho Civic Association, shown protesting unsafe construction in 1960. Courtesy of Newsday.

sence of her commuting husband, played a wide role as both home and family manager in addition to neighborhood and community activist.

It is hard to trace in historical perspective the importance and significance of the new style of suburban living. Its informality, and the degree of close contact between neighbors, stimulated numerous studies. The physical layout of suburban streets, with an openness and close proximity between buildings, allows people to observe and interact with their neighbors closely, very similar to the traditional fellowship of the small town in America. The effects of this visibility included unwritten laws in many communities, such as parking your car only in front of your own property and civic association ac-

tivism against any type of neighborhood deterioration. All of the above characteristics require considerably more investigation before historical judgments can really be made.

However, certain suburban characteristics are clearly visible and were significant elements in Nassau County's growth. One such characteristic was the strong emphasis and central role that education assumed in suburban life. Just as in the earlier 1900s, the new residents moving into Nassau County after World War II indicated that "good schools" were a major reason for their decision to move to the suburbs. Suburban schools were considered to be better for children and probably ranked as the initial major stimulus for moving, besides the physical need for better housing.

Pivotal Role of Schools

The challenges and changes of suburban life are more evident in the development of local school systems than in any other aspect of Nassau County life. Education was the continuing focus of interest and activity for residents throughout the postwar period as school systems had to be built from almost nothing in many communities. The central importance of the school system remained strong and many residents vigorously objected to any operational reductions required because of declining enrollment in the 1970s, since "we moved into this community because of the reputation of the school system."

The overriding challenge of education in Nassau County was the development of physical facilities to handle the rapidly growing enrollment. In 1947 the county's public schools contained 69,575 students. This increased to a little over 100,000 in 1950 and then a fantastic growth of 20,000 additional students occurred annually. Within five years, over 220,000 students were in the public schools. The enrollment of thousands of students in some districts where there previously had been only hundreds of students was a traumatic experience. Student population grew in all districts but the rate varied tremendously.

Union Free School District No. 5, which included most of the area of Levittown, had a grand total of 40 pupils in 1945; within ten years it contained over 19,000 students. Great Neck, during the same period, increased from 3,429 to 9,313 children. Other communities had a much slower growth; for instance, Garden City, which comprised most of Union Free School District No. 18, increased from a prewar total of 1,799 students to 3,564 in 1955. The growth continued to a peak of over 330,000 students in the county during the 1964–65 school year.

Robert Moses indicated to a planning forum in the mid-1950s: "In Nassau today there is a hodgepodge of little red and big modern schools populated by pupils some of whom are studying Mutt and Jeff . . . while others are becoming proficient in nuclear science . . . members of school boards are as numerous as members . . . of the Elks . . . [There are] too many districts of widely varying sizes and efficiency. Some are poor, others are not. The rates are scandalously unequal." Moses touched on all of the educational problems facing the suburbs, but financing was certainly the most crucial. Education expenses became the major part of all governmental expenditures and enormous funds had to be used for school support.

Initially the major portion of education cost was for capital construction. In 1945 only 2 per cent of school expenditures was for debt service and capital outlay. Within five years this had jumped to almost 40 per cent of the $49 million of total school expenditures in the county. The real increases were just beginning, however, and in 1955 almost 50 per cent of the total school expenditures of $156,500,000 was for capital and debt costs. By that time over half of the total property taxes on local homes was required for educational services. The total combined debts of the school districts in the county were $235,500,000.

In 1960 total school district debt had reached $394 million but the major bulk of building construction was completed. Thereafter, capital and debt service costs dropped to less than 30 per cent of educational expenditures. Space for over 250,000 school children was provided by these funds in less than twenty years, an achievement indicative of the citizen support of education.

During this period, complete school systems, such as the Levittown District No. 5, with fifteen grammar and high schools, were constructed. The scarcity of land in many older communities caused marginal marshland or drainage areas to be filled in for school construction in communities such as Freeport, Malverne and East Rockaway. A new style of school construction dominated most of the expansion. One- and two-story ranch-type schools were constructed rather

Jerusalem District No. 5 original schoolhouse before Levitt development.

than multistory buildings. Architects and administrators considered them much safer and more efficient, and they blended well into the suburban environment. The schools were constructed with extensive facilities including gymnasiums, cafeterias, vocational shops, physics and chemistry laboratories—some even included swimming pools and planetariums. Although there was much concern about the expenditure of excessive monies on frills and luxurious construction, most schools were well built with economical and easy-to-maintain materials.

Obtaining the financial resources to construct these school plants dominated educa-

tional needs in the 1950s. The average annual cost per student increased from $280 in 1945 to $492 in 1954. The amount ranged from $270 a pupil to over $1,000 in some affluent school districts. There was an enormous diversity of tax rates due to the varying size and type of development, including industrial and business areas, within each district's tax base. Total school expenditures increased 600 per cent in the ten years up to 1955. The escalation of operating costs began to have its effect after 1955 when the county's school districts spent $84,700,000. Within five years operations expense had jumped to $185,200,000. Local school boards

Jonas Salk Junior High and Douglas Mac-Arthur High School, one of three large high schools in District No. 5, Levittown, after

suburban growth to over eighteen thousand students.

were under enormous pressures to maintain lower tax rates, and since school district voters could directly approve or disapprove budgets, the struggles over educational tax rates became an annual community problem.

Tax rates climbed steadily from the typical rate of a little over $1 for each $100 of assessed valuation at the end of the war. By 1955 many districts had rates over $4, and even established villages such as Hempstead and Freeport, which had sizable prewar school systems, were approaching $3. Through the late fifties and sixties, rates began to increase between 40 and 50 cents a year, and then finally over $1 a year. In 1955 a taxpayer uprising rejected fifteen budgets. Even after proposing economy budgets, some districts, such as Roosevelt, had to operate under austerity budgets. The increasing financial pressure caused the independent school districts to form the Nassau-Suffolk School Board Association to provide a united front for lobbying and stimulation of additional state aid to education.

Major changes were sought in the financial basis of school financing to ensure education progress. School board officials, PTA groups and local governmental leaders persuaded the area's state legislators to support increasing state aid for local education. The School Board Association aimed to achieve a 50 per cent funding of education by the state. The average per pupil cost had risen to $692 in 1961, with a wide range still existing in the county, from as little as $506 in East Meadow to $1,096 in Manhasset. The next year, Governor Nelson Rockefeller supported increased state pupil aid to $500 but indicated that the state had gone as far as it could in helping finance local education. Pressure continued annually on the legislature to raise local aid and there were subsequent increases to $850 per pupil by 1970.

Despite the increase in state aid, school financing continued to face annual crises. In 1966 eleven school budgets were defeated in a wide range of communities including Elmont, Freeport, Plainview-Old Bethpage, Lawrence-Cedarhurst and Wantagh. By

1968, per pupil cost varied from $1,426 in Great Neck to $782 in Floral Park. Federal aid, under the new Title I through III programs, began to provide additional funding to local schools but the increasing inflationary trend of salaries and supplies drove costs ever higher. In 1971 nineteen school budgets were defeated in a major taxpayer rebellion against the projected 10 to 15 per cent increases. Some tax rates were now over $10 per $100 of assessed valuation and still rising rapidly. Despite the great inequities between school costs in different villages, little outcry was raised for the equalization of rates until the early 1970s. In 1974 a group of districts began legal action to force the state government to provide aid that would enable equalization between districts with varying tax bases. Residents seemed to feel that local control over their individual school system was of more importance than establishing new district lines or other major reorganization that might effect a fairer and more equitable financing base across the entire county. Instead of attempting such difficult restructuring, the major pressure for economic reform was placed on the state government to increase its share of educational expense.

Since the organizational basis of local school districts was well established before World War II, the enormous changes of the suburban growth did not create any major district realignments. In the late 1930s, a few central school districts had been established to provide high school services for several individual districts. The technique did not spread and most districts established independent high schools in the postwar years.

The Sewanhaka Central High School district, established in 1931 with 1,174 pupils, by 1960 had grown to over 10,000 students from the districts of Elmont, Floral Park, Franklin Square and New Hyde Park. The contrasting educational philosophies of these individual school boards, with the conflict between traditional versus modern policies and the differing rates of growth and tax rates in the individual districts, caused a serious split in 1960. There was considerable pressure to break up the central high school, with opponents urging each individual district to establish its own secondary school. The dispute continued through the sixties, and in 1974, all of the boards except Elmont's supported a proposal for decentralization, but a public vote within the four districts was 65 per cent in favor of retaining the centralized service.

Although the central district format was not expanded, internal reorganization was unavoidable. In 1954, thirty-four of the county's sixty-two districts were supervised by two central supervisory offices. As the local districts grew larger, most of the boards converted to union free status and appointed their own school superintendent. In 1961 the two supervisory school districts in the county were combined into one to provide superintendent services for the sixteen school districts that still did not have their own superintendents. With the development of a Board of Cooperative Educational Services in the early 1970s, this service was assimilated into BOCES' administrative role.

One significant change in the educational system of the county occurred because of the new religious composition of its residents.

In 1940 the parochial school system of the Roman Catholic Church had an enrollment of approximately 11,000 students. The greatly increasing Roman Catholic population of the county caused a wide expansion of the parochial school system, with parents waiting in line to enroll their children in the late 1950s. Within ten years some 23,500 students were in the county's private and parochial schools, and this tripled by 1962 to over 60,000 students. Supported entirely by church funds and individual tuition payments, the over seventy Roman Catholic parochial elementary and high schools relieved the public school systems of an enormous number of students.

Although Roman Catholic schools provided the major portion of private facilities, other religious educational institutions were established. The older St. Paul's and St. Mary's schools in Garden City continued under the Protestant Episcopal Church. Greatly expanded Lutheran congregations of the county led to the creation of several Lutheran high schools, and the new Jewish residents supported the development of Hebrew academies in several communities. Though the Catholic parochial system was able to build sufficient physical facilities to handle its initial growth, the increasing

Maria Regina parochial high school in Uniondale.

operational costs in the 1960s began to exert financial pressure on the church. Religious orders were unable to provide sufficient teachers and laymen had to be employed at much higher costs. Lay teachers increased from 34 per cent in 1963 to over 50 per cent by the early 1970s.

In the mid-1960s, efforts began to obtain state aid in limited ways for parochial school students. The initial attempt was to provide funding for schoolbooks and other special expenses. Opponents, including the Nassau-Suffolk School Board Association, contended that state aid should not go to private and parochial schools. Although the state government leadership was sympathetic, court decisions limited the scope of this funding source for the support of parochial schools. By the late 1960s, the financial burden became critical due to declining enrollments caused by the lower birth rate and changing attitudes of Catholic parents. Maria Regina High School in Uniondale was a typical example of the problem. Its tuition fee rose from $250 when it opened in 1966, to $615 in 1972. The increasing cost of parochial education was a major threat to its continuance and programs were being evaluated throughout the parishes of the county in the early 1970s.

A major educational accomplishment during this period was the development of vocational education services. The Nassau County Vocational Education and Extension Board had been created in 1928 to develop adequate training programs for local volunteer firemen. After World War II, it became evident that the many local school districts could not provide adequate vocational training courses. Out of some 25,000 high school students, fewer than 1,000 were taking vocational training available in only a limited number of school districts including Sewanhaka, Lawrence, Lynbrook, Mineola and Roslyn.

The Vocational Education and Extension Board began to develop services in this area, and in 1956 it opened a countywide vocational and technical school in an indus-

trial building near Westbury. It also established a special services school for severely handicapped, mentally disturbed, brain-injured or emotionally disturbed children. These rudimentary facilities provided a significant supplemental educational service and it became evident that the county's increasing student population would require considerably larger special facilities.

In 1962 a county commission of eleven members was appointed to study special education needs and recommended that a new type of shared services board be elected by the trustees of the existing school districts to establish such countywide services. There was considerable discussion and the State Education Department also began to develop statewide plans in this area. In 1967 the New York State commissioner of education ordered that a Board of Cooperative Educational Services be established to serve the local school districts within the county, and the Nassau County BOCES came into existence with an initial $97,675 budget. All fifty-six school districts were members and elected the Board, which supervised the BOCES program.

BOCES expanded through the 1960s, acquiring facilities for the establishment of special services programs for the different needs of handicapped students and for varied vocational training programs. By the early 1970s, its budget was over $40 million a year with almost half provided by state funding. Local districts contributed a per capita amount for each of their students who attended BOCES facilities. As the cost per student increased, concern mounted among local school boards about their relationship to the central BOCES Board and pressure grew for BOCES to be more accountable to the local school districts.

Despite the numerous fiscal problems that required the concentration of local district administrators and Board members, the school districts within Nassau County actively engaged in educational innovation. In 1963, twenty-three of the districts in the county established the Nassau Educational

Development Council to provide centralized research and methods development for educational improvement. The council received a $400,000 federal grant in 1966 and stimulated programs in the teaching of modern math, the use of television, development of upgraded elementary schools, and team teaching concepts.

All of these techniques were used in various school districts, but perhaps the most significant program was the development of open education in many elementary schools. Developed as a concept in the late 1960s, it included interage grouping, instruction geared to individual needs of children and an open space environment without rows of individual desks in the classroom, to encourage movement and interaction between the children. This experimental program was tried in many areas, such as the Merrick School District, which converted several grade levels at two of its elementary schools.

High school programs have also sought new methods to stimulate student interest and participation. The standard curriculum was expanded to provide a range of interesting elective courses. Audio-visual use increased tremendously with film, television and taped programs providing a regular supplement to normal classwork. In the early 1970s, Great Neck developed alternative programs in its high school. The Village School provided a program of independent study, while the Community School included a half day at academic pursuits and the remainder in experience at an actual job or independent study. Other general developments were remedial reading and speech programs, sex education, the new math concept and introduction of foreign languages in the elementary grades.

Another addition to the educational responsibility of school districts was the development of extensive adult education programs. Created in many districts during the Depression to provide employment opportunities, adult education programs continued during World War II to offer technical training for the many workers required in war plants. After the war, extensive adult education programs continued in almost all of the county's school districts, supported by state reimbursement and individual tuition fees for classes. The programs, with a wide range of curricula, have grown to include as many as ten thousand students at Great Neck. Vocational improvement courses, including clerical and mechanical skills, became only a small portion of the course offerings, which extended into all cultural and

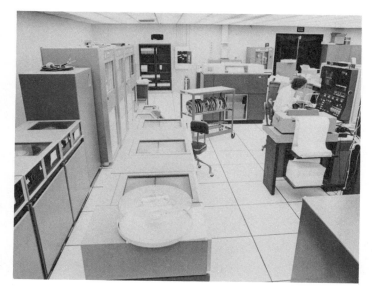

Students in the data-processing course at the BOCES county center have access to sophisticated equipment.

educational activities, including music instruction, contemporary politics, craft skills such as dressmaking, and physical fitness sessions including yoga.

The enormous diversity of the county's school population created several problem areas in which Nassau County became a testing ground for nationally significant policy decisions. By the late 1950s, the increasingly large Jewish population in many school districts was becoming concerned about the intrusion of religious activities in the local schools. The initial problem revolved around the observation of religious holidays in the schools. Jewish parents and leaders were deeply offended by Christmas celebrations and began to express such feelings to local school boards. In 1957 a Christmas play was banned in a Valley Stream school and the community immediately was involved in unpleasant dissension. The disagreement even carried over to affect the friendly relation-

ships between Jewish and Christian school staff members. By the early 1960s, most districts had effected a compromise solution and began to observe both Christmas and Chanukah holidays.

The principal area of religious dispute was over the reading of the Bible in school assemblies and classrooms. In 1962, parents of ten pupils in the Herricks School District objected to a non-denominational prayer and began a case in the courts to prevent its use. The conflict eventually went to the United States Supreme Court and in a nationwide decision the parents' contention that this was an unconstitutional activity in the schools was upheld. Thereafter, in schools throughout the country, Bible reading or prayer could not be a required activity.

The State Education Department received many complaints the following year that eleven Long Island districts were still allowing this practice. New York State Commis-

Athletic programs were expanded after World War II to include lacrosse, soccer, tennis and golf.

sioner of Education James Allen ordered the districts to comply with the Supreme Court decision and banned all prayers in local schools. The initial shock of the decision created a great deal of bitterness for many residents with strong religious convictions. But most Protestant and Roman Catholic religious leaders observed that the home and church were more appropriate places for religious experience and the antagonisms gradually faded away.

The early 1960s were also controversial years in many districts due to the problems over segregation of black students and the bussing of students to achieve racial integration. In 1963 parents in the Malverne School District appealed to Commissioner Allen to order the Malverne School District to stop the segregation of students. Allen, after studying the district's apportionment of pupils, ordered it to redraw attendance lines for three elementary schools to eliminate racial imbalance. The attempt to redraw school boundaries to achieve better racial balance was met with a cool to frigid response in the involved school districts.

There was strong opposition to changing the neighborhood school concept and instituting a system of bussing students to schools out of their immediate geographic area. That fall, supporters of desegregation, led by Long Island CORE chairman Lincoln Lynch, attempted sit-in demonstrations and registration efforts by black students in all-white schools at several districts; these attempts even resulted in arrests at Malverne. The Freeport School District took positive action and established a program with only minor public reaction. Other districts were reluctant to act. Manhasset had to be ordered by a federal judge in 1964 to integrate its Valley School. In 1965 the Roosevelt School District underwent an extensive controversy when the National Association for the Advancement of Colored People requested the commissioner to hold hearings to determine why its schools should not be desegregated. The school board's attorney defended the board's policy of drawing lines so "students could attend the school which is as close as possible to their homes." But Commissioner Allen, in viewing the racial make-up of the Theodore Roosevelt School, which had four hundred black students and four whites, concluded that the schools must be integrated and said, "The question in America today is not whether you are going to have desegregation but how." Those school districts with sizable black populations thereafter attempted to provide integrated schools although principally through the realignment of school areas or grade assignments rather than bussing.

After having conquered the initial fiscal challenges of establishing adequate physical facilities and supporting the increasing operating costs during the 1960s, local school districts were shocked with a new problem beginning in 1970. The sharply falling birth rate since that year created a declining enrollment which one official indicated "is something they don't want to talk about because they don't want to go through the trauma, the public relations problems with the community, until they absolutely can no longer avoid it." Three Nassau districts closed schools and the Plainview-Old Bethpage District, which had one of the highest tax rates in the county—over $16 per $100 of assessed valuation—projected an enormous decline in its number of students by the late 1970s. Its board considered plans for the closing of four of its eight elementary schools and their future use for special education or other rental purposes.

Other districts, such as Farmingdale, East Meadow and Levittown, all had decreases of over 500 students a year in the early 1970s. From 1961 through 1969, the total elementary school enrollment in the county dropped from 182,709 students to 164,531 students. Thus the trend continued to point toward lower enrollments. This new problem of declining enrollment required major policy study by local school boards involving the problems of the accuracy of enrollment projections, the stability of the birth rate, the utilization of surplus buildings, the community reaction to such serious changes in local districts and the unknown effect on school finances and personnel.

Initially the suburban schools were a major employment source for hundreds of college-trained teachers annually. But as enrollments leveled, demand for new teachers dropped sharply and the teachers' demands for salary increases and tenure security resulted in some strikes and unrest. Student rights and responsibilities were a major area of change during the 1960s, with more relaxed standards of dress and appearance won in court cases. These changes and the effect of lower enrollments dominated the early 1970s. The challenge of building new school systems, which had been met in the 1950s and 1960s, was shifting to the utilization and development of these systems in the remainder of the twentieth century.

Despite the unprecedented changes and difficult problems local school districts faced, they provided a consistently high standard of education. Many students from former urban families were exposed for the first time to a conducive educational environ-ment in their new suburban schools. One student who had moved from the Lower East Side to the Carle Place schools commented, "For the first time, I really want to learn. I am planning to go to college. I hadn't thought of it until we moved here."

Since some 17 per cent of the population had a college education in 1970, many families expected college study as a normal course of events. This, combined with the strong motivations of local students, produced a high percentage of students desiring further education. High school graduates from Nassau County schools jumped from 15,985 in 1960 to over 25,000 in 1970, and as high as 70 per cent indicated an interest in going on to four- or two-year colleges. This enormous number of graduates seeking college education greatly stimulated the growth of higher educational institutions in Nassau County and on Long Island. Although a considerable number of students attended universities out of the area, a strong demand began to build up in the late 1950s for increased local collegiate facilities.

The Swirbul Library at Adelphi designed by Richard Neutra.

Growth of Higher Education

The immediate impulse leading to the growth of local colleges after World War II was the return of many veterans who wanted to take advantge of the generous educational aid of the GI Bill of Rights. Adelphi College became a coeducational institution after the war to provide such facilities. Its programs, initially undergraduate and then graduate also, continued to emphasize education, social work, nursing and business administration. By 1950 it had expanded to almost 2,500 students and the local students tripled its enrollment by 1965. Its campus at Garden City was expanded, and in 1963 university status was achieved. That same year a new library, designed by the noted architect Richard Neutra, was opened.

Hofstra College, which had gained its independence from New York University just prior to World War II, limped through the war years as a liberal arts coeducational institution. Returning veterans boosted its student body and it also attracted many local students, growing gradually from some 3,500 students in 1950. The increasing number of local high school graduates pushed its enrollment to over 12,000 in 1970. The small campus, originally several quadrangles centered around the Hofstra mansion, spread out across the open plains land.

Hofstra became a university in 1963 and six years later was one of the seven universities and colleges in the United States cited by federal Commissioner of Education Earl McGrath for "innovation in higher education." The campus had by then also expanded across Hempstead Turnpike to a portion of Mitchel Field and represented over a $60-million capital investment. A new library was constructed on the south side of the turnpike and a covered walkway across the roadway connected it with the student union building and a series of high-rise dormitories on the north side.

With the addition of dormitories, out-of-state students added a new dimension to the growth of the university. In 1970 a law school was instituted, providing the only local university facility for such studies. The large number of local graduates of the university undertook a significant leadership role in Long Island professions, education and government. The university had taken an active role in providing major community resources such as its Center for Business and Urban Research, the Emily Lowe Art Gallery, and its renowned annual Shakespeare festival, first initiated by university president John C. Adams.

The rising demands for new college facilities, due to increasing population on Long Island, led to the creation of several other major institutions. In 1955, C. W. Post College opened on the former estate of heiress Marjorie Merriweather Post in Brookville. A branch of Long Island University, the college developed an extensive campus with new classrooms and dormitories in the 1960s. From an initial student body of 121, it grew to over 3,000 in 1960, expanding rapidly to almost 12,000 by 1970.

C. W. Post provided a general liberal arts curriculum although library science and business courses have supplied many graduates for Long Island organizations. An extensive program of evening classes and an innovative weekend college have provided unique opportunities for adult residents on the island. Extension into the community has also been provided by special programs of business management and a popular annual American theater festival.

The need for lower-cost educational opportunities led in 1960 to the creation of Nassau Community College as part of the expanding New York State University system. The operating budget of the college was funded equally by the state of New York, the county of Nassau and student tuition. The college opened with a modest 640 students in a county building adjacent

Hofstra's unique reproduction of Shakespeare's Globe Theatre.

to the courthouse. In 1962 it moved into temporary campus facilities in the major portion of the remaining Mitchel Field Air Force Base buildings and immediately began a rapid expansion to almost 7,000 students by 1965. In the early 1970s its student population had doubled, with over 7,000 out of 16,000 attending daytime classes. The college provided an extensive two-year curriculum and some 80 per cent of its graduates continued on to four-year colleges. It provided a means for students from modest-income families to begin their educational experience and enabled many older individuals to retrain themselves in evening classes. An enormous new campus was planned for the site, with construction under way in the early 1970s.

The expansion of the state university system provided other public higher education facilities. The old agricultural school at Farmingdale was transformed into the SUNY at Farmingdale with a $40-million building program. A broad program of technical training courses, ranging from recreation to police science, was established. The State University of New York at Old Westbury was organized in 1967 with an unusual academic program. Designed to provide education for those students traditionally bypassed, the college sought black, Spanish-speaking and economically underprivileged older students. After a controversial experimental period in the early 1970s, plans were developed for expansion of its student body and development of a course of studies including extensive community contact and work experience.

In addition to these major universities and colleges, specialized institutions were also founded and developed in the county. In 1943 the United States Merchant Marine

Residence towers of Hofstra University rise above the Hempstead Plains.

Cub Scouts tour the Merchant Marine Academy Chapel at Kings Point. Courtesy of Newsday.

Academy was established on the former Walter P. Chrysler estate in Kings Point. Federally funded, this service academy trained future officers for the commercial merchant marine services of the United States. Just after the end of the war in 1947, the Webb institute of Naval Architecture, founded in 1899, moved to Herbert L. Pratt's estate in Glen Cove. This unusual institution provides an engineering college with its sole curriculum in the field of naval architecture and marine engineering for an elite enrollment of eighty full-scholarship students.

One institution of higher learning was developed committed solely to the education of women. Molloy Catholic College for

Women, founded in 1955, provided courses in liberal arts and the humanities. Its student body grew from a little over 300 in 1960 to over 1,500 in the early 1970s, and could study specific career fields in nursing and teaching. The New York Institute of Technology established a campus on several adjacent estates in Old Westbury in 1964. The college provided specialized training particularly in fine arts, audio-visual and technical fields for 3,000 students in 1970. The Polytechnic Institute of Brooklyn also started a small branch for technical courses in the aerospace complex near Farmingdale.

By 1970 the county's eleven colleges and higher educational institutions had an enrollment of almost 70,000 students. The increasing number of local high school graduates provided the basic student body and established a long-range demand for higher education located nearby. Rising costs of private college tuition led to establishment of a public community college and demands for state aid to private universities. Such aid was begun in the late 1960s to diminish the cost difference between units of the state university and local colleges. The development of these extensive private and public collegiate resources created excellent higher education opportunities for local high school graduates, enabled many older residents to complete college programs, enriched the county's cultural resources and provided specialized technical services to the business community.

Paralleling the school and college expansion of the postwar period, an extensive development took place in the growth of local public library services. In 1940 there were thirty public libraries scattered throughout Nassau County. During the growth years between 1945 and 1960, fifteen libraries were established, most of them encompassing school district geographic areas. The older Great Neck Library was the county's largest in 1960 with over 160,000 volumes. Indicative of the strong citizen interest, the new communities of East Meadow and Levittown both established major libraries that rapidly grew to challenge Great Neck's col-

Levittown Library's sparkling interior symbolizes the contemporary service of the county's local libraries.

lection size. The circulation of libraries varied from a high of twenty-nine volumes per resident in Oyster Bay to as low six for each resident in Hicksville. Great Neck's budget was almost $300,000 and Levittown's was not too far behind with $250,000 in expenditures. The total expenditures of all libraries was over $3 million in 1960.

Throughout the sixties, this growth continued so that by 1970 the three largest libraries were approaching almost $1-million budgets. Libraries were highly individualistic, utilizing a variety of buildings, from a former Methodist church in Sea Cliff to a section of a public school in North Merrick. Predominantly organized on a school district basis, some were under village boards, and a new Shelter Rock Library served an unincorporated area stretching from New Hyde Park to Herricks.

As part of a statewide program to improve library services, a Nassau Library System was organized in 1959 under a board of trustees chosen by member libraries. Thirty-two of the county's libraries joined the system to establish a central book-processing facility, provide special technical services and institute direct access for patrons between all the libraries. By 1970 all fifty-three libraries in the county were part of the system, which operated under a $1,500,000 budget, principally from state aid. The county of Nassau, in its development of the Mitchel Field area, also included plans for a central Nassau County Research Library. A small staff was at work in the early 1970s to create this major reference resource for the entire county.

As the central public facility in many of the new postwar communities, the public library provided a much broader role than the prewar book depository. Books and periodicals were still the principal emphasis, but new materials including records, movies, microfilm and paperbacks provided broader resources. As community centers, libraries provided meeting rooms used daily by the many local civic-educational organizations of suburbia. In addition to this public use, libraries provided film programs, drama performances and art exhibits, extending educational and cultural services to their local audiences.

Good library resources, the extensive college and university system providing evening and weekend courses, adult education programs in school districts, and the highly developed elementary and secondary schools in the county created an exceptional educational resource for county residents after World War II. The network of educational facilities is very visible evidence of the significant role education assumed in suburbia. Public support and participation in the tremendous development of all educational facilities was a major part of the postwar growth in Nassau County. It was a central factor of the area's ethos and initially focused on the new resident's great concern for better schools for his children.

Increasingly, however, the adult portion of the population became active users and participants in all areas of local educational activities, creating a new thrust of institutional development and resources. Strong and persistent citizen leadership, exercised by hundreds of school board members, enabled the creation and funding of entire new school districts. Despite a general desire for fiscal economy, local residents provided the necessary resources for the expansion of a strong higher education system and public libraries. Hofstra University grew to prominence without a major endowment fund, and Levittown, a community with one of the county's lowest tax bases, supported creation of one of the area's major libraries. Education was, to a very great extent, the core of Nassau County life.

CHAPTER VII

A MATURING SUBURB

The Leisure Revolution

The Salisbury Golf Club, with four golf courses in Westbury, was among the parcels of land that reverted to county ownership for delinquent taxes in 1940. County Executive J. Russel Sprague decided to have the county absorb the $190,000 in back taxes and keep the large tract of land in the center of the county. During the war years he mulled over the future of the property and finally proposed a major public project in April 1944.

In a twelve-page prospectus, Sprague urged that a Nassau County public park be constructed on the old golf club property. He indicated, "Postwar plans for our county would not be complete without envisioning county-owned recreational facilities. We propose to proceed with the establishment of a Nassau County park at Salisbury . . . which one day will be to Nassau County what Central Park is today to New York City."

The report was a strong justification for the use of the property as a park, which Sprague felt was "the only farsighted, provident way of reaping ever-increasing public benefits from it." He conservatively indicated that the income from the golf courses would support the facility and that this was a prudent, fiscally sound plan. The county had been operating the courses to prevent their deterioration and in 1944 had collected $21,-

Unveiling of Nassau County Park dedication plaque at lakeside flagpole by County Executive J. Russel Sprague, October 1, 1949.

ooo in golf course revenue. The development of a public park on the property was part of over-all plans which the county government had made for vital postwar public works in response to Sprague's estimate that "Nassau's population will double in the twenty years following the war."

Since the county government had never previously undertaken a project of such magnitude, it was regarded as an enormous venture. Voices of caution were raised, and few people then imagined that Sprague's prediction of a doubling of the county's population would fall far short of the mark—the population would actually triple within the next twenty years. Others scoffed at the whole idea of the project, such as the skeptic who wrote a letter to the editor of *Newsday* and complained, ". . . in the meantime, here in Nassau they're building a new park on the old Salisbury Golf Links. It's a joke. We are surrounded by water and beaches and every backyard is a park. I'm sure I'm not going to pack a lunch and run out to Salisbury and eat it, are you? . . . Why wasn't it sold for land and home improvement?" Only fifteen years later he would readily get his answer any summer weekend from the golfers lined up at the park's three golf courses at 5 A.M. and the crowds filling the nearby picnic areas by late morning.

Despite the criticism, Sprague continued to move ahead to develop the park carefully. Robert Trent Jones, a nationally famous golf course architect, was hired to provide a plan for the facility, and architects were also hired for a new clubhouse. In 1947, district engineer George H. Peters, who was in charge of the park's development and later became the county deputy commissioner of public works for parks, made an extensive speaking campaign before civic groups throughout the county to explain the park's future development. Natural springs were found on the property and an artificial lake was established which became a popular winter skating spot. Perimeter fencing was installed and the first of some fifteen thousand trees were planted on the large acreage. Public interest grew and the American Legion urged that the park be dedicated to the veterans from Nassau County who had served in the armed forces.

The park was formally dedicated as a memorial to the county's dead in our nation's wars in October of 1949, as part of the fiftieth-anniversary celebration of the county. A major ceremony, with a parade of some nine thousand marchers, was climaxed by a flight of jet aircraft from nearby Mitchel Air Force Base. Development gradually continued, including extensive picnic areas, athletic fields, a major clubhouse completed in 1958, a veterans memorial, a historical museum and other recreational facilities. In 1971 the park was renamed Dwight D. Eisenhower Memorial Park in honor of the late President of the United States. Creation of the park and its development were indicative of the great public interest and support in the county for recreational and leisure activities. Suburban life, to the new Nassau residents after World War II, was not just a new home and community, but also a new lifestyle with a strong concept of leisure fulfillment.

Leisure activity was a major characteristic of suburbia in American life. Nassau was no exception and also felt the national trends of the reliance on the automobile as the major

Eisenhower Park: Salisbury Club House on left, Veterans Memorial center, Lakeside Theatre on right.

transportation means, the construction of enormous shopping centers to provide every form of material convenience, and the development of political independence. While these qualities of life were new predominant factors, recreation had always been a major part of Nassau County life. An extensive range of community organizations and recreational facilities for residents was evident in the initial suburban development of the county prior to World War II, and was greatly expanded by the postwar growth.

An endless variety of community organizations developed within three general areas of interest, providing community activities, charitable needs and cultural outlets. Organizations in all of these areas created social contacts for residents and means to accomplish socially desirable goals. Participation was greatest in the large variety of community-improvement activities. A vast number of these organizations related to children and home ownership.

The local civic association became a major force in almost every area of the county. Generally organized in a contiguous area of one to two thousand homes, the civic association was the most powerful means for residents to express their views concerning local problems. As unincorporated areas were developed, the civic associations also initially provided a means to meet and socialize with neighbors. As areas matured, their activity began to fluctuate in accordance with the extent of issues and leadership in an area.

Numerous other organizations also focused on the improvement of local life or existed to provide special services. The long tradition of volunteer fire departments was eagerly continued by newcomers and the system of volunteer fire protection formed rapidly in all the newly developed areas, while established departments readily expanded to cover the growth in older communities. Fire protection was well provided by seventy-one independent departments with over ten thousand vol-

Enjoying the park playground.

Firemen in practice session at Nassau County Firemen's Training Center, Old Bethpage, 1961.

unteers who received training at the Nassau County Firemen's Center constructed in 1961 at Old Bethpage. Volunteer ambulance corps and auxiliary police units were formed in many localities to provide supplemental public services on a voluntary basis. Military service groups, including the American Legion and the Veterans of Foreign Wars, provided a meeting ground for veterans and assistance in solving their problems.

A host of child-centered organizations provided extracurricular activities for youth, including the Little League, Midget Football, the YMCA, the Boy and Girl Scouts and other sports or crafts groups. These all required extensive adult leadership and participation. For thousands of youngsters, such activities provided an enormous range of experience, from business methods in Junior Achievement to musical training in the many drum and bugle corps.

Another major portion of citizen energy

was directed into the creation of many new charitable and humanitarian groups. A key development in this area was the formation of a United Fund of Long Island. Originally founded by Grumman Corporation president Leon A. Swirbul in 1951, the Long Island Industry Fund raised monies to assist in meeting the critical shortage of hospital facilities in Nassau and Suffolk counties. By 1958 the Fund had expanded to include a wide range of health and welfare agencies and began to raise over $1 million annually. Most of the money was raised through payroll deductions of the employees in participating companies. Renamed the United Fund of Long Island in 1965, support was extended to additional service organizations including some seventeen voluntary hospitals, thirty-nine health and welfare agencies, the Boy and Girl Scouts and four local community chests. Although the Fund's unified drive raised considerable money, individual

Association for the Help of Retarded Children vocational training center in Freeport, *where more than three hundred retarded adults are employed.*

charities still found it necessary to perform independent fund raising to support their activities.

Many of the new charities developed after World War II were in response to the need for medical research and training for specific illnesses, including the Mental Health, Heart and Muscular Dystrophy associations, the Association for the Help of Retarded Children, the Multiple Sclerosis Society and the American Cancer Society. Organized in 1948, the United Cerebral Palsy Association, which opened a major training center in Roosevelt four years later, was a pioneer national endeavor. The center provided a school with extensive training and therapy programs for cerebral-palsied children. The activities were financed through an annual fund-raising telethon and were assisted by the services of five hundred volunteers. Another unique organization was Abilities, Inc., founded by Henry Viscardi, a paraplegic.

This facility for the handicapped provided both educational training and employment opportunities. Older traditional organizations, such as the Salvation Army, the American Red Cross and the Industrial Home for the Blind, continued to receive strong private support.

The institution of new cultural pursuits caused expansion into a third broad activity area. Before the war, there were many multiple-purpose clubs that included cultural activities as part of their program. The multiplicity of interests in the much larger postwar population led to the creation of specialized cultural groups in local communities. These ranged from arts councils providing a wide range of classes in art, dance and music to clubs specializing in one specific medium. Choral societies, theatrical and musical organizations became popular permanent organizations in many communities. Almost all of these groups were composed of

The Mineola Theatre under Dr. F. Calderone's ownerhsip attempted to provide live theater in the 1960s.

amateurs, but the increasing sophistication and training of residents provided a very high standard of performance, which in some cases approached professional quality.

The high income level of Nassau residents and additional leisure time increased the demand for cultural activities throughout the county. Almost all of the local universities provided significant art and drama facilities open to the community. Commercial facilities such as the Westbury Music Fair offered popular musical and dramatic entertainment. However, efforts to establish permanent serious theatrical and musical enterprises failed repeatedly due to the availability of the facilities and professionalism in New York City. Overall the extent and scope of cultural activities was impressive in terms of individual participation and variety, despite the inability to match the higher standards of urban cultural performances.

Local governments at the town and county level established cultural development programs to stimulate performing arts activities and bring major professional groups and star performers before local audiences. The county government also established, under the Nassau County Museum, a comprehensive museum system within its parks and recreation program. Over 1,500 acres of land was reserved for nature preserves, with several natural history museums and historical facilities including Falaise, the Gold Coast estate of Captain Harry Guggenheim. The

Entrance gates to Falaise courtyard, a vision of the Gold Coast.

Nassau County Museum also established and completed the first stages of the Old Bethpage village restoration as a major outdoor village restoration of rural life in America a century ago. A wide program of historic preservation and interpretation was developed in the 1960s by over a dozen local community historical and preservation societies such as the Roslyn Landmark Society, which successfully stimulated preservation of its historic village environment.

Long Island continued to live up to its earlier reputation as a major recreational area despite the encroachment of suburbia.

Old Bethpage village restoration located off Round Swamp Road in Old Bethpage is a major outdoor re-creation of a Long Island farm village of the early 1800s. Over thirty historic buildings have been moved to the site. A year-round program of activities enables visitors to see the rural crafts of yesterday, from blacksmithing to a complete operating farm with animals.

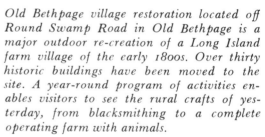

The monkey mountain was a major attraction at Frank Buck's zoo in Massapequa before World War II.

The *Long Island Daily Press* proclaimed in 1959, "You've got the finest pick of parks, white-sanded beaches, peaceful harbors for boating and fishing, golf courses, tennis courts . . . any of a long list of fun facilities all right nearby." The initial availability of plentiful open space was rapidly threatened by the march of housing developments across fields, marshes and woodland. In 1956, Robert Moses warned that even though many facilities had been set aside, actually "very little has been done in the case of municipal parks and playgrounds in the very suburban areas where postwar increases in population have created unprecedented needs, raised property values, imposed heavy burdens for all sorts of urgent services and utilities and made acquisition of adequate park areas costly and difficult if not prohibited."

The over 1 million population in the 1960s, including a high percentage of young adults and children with considerable leisure time, created an enormous demand for recreational facilities. Although much leisure activity centered on the homeowner's property and its gardens, back-yard barbecue, basketball hoop and lawn sports, residents needed major physical resources.

Pre-World War II facilities, such as Frank Buck's zoo on Sunrise Highway at Massapequa, had disappeared. New facilities were required for the much broader participation a new generation desired in sports activity. Due to economic factors, polo had decreased so that only one field survived and private golf clubs numbered less than forty, versus the sixty prewar clubs. Local woods and vacant lots that had provided playgrounds for children disappeared in the demand for building lots and were replaced by split-levels or gasoline stations.

The need was obvious and government at all levels took action. Eisenhower Park became the central facility of an extensive county park system. The county government concentrated on major regional facilities such as Cantiague Park in Hicksville, which contained an indoor ice-skating rink, tennis courts, pool, athletic fields and play fields for all age groups. Regional facilities with pools were developed in Manhasset, Wantagh, North Woodmere and Morley Park in Roslyn. The county government also built the Veterans Memorial Coliseum at Mitchel Field. Opened in 1971, the arena provided a regular home for two major-league teams, the basketball Nets and the hockey Islanders. Over fifteen thousand fans could attend a wide range of functions from rock festivals to the circus.

Town governments also developed some major local facilities, such as the Town of Hempstead's major parks with extensive athletic fields and pool facilities including an indoor pool complex in West Hempstead. Many villages developed broad recreational programs, such as Rockville Centre, which had its own recreation center, and the Village of Freeport, which constructed a major recreational complex including an indoor pool in 1974. Professional recreational personnel expanded municipal park operations and the concepts of recreation were broadened to include special programs for senior citizens and the handicapped. Parks also became a major site for entertainment and cultural activities, utilizing elaborate mobile

Action is always exciting at Islander games on the Coliseum ice.

The Nets won the American Basketball Association championship in 1974.

bandstands, along with the traditional sports and picnicking.

Private enterprise also responded to the increased demand for recreational activities. Motion picture theaters, which provided regular Saturday entertainment for children in the 1930s and 1940s, kept pace with increasing population. Although some older main street theaters closed due to the competition of television, new ones at major shopping centers provided over seventy-five movie showplaces. Television assumed a major role in entertainment by the mid-1950s. Despite the availability of more than one set in each household, television, although a pervasive and tremendously appealing medium, could not provide actual participant thrills.

Until the opening of the Coliseum, spectator sports were a minor part of local entertainment. Motorcycles and midget car racing had begun in the early 1930s at Freeport Municipal Stadium, and the roar of racing cars, modified and late models,

Demon Hanover driven by Harrison Hoyt and Proximity by Clint Hodgins race toward an exciting finish at Roosevelt Raceway.

Andrew Varipapa, Nassau's leading bowler, twice National All-Star Champion, at age fifty-six in 1947.

The modern grandstand at Roosevelt Raceway began a new era for harness racing in the late 1950s.

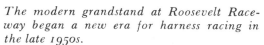

thrilled thousands through the postwar period. People were interested in actual participation and increasing wealth and leisure time led to greater individual activity. Bowling became one of the most popular participant sports and bowling alleys increased from fewer than a dozen in the prewar years to more than fifty by 1970. Some 1,500 leagues enabled competitive action for over 50,000 enthusiasts. The increasing popularity of tennis led to the building of several dozen new indoor facilities with over one hundred courts in the decade of the sixties. Industrial recreation became a significant factor of life for employees of Grumman and other major corporations, which provided extensive bowling, softball, travel and other organized activities for employees.

The traditional recreational appeal of horse racing continued in popularity. Belmont Park, which underwent a $30-million renovation in 1968, remained a magnet for racing enthusiasts, with crowds exceeding 75,000 people. Roosevelt Raceway, which was founded as a harness-racing track by George Morton Levy at the beginning of World War II, barely managed to survive the transportation limitations of the war. However, continued promotion spread the appeal of a night at the trotters. A mobile starting gate was developed, and in 1957 a brand-new $20-million grandstand building was erected. By the early 1970s, evening crowds added up to over 3 million visitors a year, wagering upward of $300 million. In addition to their recreational effect, the race tracks provided considerable governmental funds through pari-mutuel tax percentages. Relaxed societal attitudes toward gambling also allowed regular bingo games as a community activity by charitable organizations.

The exploitation of Nassau's marine shorefront for recreational purposes expanded the use of local waters beyond any old bayman's imagination. Jones Beach continued to add parking areas along more than five miles of glistening white sand—one of the great public ocean bathing beaches in the world. With facilities for over twenty thousand cars, the

The new marine theater constructed in 1952 at Jones Beach attracted millions of visitors to wonderful outdoor musicals produced by long-time Freeport resident Guy Lombardo.

beach became a major recreational resource for the entire metropolitan area. From fewer than 4 million visitors in 1940, use had grown to over 10 million visitors annually. The extent of visitors generally required closing the area to additional traffic by 11 A.M. on summer weekends.

To provide surf bathing for local residents, the Towns of Hempstead and Oyster Bay both acquired oceanfront beach areas. The county of Nassau also acquired a portion of the barrier beach between Long Beach and Point Lookout as an oceanfront recreational resource only for county residents. A county beach at Port Washington and several town facilities also provided Long Island Sound public beaches.

Boating maintained its long-time popularity and the former marshlands across the south shore were lined with bulkheaded canals for dockage space. More than 44,000 inboard powerboats were registered in Nassau County in 1970, plus hundreds of thousands of other sailing vessels, rowboats and outboard-powered craft. Over forty marinas and public launching sites were available on the north and south shores to service maritime needs. Party boats leaving early in the morning from Freeport docks afforded deep-sea fishing for tuna, bluefish, fluke and weakfish, while surf fishing remained a popular sport. The bay was crowded on weekends from June through September as residents enjoyed a wide range of water sports from fishing to water skiing. On the north shore many yacht clubs served as home base for sailboats, which afforded the same thrills to sailing enthusiasts that several generations had enjoyed.

Over fifteen thousand acres of park land, lush golf courses and miles of shoreline created unequaled recreational opportunities in Nassau County. Despite massive suburban encroachment, the Sunrise Homeland was still alive and well—suburbanites enjoyed a close proximity to nature and its verdant woodlands, meadows and waterfront. A popular Freeport High School song of that south shore community in the earlier part of the century included a lilting refrain, "Out on the Island, where the breezes blow." The breezes still carried a salt spray tingeing the air for space-age suburbanities in Nassau County and reminding them of their beautiful natural resources.

Public Works Response

A major postwar characteristic that suburban Nassau County shared with other similar localities in the United States was the great suburban love affair with the automobile. Even during World War II, officials of the Nassau County Department of Public Works were studying the problem of providing an adequate highway system after the war. A report in 1945 indicated that "the highway users of Nassau may well have been lulled into a feeling of false security by the decrease in traffic during gas and tire rationing but with the coming availability of new cars, trucks and tires, the inadequacy of the existing highway system will all too soon be reflected in serious traffic delays and accidents . . . motor vehicle registrations exceeded 150,000 in 1941 . . . to what extent it will increase is unpredictable but rather appalling to contemplate." The increase was beyond anyone's imagination.

Up to 1950 the growth was moderate, with 210,025 cars registered to Nassau owners. In the next decade, car ownership leaped to almost 500,000 vehicles; 214,300 households had one automobile, while over 100,000 homes had either two or three cars. The growth continued to a total of 693,176 registered vehicles in Nassau County during 1970. The predominant number of households contained more than one automobile. There were 164,700 two-car families, while 32,900 households had three cars, and only 170,100 single-car households remained.

The major burden of providing road systems for Long Island traffic had been assumed by the state government even before World War II. The Long Island State Park Commission continued to play a significant role in this road development. In 1955, Southern State Parkway was widened along the south shore, funded by a ten-cent toll which was established on the parkway for passenger cars going in either direction. During the first year of toll collections, over 26 million dimes were collected. Throughout the fifties and sixties, additional improvements were made on the parkway system, including the extension of Meadowbrook Parkway to link into Northern State Parkway and the major widening of all three parkways.

In addition to these improvements by the Long Island State Park Commission of its parkway network, the state government also provided a major renovation and expansion of other arterial roads. Sunrise Highway was widened throughout the county and other major east-west routes such as Hempstead Turnpike, Jericho Turnpike, Northern Boulevard (including construction of a long viaduct over Roslyn Harbor) and north-south

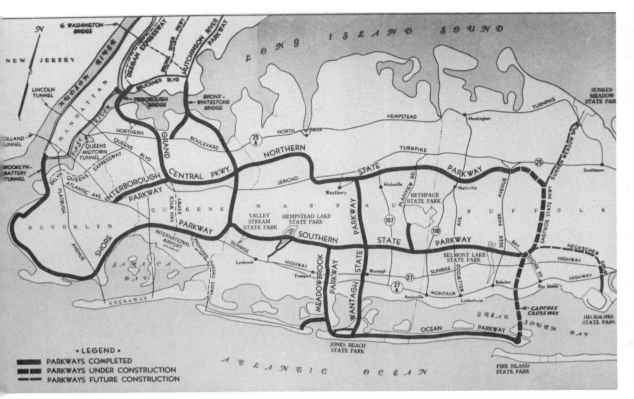

The Long Island Parkway system in 1950.

Sunrise Highway after widening at Lynbrook in late 1950s.

*The Long Island Expressway with rush-hour traffic at New Hyde Park.
Humorists have labeled it the world's "longest parking lot."*

Routes 106 and 107 were also widened and improved.

The increasing growth in the central and northern portions of the county out into Suffolk County created additional traffic on Northern State Parkway. It was evident that a new thoroughfare would be necessary through the center of the island, particularly for transportation access required by commercial vehicles. The State Transportation Department initiated construction of the monumental Long Island Expressway. Beginning at the East River and extending eastward to Riverhead in Suffolk County, it was planned as the major east-west route for trucks and commercial vehicles on the island. A section to Shelter Rock Road was opened in September 1958, and by August 1962 the expressway had been completed through Nassau County up to the Suffolk County line. This and the other road proj-

ects required major state funding, since construction costs frequently exceeded several million dollars per mile. Although critics have referred to it as "the longest parking field in the world," the six-lane highway provided a major boost to the industrial development of the central area of the island.

Increased road congestion due to population growth also required improvement in the north-south highway system in the county. The State Transportation Department planned the Seaford–Oyster Bay Expressway to reach from Wantagh on the south shore to Oyster Bay on the north shore. Construction was initiated in the early 1960s, and completed from the south shore up to Jericho Turnpike by the end of the decade. At that point, construction was stopped, since future plans depended on whether a bridge connection would be constructed to Connecticut or upstate New York. Planning

Construction of the Atlantic Beach Bridge linking Long Beach and the Rockaways, early 1950s.

wizard Robert Moses had proposed such a connection for many years. Other planning agencies also viewed it as an absolute necessity to provide adequate egress from the island and to ensure the island's continued economic development. Governor Nelson Rockefeller supported efforts to build such a bridge, and an Oyster Bay-Rye route was finally proposed as the most adequate solution. However, tremendous opposition by local residents on Long Island and in Westchester County caused the proposal to be dropped in the early 1970s.

The county government also provided significant improvements in the local road system. Peninsula Boulevard was created as a divided highway from Hempstead to Inwood, enabling access to the congested Five Towns area. In addition, the county built a new bridge on the main road from Island Park to Long Beach in 1956. A local Nassau

County Bridge Authority was created to build the Atlantic Beach Bridge between Rockaway and Long Beach in 1950. The county also improved many roadways and an enormous amount of local street mileage was added to town and village governments by the massive residential development. Developers who turned vacant land into subdivisions were required by law to build interior roads in accordance with county specifications. Between 1945 and 1970, over eight hundred miles of streets were built by developers in the unincorporated sections of the county and turned over to the townships for ownership and maintenance.

Despite all of the massive road building, the highway system in the early 1970s barely managed to handle the congestion of commuter-hour traffic. In 1960 only 62 per cent of Nassau workers used their automobiles for transportation to work, but by 1970, over 71 per cent drove. The increase from 293,895 auto users to over 398,000 created a tremendous strain on roadways during rush hours. Traffic on Southern State Parkway increased over 80 per cent from the initiation of the toll in 1955 to 1970, despite the Long Island Expressway's use by over ninety thousand vehicles daily.

Residents, however, increasingly began to feel that enough cement and concrete had been poured on the island. Government leaders echoed these concerns, and in the early 1970s, attention turned to the enhancement and development of railroad and bus transportation, which created less pollution, enabled more economical use of resources and would alleviate the growing energy crisis of the seventies.

The trail to the Sunrise Homeland had been established by the Long Island Rail Road in the early years of the 1900s. Although the spread of automobile ownership assisted the initial suburban growth after World War I, it was the railroad that provided the major means of transport for Nassau workers commuting to their occupations in the city. The increased commutation from Nassau and Suffolk brightened prospects for the railroad's future, but in 1939 the line received a major financial setback when the Independent subway system was extended to Jamaica. The railroad lost 80 per cent of its former passenger traffic to Queens County.

The onset of World War II ameliorated the immediate effects of this slash in the railroad's income. Greater traffic, due to gasoline shortages and wartime freight demands, gave the railroad its first profitable years. However, since fares had remained at the same level as in 1918 and material resources were not available, the Pennsylvania Railroad was unable to make major capital improvements on the Long Island.

Although the initial postwar suburban residents of Nassau County were principally commuters (some 75 per cent of the original Levittowners traveled to employment in New York City), the line was unable to obtain sufficient funds for its operations. Fares were

Double-decker trains were a postwar innovation on the elevated south shore runs of the railroad.

finally raised in July of 1947, but the additional income came too late to improve the railroad's position. The following December a heavy snowstorm completely paralyzed the line and commuter complaints crescendoed over the inadequate service. The railroad needed new cars, which required a massive capital expenditure, while income was not sufficient even for current operating expenses. In March of 1949, the Long Island Rail Road was declared bankrupt when it was unable to pay off some $60 million in bonds. The courts appointed a bank trusteeship of the line and operations continued to decline.

In 1950 the railroad was struck by a series of major accidents that caused a strident public demand for action. On February 17, at Rockville Centre, where a grade crossing elimination program was in its final stages, two trains collided at 10:30 P.M. in an almost head-on collision. One of the speeding trains should have been held up while the other went through the section, but due to signal errors, both trains proceeded. The first two cars on each were almost completely demolished, with others derailed. It was a chaotic scene with some twenty-nine passengers killed and over one hundred injured. Later that year, there were several other serious accidents at Huntington Station and Richmond Hill which completely demoralized commuter confidence in the railroad line.

Despite these problems, the railroad was essential to the transportation needs of Nassau residents. In the period from 1936 to 1946, commuters had increased from 4,706 to 6,079 from the Hicksville station and continued to increase in the early 1950s. Using its limited resources, the railroad attempted to make improvements and in 1951 installed a completely automatic electronic control system to prevent any future accidents. Various governmental study groups were established at both the local and state levels to determine how the railroad could continue to perform its essential services.

In 1954, a railroad development corporation was organized under state law, replacing the bank trusteeship. A twelve-year development program was mandated, with some $65 million of state funds to be used for a complete rehabilitation of the line. The line was exempt from taxes during this period and also received a Pennsylvania Railroad loan of $5,250,000. Within five years, over four hundred railroad cars were rebuilt and two hundred new air-conditioned cars were running on the line. Throughout the fifties and sixties, there was also an active program of elevating railroad tracks, particularly along the south shore line, so that the railroad operations did not interfere with local auto traffic at grade crossings. This work was also stimulated by the unsafe nature of grade crossings in the highly congested areas. The state government provided millions of dollars for these elimination projects, which were considered general public improvements.

Although the railroad made considerable improvements during the development program, the increased use of automobiles severely cut its use and commuter traffic was insufficient to provide adequate revenue for the line. Commutation rates increased regularly. The 1918 fare from Hicksville had grown from $12 to a monthly rate of $21 in

Sleek, air-conditioned Metropolitan cars of the early 1970s.

1951, and increased to $35 by 1960, with additional increases to $47 by 1970. There were difficult problems between the railroad's various labor unions and its management, with several costly labor settlements adding to the line's financial problems.

In 1966, after expiration of the development corporation act, it was obvious that government ownership of the line would be the only way to ensure its continuance. The state legislature created the Metropolitan Commuter Transportation Authority and it purchased the railroad from the Pennsylvania for $65 million. State responsibility for mass transit became final on March 1, 1968, when the Metropolitan Transportation Authority was created. The MTA immediately began an extensive development program that was to cost several hundred million dollars with an initial appropriation of $45 million. Electrification was extended along the center line to Hicksville and along the Port Jefferson line. A completely new high-speed railroad car was designed and by the early 1970s, over seven hundred of the sleek stainless-steel Budd cars were in service. Despite the improvements, commuters increasingly were reluctant to put up with the three-hour round trip into the city. They echoed old complaints that although the service had improved, it "was at least at a point where you can call the service dreadful!"

The great road construction on the island made commutation by car feasible and the movement of industry and business to the island also reduced the possible number of commuters. The 81,900 Nassau commuters who used the railroad line in 1960 had declined to fewer than 75,000 by 1970. The decrease in business caused larger deficits for the line, and in the early 1970s, annual deficits over $10 million had to be met by state and local subsidies. The MTA received funds in excess of $5 million annually from Nassau County for the maintenance of the railroad stations in the county. Despite all this extensive governmental support, the railroad's inability to improve rapidly after World War II had severely hampered its ability to retain users. The eventual commitment of government to its continual development was a major effort to provide alternative, more efficient means of mass transportation than the automobile.

While the railroad fought its decline, private bus companies, which provided public intracounty mass transportation, were also unsuccessful in meeting the requirements of suburban transportation. There were some nineteen independent bus operators in the county in 1948, providing over 45 million rides to local passengers. Only a few were able to make a profit on their activities, and in the next twenty years, although population increased spectacularly, bus passengers decreased 50 per cent.

Despite the efforts of a county Department of Franchises to improve bus routes, the consistent decline of passenger traffic caused bus companies to decrease operations, and over half of them went out of business by 1970. The lack of bus usage was evident even in lines serving shopping centers such as Roosevelt Field and Green Acres, where only some two or three hundred passengers a day were carried.

In 1971, the necessity to boost fares and eliminate unprofitable routes including Sun-

New buses of the Metropolitan Suburban Bus Authority are part of an attempt to stimulate mass transit use.

day service threatened this transportation resource of some thirty thousand autoless families in the county. The Nassau County Department of Public Transportation was created and established a stopgap bus subsidy program. After a year, with the assistance of a $9-million grant from the federal Department of Transportation, it acquired the assets of the remaining ten private bus companies. A special subsidiary corporation of the Metropolitan Transportation Authority was then created to reorganize and redesign a suburban bus system.

The failure of both railroad and bus transportation systems caused the automobile to assume the predominant role in local transportation. Increasing concern over its wastefulness as a commuter mover, the inability to move any more cars during rush hours and the unmet transportation needs of the young and elderly caused the state government to assume the responsibility for better mass transportation. The county government also was required to subsidize such facilities though major financial contributions, in addition to its traditional road and highway programs.

Besides the complete transformation of transportation means within the county, the expansion of Nassau's population required other extensive physical improvements. Thousands of acres of vacant farm land had been rapidly subdivided, requiring local government to install adequate residential water supply and waste disposal systems. Although a start on these problems had begun in the latter part of the Depression, most public works construction had halted completely during the war. However, planning continued and at the end of the war, nearly $30 million in county public works projects had been approved to modernize highways, provide drains and install sewers as essential physical improvements for the rapidly growing county.

Since the construction industry was a major source of local employment, the projects also were a strong economic stimulus. Labor constituted a high proportion of construction expense, and the great increase in public works provided considerable employment, while the private sector of the economy was gearing up for the postwar period.

A countywide sewerage system had been recognized as a public works priority in the 1930s when the county Department of Public Works began the design and planning for such a system. At the end of the war, seven existing village governments in Nassau County had small treatment plants but the vast unincorporated area had no waste disposal system. Although septic tanks and cesspools could fill immediate needs of new residential buildings, a sewerage system was required to maintain the purity of underground water resources.

The development of Nassau's countywide sewerage system was one of the largest public works undertakings in the United States. Plans drafted during the war called for priority to be given to Sanitary Sewer District No. 2, covering the southwest portion of the county except for Inwood, which was already covered in a small district. In the years between 1952 and 1963, an average of nearly one hundred miles of pipelines were laid annually. The total cost for these lateral lines and larger interceptor lines connecting to a new sewerage system treatment plant built at Bay Park in East Rockaway was in excess of $100 million. This plant was completed in 1951 at a cost of $30 million with a capacity to treat 27 million gallons of waste water per day, and although capacity was doubled in 1958, further expansion was under way in the early 1970s. The completion of this project provided sewerage facilities for approximately one third of Nassau County by 1960.

Plans continued for the remainder of the county, and in 1964 the next major phase began with the creation of District No. 3, covering an area roughly bounded by Meadowbrook Parkway, east to the Nassau-Suffolk county line and north to Jericho Turnpike. Construction work advanced toward the eventual 1,800 miles of pipelines that this district required. From the new Wantagh water pollution control plant, a two-and-a-half-mile underwater outfall pipe was built at a cost of over $60 million to take the treated effluent for disposition into the Atlantic Ocean.

By 1970, the county government had assumed an indebtedness of over $300 million for its share of this sewerage system, with the complete costs reaching three times this amount. A large proportion of the total construction costs for the sewerage districts had been received from the federal government. Local residents within each district paid special tax rates to cover the county share. Although this construction meant sharply increasing tax rates, most residents were pleased to solve the annoying problems associated with individual septic tanks or cesspools. The extension of sewers did not meet any public opposition until the north shore portions of District No. 3 were reached. After strong protests by local officials and residents in 1974, the Board of Supervisors voted to halt the north shore extension of the countywide sewerage program in the

Construction of sewer interceptor lines caused temporary disruption of many areas but filled an essential public need.

The Bay Park treatment plant through a complex technical process provides essential purification of waste waters.

A major sump or recharge basin at intersection of Old Country Road and Herricks Road in Garden City.

Manhasset-Kings Point and the Sea Cliff-Roslyn Harbor areas. The opponents contended that their area had less need for sewers due to lower population density and that the costs in terms of public value were too high due to hilly terrain and costly right of way.

A principal reason for the installation of a sanitary sewerage system was to protect the county's water supply from contamination. All of Nassau County's drinking water was supplied by deep wells. There were two serious threats to this water supply as the county underwent rapid suburbanization after the war. One was the danger of seepage from cesspools that would contaminate the underground water supply. A second threat was the decreasing amount of farm and vacant land area in the county and the increasing area covered by buildings, concrete and development. This reduced the amount of surface water that was able to penetrate into the underlying strata where wells could pump it back for the use of Nassau's growing population.

The imperative need to drain off storm flood waters and conserve rain water was recognized in the 1930s. The county Department of Public Works initiated the development of sumps or recharge basins throughout the county to accomplish this purpose. Storm water was diverted from road and natural drainage areas into these large basins. This water percolated into the earth rather than being lost by processing through sewerage plants or draining into the ocean and Sound. Although the war caused a halt to the building of sumps, construction continued afterward in pace with the county's development, and over five hundred sumps were provided to return into the ground in excess of 14 billion gallons of water a year.

While these two major efforts at conserving and treating water sources were planned on a centralized basis for the county, the supply of water was handled on a local basis. Nassau County was fortunate in having a relatively high water table with very pure drinking water. By the early 1950s, over thirty municipal water supply companies and seven private companies were providing water resources for individual communities. In many of the unincorporated areas, special water districts were created under the auspices of the town governments to provide drinking water and fire hydrant services. Such public water systems provided about two thirds of the county's need, and private companies the remainder.

In the late 1940s, a little over 40 million gallons of water per day were being used in the county. This demand increased to over 120 million gallons by 1960. Some 260 additional wells were installed during this time to satisfy residents' demands for water. In the 1960s, an extensive study of water resources was undertaken with federal and state aid to ensure available underground water resources for future demands. Water use had doubled in the decade to 1970 and estimates indicated that unless there was a decrease in water consumption, the county's resources would have to be augmented by water from Suffolk County or upstate New York later in the century.

Since the major portion of new housing development was in the unincorporated areas of the towns, the disposition of refuse and garbage required immediate action. Although private carters attempted to provide services, it became evident that only governmental efforts would be able to handle the problem satisfactorily. Therefore special sanitary and refuse districts were created in the three townships to provide this essential public service. By 1970 over 800,000 people were serviced by these districts—the remainder by individual villages and cities. The Town of Hempstead had over a half-dozen districts, with one large district serving most of the newly developed unincorporated areas in the central portion of the county. The Town of Oyster Bay also created several districts with District No. 1 providing coverage for most of the new southern and central portions of the town developed in the 1950s.

In the first five years of the 1950s, each of the towns built huge incinerators with a combined capacity for burning over 1,300 tons of garbage per day. In addition, the city of Long Beach also built a 200-ton-per-day incinerator. In the mid-1960s, each of the towns built an additional incinerator and made improvements on existing facilities to

Modern incinerator operated by the Town of Hempstead in Oceanside.

handle almost 2,000 additional tons per day. The tremendous growth in refuse due to disposable containers and new products put continued pressure on existing facilities in the late 1960s. The towns began the reclamation of newspapers and explored new methods of processing refuse.

In addition to the essential physical services provided by government, the expansion of utilities was required for the larger population. The Long Island Lighting Company, which had been well organized before World War II, faced greatly increasing demands. In 1946 with a capability of about 215,000 kw. of electric generation, LILCO installed an average of six thousand meters a year and by 1950 reached a level of twenty-eight thousand meters. The new demands for power by old customers as well as the new population required additional generating units, most of which were added at Suffolk County locations. In 1952 two additional 115,000 kw. generating units were installed in the Glenwood Landing plant and a complete new generating plant was built on former marshland in Island Park to provide 185,000 kw. in 1956. By 1958 LILCO was generating over 1,000,000 kw., over 2,000,000 in 1967, and at the end of 1973 the company had a generating capability of over 3,200,000 kw.

The company also extended gas lines throughout the county to provide for cooking and heating services. Natural gas was brought from Louisiana and Texas in 1946 and by 1958 the company had completely converted from manufactured to natural gas. A considerable campaign was launched in the 1960s to have customers convert to gas heating from oil-burning units, which provided the majority of home heating systems. However, with the onset of the energy shortage in the early 1970s, residential use of gas had to be greatly restricted. The company also initiated construction of an atomic energy power plant in Suffolk County to meet future needs and was planning to satisfy much of future demands by nuclear-fueled plants.

Oyster Bay town supervisor John Burns places direct dial call, June 1960, ending manual phone service in Nassau County. Courtesy of Newsday.

The New York Telephone Company was under tremendous pressure during these years to keep up with the growing demand for telephone service in the metropolitan New York area. At the end of the war, there were 130,800 telephones in the county. This rose to 246,700 instruments by 1950 and jumped spectacularly to 505,000 only five years later. The company continued to improve communication technology, initiating dial service in Floral Park in 1949 and then extending it throughout the county with direct distance dialing available by the early 1960s. Many new customer service and technical support facilities were constructed throughout the county.

In the early 1970s, a new electronic switching facility at Roosevelt Field was being completed as one of the world's largest single-level communications centers. Telephone

North Shore Hospital, a new private institution which raised significant gift funds, shown after expansion in 1964.

Meadowbrook Hospital in East Meadow showing before and after views of new support units in rear and main tower patient care center added during early 1970s.

use in Nassau County rose to over 882,000 instruments in 1965, and the great volume of calls, particularly traffic in and out of New York City, caused delays and dissatisfactions with service in the late sixties. The company responded with major capital investments, technical service improvements and personnel training to recover its high standards of service.

The great tide of new people also necessitated extensive physical facilities for medical and health services. Most of the prewar hospitals were expanded to augment their capacities. South Nassau Communities Hospital underwent several renovations including a major addition in the early 1970s. Mercy Hospital had moved into a new building on the northern edge of Rockville Centre at the beginning of the war in 1941. It expanded several times so that by 1965, it reached a capacity of 390 beds. Both Nassau Hospital in Mineola and Community Hospital in Glen Cove also were modernized and enlarged to improve technical facilities and treat more patients.

Between 1950 and 1974, the number of hospitals increased from ten to sixteen and beds rose from 995 to 4,120. A series of smaller independent hospitals was built in many of the new growth areas of the county, including Syosset, Massapequa, Manhasset, Mid-Island in Bethpage and Central General in Plainview. The North Shore Hospital was opened in Manhasset in July 1953, and grew into a major medical center with a wide range of community services and highly specialized care facilities. In 1973 it was renamed North Shore University Hospital in recognition of its service as an academic health center.

The county government also moved ahead vigorously with public medical facilities. The old county home for the aged, sick and infirm in Uniondale was replaced in 1961 by an 875-bed hospital care facility named in honor of former county executive A. Holly Patterson. Meadowbrook Hospital was enlarged several times and by 1968 had a bed capacity of 650, a comprehensive rehabilita-tion medical center, a speech and hearing center and major medical emergency facilities. On March 9, 1970, the hospital officially became the Nassau County Medical Center, and in October of 1973, the Dynamic Care Building, a nineteen-story structure, was completed. A highly sophisticated and modern health care facility with capability of use for medical teaching, the new hospital included over 770 beds. The development of these facilities and many local medical centers extended medical care throughout the county.

Economic Independence

Even before the war was over, plans were prepared to build new commercial facilities for residents. The management of the Franklin Simon department stores announced in June 1945 a plan to build a branch store in Garden City just as soon as war priorities permitted the availability of materials. This was the beginning of a suburban movement by New York department stores and the development of radically different retail services. The automobile was a key part of this postwar growth, since it allowed the suburban housewife to move more freely and widely. This enabled major facilities drawing on a broader geographic area than the former main street sections of villages.

The shopping center became the new retail hub of the suburbs. In 1945 construction began on the Strathmore Center on Northern Boulevard in Manhasset, and a unique regional center developed along this thoroughfare through Manhasset. This string of fine shops, including several department stores, was termed the "Miracle Mile." The development of Levittown had also shown the need for small shopping centers. Village greens were installed throughout the area, each containing a supermarket with ten small convenience and service stores. However, the initial success of these small centers was eventually overshadowed by the completion of major community shopping centers on Hempstead Turnpike which provided one-stop shopping for the busy suburbanite.

During the two decades from 1950 to 1970, total retail sales in the county rose from less than $1 billion to over $3.8 billion, to rank Nassau as the fifth largest retail sales area in the nation. The greatest proportion of these sales occurred in the numerous shopping centers that had been built in Nassau County. From three centers in 1950, additional units were added each year, with a peak reached in 1956 when 22 centers were built. By 1970 over 141 shopping centers provided groups of commercial establishments and shops with convenient on-site parking throughout the county.

Some 102 neighborhood centers comprised the majority of these facilities. Serving an area within two miles, the neighborhood center contained a supermarket and an average of eleven stores providing convenience goods and personal services. Larger community shopping centers developed around a major variety or department store with additional clothing, appliance and other shops.

The most significant impact on retail sales was the creation of regional shopping centers, which were major retail centers with two or more department stores that drew customers from an extended area of thirty or more minutes' travel from the center. In 1956 there was the simultaneous opening of three such regional centers. The Mid-Island Center in Hicksville provided two major department stores and some one hundred other small shops. Sears Roebuck added to this center in 1964 when it built an enormous adjacent department store. Since it was close to the New York City line, the Green Acres Shopping Center in Valley Stream attracted many shoppers from the city to its one hundred stores and over 1.2 million square feet of retailing space. The largest

Roosevelt Field Shopping Center in late 1950s.

Abraham & Straus, Hempstead Turnpike, Hempstead, the county's largest department store.

center was constructed at Roosevelt Field on one hundred acres of land. By 1970 it had grown into a major retail complex of almost 2 million square feet with department stores operated by Macy's, Gimbels, J. C. Penney and Alexander's with some 3,500 employees for over 135 shops. In 1967 these three centers alone accounted for 8.5 per cent of the total retail sales in the county.

The older Miracle Mile expanded into a regional complex, and in the early 1970s, the Sunrise Mall, with four major department stores and over 1 million square feet of space, opened in Massapequa close to the Suffolk County line. The regional centers were originally constructed with open malls between the major building components, but in 1968 the concept of a covered mall enabling an all-weather interior was developed. All of the centers thereafter added protected malls and the Roosevelt Center even built double-deck parking facilities to provide space for over 9,500 cars. The Sunrise Mall added the new concept of a multi-level retail space with major decorative plazas.

The giant department store was the major element of the shopping center. Macy's at Roosevelt Field contained over 400,000 square feet of retailing space and there were

dozens of other department stores exceeding 200,000 square feet. The largest in the county was Abraham & Straus at Hempstead, which was enlarged several times to exceed 550,000 square feet with extensive retailing space in almost every line of goods. Since thirty-three of the thirty-nine major retail stores in the county were within shopping centers, they provided the major attraction for consumers.

As the centers grew in importance, the sales volume fell off in stores in the older central business district and main streets of established communities. The combination of traffic congestion, inadequate parking and less attractive older buildings reduced business volume. Retail shops closed down and deterioration accelerated in most of the older central business districts of the county. New uses were sought for their future development. An extensive urban renewal project in Hempstead was undertaken to renew its downtown area. The vigorous development program, combined with construction of a new Times Square department store and the enormous business of Abraham & Straus, still provided over $200 million in sales to maintain Hempstead's position as the leading commercial center of the county. Glen

Meadow Brook National Bank in Merrick, the beginning of the National Bank of North America.

Cove also began a major urban renewal in the late 1960s to rehabilitate its commercial center. Many communities such as Freeport attempted to provide off-street parking and promotional campaigns to win back retail business, but the shopping center competition was extremely heavy.

Accompanying this great commercial growth, the banking system within the county expanded to provide necessary financial resources and money services. Due to restrictive state regulations, only two new banks had been started in the year from the Depression until 1960, the Central Bank and Trust Company of Great Neck and the State Bank of Long Beach, both during the 1950s. Through that same decade an extensive series of bank mergers occurred that completely transformed the local banking system. The number of existing individual banks was reduced by consolidations and mergers from sixty to fewer than twenty by 1960.

The Franklin Square National Bank, under Arthur T. Roth's direction, grew from a small prewar bank with some $18 million in assets to one of the fifty largest banks in the United States by 1960, with over $600 million in assets. Augustus B. Weller developed,

in less than a decade, a small bank in the south shore community of Merrick into the Meadow Brook National Bank with over thirty-eight offices including a six-story headquarters in West Hempstead. Meadow Brook expanded to over $450 million in assets by opening branches in shopping centers and the new growing residential areas. The great extension of these two major institutions and other commercial banks provided over 116 banking offices throughout the county in 1960.

During the 1940s, small savings and loan associations continued to grow, assisting in realty financing and providing a stable savings investment for local residents. County Federal Savings & Loan Association, which had opened in 1937 in Rockville Centre, had under $10 million in assets in 1945. Assets jumped from $52 million to $94 million in 1952 as a result of its high dividend offering of 3 per cent, which attracted funds from the entire metropolitan area. It continued to grow into the largest association in New York State, with over $400 million in assets by 1968. Some twenty other savings and loan associations in 1960 provided $700 million in resources.

During the postwar growth there was continual pressure by city financial institutions to obtain a change in the state law restricting the entrance of new banks into Nassau County. Local banks strongly resisted any legislative change but the New York State legislature passed a bill in 1960 allowing New York City commercial and savings banks to open branches in Nassau and Westchester counties. Although they were restricted from villages where a local independent bank had its home office, city banks initiated a new wave of bank expansion in the county. While New York City commercial and savings banks began to move into the suburbs, the giant Meadow Brook, which became the National Bank of North America, and Franklin National Bank moved into the city. By 1970 the intrusion of New York City banks had completely transformed local banking facilities and out of some 313

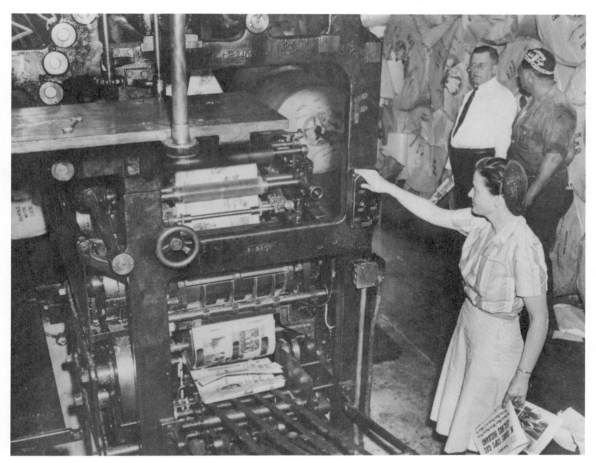

Alicia Patterson, Newsday's *first editor and publisher, starts presses for the first issue of* Newsday, *September 3, 1940. Courtesy of* Newsday.

Newsday *was awarded three Pulitzer Gold Medals for meritorious public service in 1954, 1970 and 1974 with stories exposing corruption on Long Island and a thirty-two-part series on the movement of heroin from poppy fields of Turkey to the streets of Long Island. Courtesy of* Newsday.

offices, over a third were branches of New York City banks. The monthly clearings of these institutions averaged over $1.2 billion in 1970, which was four times the activity of the previous decade. There were also thirty savings bank offices, which were almost all branches of New York City institutions. Since 70 per cent of local home mortgages were held by these institutions, these savings banks had provided a major role in the development of the county.

The growth of population and retail business was accompanied by a correspondingly rapid growth in the communications media serving the county. The most dramatic development was the creation and expansion of a new daily newspaper—*Newsday*. The new tabloid began publication in September of 1940 with an initial press run of thirty thousand copies. Its editor and publisher, Alicia Patterson, infused the paper with a vivacious, inquisitive and human-interest focus, compared to the older, more staid and informative *Nassau Daily Review Star*.

There was bitter competition between the dailies through the 1940s. In 1947 a protracted strike severely affected the *Review Star* and it was never able to recover. James E. Stiles sold the newspaper to S. I. Newhouse, who also owned the *Long Island Press* in Jamaica. The *Nassau Daily Review Star* continued the competition but finally in 1953 it was merged into the *Long Island Daily Press*. *Newsday* continued its phenomenal growth, based on display advertising of the burgeoning retail businesses in Nassau and Suffolk. By 1974 it was the fourth largest evening newspaper in the nation with a daily circulation reaching three out of five families on Long Island. Harry F. Guggenheim, who was president of *Newsday* from its inception and owned the controlling interest in the paper, continued as publisher after his wife Alicia Patterson died in 1963. In 1970 he sold his interest in *Newsday* to the Times Mirror Company of Los Angeles, so that both local daily newspapers had reverted to outside corporate ownership. Mr. Guggenheim died in 1971. *Newsday* launched a Sunday edition in 1972.

In addition to the local dailies, New York City newspapers, particularly the New York *Times* and the New York *Daily News,* provided a major news source for local residents. The *News* was second to *Newsday* in daily circulation and first in Sunday circulation. Both city newspapers maintained full-time correspondents in Nassau and included limited special sections devoted to Long Island news. Although some families read none, Nassau was a fertile area for newspapers. Daily circulation exceeded 530,000 copies as compared to approximately 400,000 families in 1970, indicating that many families read two newspapers.

Since daily newspapers had limited news space to cover local activities, weekly newspapers, with their emphasis on local personalities, conflicts and events, prospered. Growing along with their communities and providing detailed coverage of village happenings, more than seventy weeklies existed in the late 1960s. Editorial quality varied widely but the home-town flavor was most important to readers surrounded by more impersonal media. The size and importance of local commerce and industry is reflected in the success of the specialized *Long Island Commercial Review,* founded in 1953, which grew into a daily business paper. Locally edited and produced magazines were issued sporadically but met with less success. Nassau was, however, considered an excellent magazine market by the national publishers. *Reader's Digest,* for example, had a 120,000 circulation in Nassau, reaching almost one third of all households.

As in the rest of the nation, television had a strong postwar impact on Nassau. With access to seven New York VHF channels— and in some areas of the north shore to Connecticut channels as well—set ownership rose rapidly to virtually 100 per cent of households. As a source of free entertainment and graphically presented national news, television reigned supreme as an entertainment medium. However, coverage of Nassau news on the city TV stations was extremely poor, ranging from spotty to non-existent. Local educational television programing began in

Endo Chemical Laboratory structure by noted architect Paul Rudolph in Garden City.

1969 by Channel 21 at Mitchel Field, a public UHF station supported by the county government, viewers and local interests. In 1974, Channel 67 in Suffolk became Long Island's first commercial TV station.

Nassau's first radio station, WGBB, began broadcasting in 1924, the pioneering days of radio. The late 1940s saw WHLI and WTHE begin broadcasting, followed by WHLI-FM and WLIR-FM. Concentration on local news, personalities and events, even including broadcasting descriptions of lost pets, and the increase in Nassau-employed workers who listened while driving to work, enabled the local stations to compete successfully with stations based in New York City.

The media bombarding local residents had become so complex and varied by the early 1960s that it was no longer possible to determine with any certainty the relative degrees of influence of any single medium. Nassau had entered a new era of extensive news and advertising coverage, but the enormous quantity and extent created difficulties in the communication of essential information.

As the county's population expanded through the 1950s, its economy began to take on a new dimension and pattern. It followed somewhat the classic economic development scheme with a basic industry providing an area's chief income source, and

then the employees passing this income into a broad spectrum of personal service businesses. The aerospace industry had provided a major thrust to the county's economy in World War II, and defense business continued to provide a major influx of income into the area. Following the uncertain decade after the war, employment within the defense industry during the sixties was relatively steady, dropping to a low of 32,600 employees in 1963 and reaching a peak of 49,803 in 1968. In the postwar years up to 1970, 33 to 42 per cent of manufacturing employees received their income from federal contracts, providing a strong economic base for the county's economy. This income flow then went into numerous retail and personal service facilities.

Nassau County also had a unique economic resource in the many professional, technical and managerial personnel who lived in the county but commuted daily to New York City. In 1960 almost 40 per cent of the county's working population, including some 182,699 workers, commuted to the city. Although this had declined to 173,682 workers or some 30 per cent by 1970, commuters still provided a strong base of high-income wage earners within the county.

Although initially a great many of the residents moving to the county in the postwar period were commuters to outside areas, the

Landscaped roadways create an attractive environment at Crossways Industrial Park in Woodbury.

rapid growth of the county's economy provided employment for over 50 per cent of local residents by 1960. Over 110,000 residents held manufacturing jobs, with many employed within the county. Significant increases in local manufacturing employment occurred during the 1960s as small industry expanded, providing some 3,500 additional jobs in the years between 1963 and 1969. By 1967 there were 2,271 industrial plants in the county, with some 70,000 production workers. All these were not county residents, but the continued healthy growth of local small industrial plants provided additional employment opportunities for county residents.

A major portion of this industrial growth was along the route of the Long Island Expressway, which provided easy truck transportation access for small manufacturers. Plainview, Syosset, New Cassel, Jericho and the industrial area around Roosevelt Field were developed with a wide variety of industrial plants. Hicksville and south Farmingdale also continued as major manufac-

turing centers around the aviation facilities which had been developed during World War II.

The production of electrical equipment and instruments was the major industry in the county, with almost $700 million worth of shipments in 1969. Manufacturers of machinery and fabricated metal products provided employment for over ten thousand employees, while apparel and textile factories, chemical, paper and printing facilities created a diverse small industrial base. Manufacturing provided the most significant amount of employment, with over $1 billion in personal income in 1967 for county residents.

The changing thrust of the county's economy also moved wholesale and retail trade into the second major income source, with $672,500,000 in personal income for almost 130,000 local residents. From the great department stores to the small family delicatessens, retail business followed manufacturing in economic importance. Automobile and repair service organizations doubled their business in the period from 1958 to 1970. Considerable increases occurred in mail-order operations, vending machine companies, groceries, retail stores specializing in books, farm and garden supplies, liquor, sporting goods, hardware, furniture, appliances, clothing and antique shops.

Varied service establishments necessary for the burgeoning population were a continually expanding portion of Nassau's economy. Total service employment in the county had risen to 162,700 employees out of a total labor force of 592,331 in 1970, providing the largest amount of local employment. A considerable portion of this was seasonal or part-time, however, and it provided only the third highest source of personal income of half a billion dollars. The principal areas of service growth were in hotels and motels, which increased in number from 106 to 146 during the 1960s. Various personal service businesses increased from 2,807 to 3,107 during this same period so that by 1967, there were a total of 8,808 small service establishments with sales of almost a half-billion dollars.

Another new aspect of local business developed during the 1960s with the expansion of wholesale distributors in the county. The ease of access to the entire metropolitan market made Nassau a natural place for warehousing facilities. By 1967, there were almost 28,000 employees in some 2,685 wholesale establishments, providing the third highest concentration in New York State, with sales over $3 billion.

For many decades, construction had provided a consistent steady employment for county residents. From some twenty thousand employees in the early 1950s, the construction work force grew to approximately thirty thousand in 1960 and maintained that level to the early seventies. The tremendous expansion of residential housing originally provided the basis of this employment. Between 1960 and 1970, residential construction was in a steep decline due to sharply rising prices, credit costs, national credit restrictions and the scarcity of desirable build-

An unusual office use was the conversion of a portion of the Sperry Gyroscope Lake Success plant as temporary headquarters for the United Nations in 1946.

ing sites. The total value of residential construction declined from over $100 million annually to less than $50 million at the end of the decade for a ten-year total of $834,046,000.

While residential construction was declining, construction of industrial and commercial buildings took up the slack and maintained a steady pace with an average of over $70 million worth a year during the decade. The total of non-residential housing during the decade was $772,137,000, with industrial buildings, stores and offices each making up about 20 per cent. Schools, churches and hospitals were other major sources of new construction.

The significant increase in office buildings was a direct reflection of the expanding service, public administration, finance and insurance organizations in the county. Before 1965, there were fewer than fifty office buildings in Nassau County, with a total of 1,750,000 square feet of space. In the remainder of that decade over eighty addi-

Levitt & Sons built residential developments throughout the world and maintained their headquarters at Lake Success.

tional office buildings were constructed, more than doubling available space. Office construction hit its peak in 1969, when twenty-four structures were completed. Growth continued at a fast pace in the early 1960s, with some very large buildings completed. After 1972, demand for office space eased considerably and construction fell off sharply.

During this great building spurt, an office complex at Lake Success containing some fourteen units, with over 1 million square feet, provided the largest concentration of such facilities. Garden City also experienced considerable construction, with some twenty new office buildings. Although most of these structures were multi-floor units, only a few were higher than five stories, including several seven-story structures in Hempstead. From 1960, total office space grew from 900,000 square feet to over 8 million by 1971, adding another new ingredient to the economic life of the county.

Although there had been a serious decline in agriculture before World War II, production was maintained through 1950.

There were still 27,334 acres in use on some 618 working farms in the county. Over 300,000 tons of potatoes and vegetables were produced annually in the late 1940s on these farms. The march of homes and community development across the Nassau landscape took a direct toll of this farm land. The decline of agriculture was also hastened after 1941 by the discovery of the golden nematode worm in local farm fields, which prevented the continuation of potato production. Many local farmers sold out to building developers and moved to Suffolk County. By 1954 there were fewer than 13,000 acres of farm land.

As suburban development continued, acreage dropped below 7,500 in 1960 and to less than 5,000 in 1965. By 1970 agriculture had almost disappeared, with fewer than a dozen farms left in Nassau County on some 1,000 acres. These remaining, such as John Youngs's in Glen Head, were principally in the Town of Oyster Bay and sold fresh produce from their own roadside stands to local residents.

Although agriculture had almost disappeared from the county by 1970, the local horticultural industry continued to provide related work opportunities. Many nurseries and greenhouses produced enormous quantities of plants to supply materials for home landscaping and gardens. In 1960 Nassau County was the fifteenth top-producing horticultural county in the United States. Agriculture and the small commercial fisheries industries, which still continued to a minor extent in oyster beds off Oyster Bay, and commercial fishermen along the south shore provided only 3,500 local jobs in 1970.

The traditional pursuits which were the basis of local employment in the early part of the century had declined to insignificant parts of the county's economy in its postwar growth. Nassau's work force by 1970 had grown to 592,331 employees, with some 40 per cent female. Professional, technical and clerical employees provided the bulk of county employment skills. The high educational level and ability created a median income of $14,632 by 1970. This tremendous increase from a median income of $8,515 in 1960 had major ramifications in the retail and service areas of the county's economy.

Suburban development after World War II continued to be influenced by the manifold recreational opportunities in Nassau County. Although the decline of natural areas created a different environment, the expansion of public parks and recreational areas enabled new leisure activities. Transportation was a key element in growth patterns and the automobile assumed a

Throughout Nassau County in the 1950s and 1960s, residents became familiar with the county Department of Public Works standard project sign proclaiming "Nassau County Fastest Growing County in U.S." Here County Executive A. Holly Patterson breaks ground for new structure at Volunteer Firemen's Training Center in 1960.

dominant role. Government recognized the vital necessity of mass transportation and assumed control over the Long Island Rail Road and local bus services.

The county's highly skilled and technical work force was among the highest paid in the nation and had a disposable income which influenced extensive retail and service business growth. Nassau's local economy had matured greatly and over 50 per cent of the residents were now employed within the county. Small manufacturing and office employment opportunities created a new economic vitality within the county. This economic development was a healthy accompaniment to the extensive residential growth of the area and supplied the necessary tax base for the community improvements required as Nassau became America's major suburban county.

CHAPTER VIII

GOVERNMENTAL REACTION

Political Upheaval

Nassau County's seventy-fifth anniversary as an independent county was marked by brief ceremonies at the year's first meeting of the Board of Supervisors on January 7, 1974. County Executive Ralph G. Caso accepted a gold and blue banner proclaiming the anniversary with the dates 1899–1974, and was surprised by an outburst from the audience. Carl W. Schmitt, a regular public visitor to Board meetings and ardent fiscal critic, enthusiastically recalled, "My father took me to Mineola when I was four years old, and I remember watching Teddy Roosevelt." Caso happily invited Schmitt to pose for a photograph in front of the banner, and the county's seventy-fifth birthday year began with an incident of warm good humor.

The Board meeting was of even greater historical interest since it was the initial meeting for the first elected female supervisor. Mrs. Hannah Komanoff, a veteran school board member of the city of Long Beach, became one of two Democrats on the Board. In her opening remarks, she stressed harmony and a desire to work for the best interests of the county.

She voted in agreement with the Board on a long agenda of items which clearly reflected the tremendous changes and growth of county government since its beginning,

Nassau County Executive Ralph G. Caso welcomes in County's seventy-fifth year with Carl W. Schmitt, regular attendee at Board of Supervisors' meetings.

and particularly in the decades since the end of World War II. The scope of the Board's approvals included establishing a Nassau County medical emergency services program, funding a youth delinquency prevention project, acquisition of historic costumes for attendants at the Old Bethpage village restoration and studying "the needs of welfare youth in transition from motel settings to other places of abode." Although Schmitt, in his usual form, charged the Board was spending too much money on a new Office of Gaming Services, major financial commitments were routinely approved. The Board scheduled approval of a $36-million bond issue for construction at Nassau Community College and adopted various leases, small construction contracts and land acquisitions. This wide range of medical, educational, social service and public works activity was indicative of the county government's involvement in so many aspects of Nassau County life.

The governmental reorganization, after the County Charter Act of 1938, assumed increasing significance as local government had to supply additional services for the rapidly growing postwar suburban population. Under the charter, the county government was responsible for the major necessary public physical facilities. Roads, drainage and sewerage systems were public works projects requiring major capital expenditures that could not be funded out of current revenues. The county issued over $575 million in bonds for an extensive construction program, one half of which was required for the sanitary sewerage system. This surpassed the total debt of all other governmental units (schools, towns and special districts) in the county, but was still well below the legal indebtedness limit. Initially the county government had been able to maintain relatively modest budgets. In 1950 total county expenditures were $28 million, which gradually increased to $72 million by 1960. Services had to expand rapidly for the burgeoning population, and by 1965, a $123-million budget was required, with both police and social service costs in excess of $25 million. In the next five inflationary years, as new facilities and programs were opened, county government expenditures rose to an annual budget of over $380 million.

The major portion of this growth occurred in the area of social services as expanded programs and higher costs raised welfare expenditures to over $160 million a year with annual increases in the sixties exceeding $20 million. Other sizable raises occurred in police services, Nassau Community College, which was an entirely new function, and in debt services, which jumped from an average of $20 million a year to $30 million in 1968. Higher expenditures required repeated real estate tax increases throughout the 1960s. The great inflationary pressure of the early seventies pushed county government expenditures over $400 million in 1972, but an income of over $100 million from a newly imposed local sales tax and some $96 million in federal aid provided some relief to the local real estate tax burden.

Although the county's population leveled off by 1960, the county government then began to experience the service demands created by its greatly enlarged population. A change in political control of the county administration also marked the new decade. A. Holly Patterson turned over the reins of the county government to Eugene H. Nickerson after the latter's upset victory in 1961. Despite widespread changes in major official positions, the majority of civil service staff members provided governmental continuity. Nickerson also adopted and followed

through with many major projects and plans initiated during Patterson's administration, particularly in public works and park development. The new administration, however, was faced with a wide diversity of demands for increased governmental services.

Social needs became particularly insistent, with an expansion of support activities required and an extension of services into new problem areas. Aid to the elderly, dependent children and unemployable residents required greater expenditures as the cost of living rose. Despite increased state and federal aid for such assistance programs, the local share of such funding ascended. New areas of need in social services were served, including a county youth board, neighborhood youth corps and youth centers. Countywide health services for the larger population were augmented by the expansion of Meadowbrook Hospital, the creation of a mental health program through over twenty local community clinics, drug and alcohol addiction prevention and extended clinical health services.

Providing protection and court services required a doubling in the county police force to almost four thousand men in the early 1970s. The court system, which was reorganized by the prewar charter, had to be greatly expanded. In 1945 there were only four Supreme Court justices serving the county, and by 1970, increasing case loads required twenty-seven justices. County Court judges increased from one to a dozen during this same period. The District Court system grew from seven judges to over twenty-four, while a separate Children's Court, established in 1950, was changed in 1962 to the Family Court, with five judges to handle increasing matrimonial and domestic disputes. Greater criminal activity required the construction of a separate children's shelter, expansion of the county jail and massive courtroom expansions.

The county government also began to function in new social and cultural areas that had not been required before the extensive growth. A Commission on Human

Expansion of judicial system required construction of new Supreme Court building in 1960s. County Executive Eugene Nickerson checks construction of the building with Commissioner of Public Works Eugene Gibbons.

Rights was established in 1963, and other specialized areas of public service were furnished by a Department of Commerce and Industry, Department of Transportation, Department of Consumer Protection, Department of Recreation and Parks, and Office for the Aged.

Continuing the trend of the prewar years, special districts also proliferated to enable essential local municipal services within given geographical areas. The majority of new housing developments were in the unincorporated areas of the towns. The creation of villages was uneconomical and legally difficult due to restrictive state legislative regulations after 1938. Therefore, special districts, which were established and administered by residents and the town boards, became the major means of provid-

Special governmental districts provided many needed public services to developing areas, such as water supply.

ing local sanitary, water, lighting, parking and other special needs.

From 1945 through 1955, special districts in the county increased in number from 173 to 268. After this rise, creation of new districts leveled off and some consolidations occurred. Their accumulated debt of $107 million exceeded the total of the three town governments, and administration of the districts was a major portion of town governmental activity. The towns began to provide more direct control, and in 1961, the Town of Hempstead consolidated thirty-two street lighting districts into a centrally administered district.

The town governments continued to handle their traditional local road maintenance, garbage disposal, central record keeping, zoning and building code enforcement functions. They also began to establish extensive recreational and park programs in the post-

war period to provide unincorporated areas with a wide range of leisure activities. In a unique cooperative venture, the towns of Hempstead and Oyster Bay established a joint park district to serve the parks and pools in the new communities of Levittown and Island Trees, which encompassed portions of both towns. They also responded to the increase in older residents by opening senior citizen centers and housing developments. Despite the great growth in population, the town governments made a real effort to remain responsive to residents, and Hempstead officials proclaimed: "You can still get into your car, ride to town hall, park nearby, and drop in on your town officials. And, you can have your say about any town matter."

One of the major problems of the postwar era was the coordination of governmental planning. The Nassau County Planning Commission, which began to function immediately after the war, had the power to review and supervise the installation of public improvements in all subdivisions within the unincorporated areas of the county. Therefore uniform standards were followed during the tremendous expansion of the period, and the commission approved subdivision maps on over 25,000 acres in the years between 1945 and 1960. Ensuring uniform standards within these subdivisions was a major achievement during this period. The commission also provided considerable technical and research advice useful for educational and business planning.

In 1965 Nassau joined with Suffolk in the creation of a Bi-County Regional Planning Board. The Board prepared a comprehensive master plan to guide future economic development and land use. Since the County Planning Commission had no zoning authority, individual township and village zoning boards were responsible for land use planning and zoning. Although the Town of Hempstead established a zoning ordinance in the early 1930s, land use controls allowed construction on small plots throughout most of its area and considerable portions of the

Interior of the new Town of Hempstead indoor pool at Echo Park, West Hempstead, a major facility of an active program implemented by Supervisor Francis Purcell.

Town of Oyster Bay. While this resulted in greater availability of housing, lack of central planning created less controlled development of land zoned for business use. Consequently, many major roadways haphazardly developed into uninviting commercial strips.

One of the major planning problems of the postwar era was development of the former Mitchel Air Force Base. In 1961, County Executive A. Holly Patterson named a commission, under chairman Robert Moses, to plan the development of the base in the best interest of the county at large. The commission and public officials had to contend with the Federal Aviation Agency, which felt "a need for a public airport to serve general aviation in Nassau County . . . a portion of Mitchel Field will satisfactorily and safely serve this purpose." The commission was successful in opposing further aviation activities and its initial report recommended the area's development as an educational, light industry, civic center and recreational facility. Limited residential use was to be developed in the old Santini area, formerly used as a housing annex to the air base.

County political leaders fought to obtain as much of the land as possible from the federal government, with a major portion to be used for educational purposes by Nassau Community College and Hofstra University. The federal government initially was reluctant to give up a major portion of the property and wanted to retain it for future federal purposes. In 1962, newly elected County Executive Eugene H. Nickerson endorsed the general plan of the commission, and in the next year, the county purchased over four hundred acres of land at Mitchel for some $13 million. The new county executive named a Mitchel Field Planning Commission to develop a detailed plan for the property.

During the remainder of the 1960s, various proposals were made for the development of the property. In 1966, the County Planning Commission urged that ten thousand apartments be constructed at Mitchel so that a central residential area could be created there; and three years later Marcom, Inc., a professional planning consultant, called for the creation of a main center for the county at Mitchel with some seventy thousand workers and thirty thousand residents. The John F. Kennedy Educational, Civic and Cultural Center was also proposed, with a coliseum, central library, concert hall and theater, museum and planetarium.

The Board of Supervisors did not agree with the complete concept of these proposals and no major plan was adopted. Construction of the Nassau Coliseum was approved, and it was finally opened in 1972. Plans for a central reference library on the site continued to be advanced in the early 1970s, and the development of Mitchel Park, a major hotel, and light industrial areas was initiated in the early seventies. After the election of Ralph G. Caso as county executive, the Mitchel Field Planning Commission was dissolved and county government agencies took over the future planning. County Executive Caso agreed with the Board of Supervisors on the exclusion of major housing in the area, and court litigation was initiated by housing supporters. As the county government ended its seventy-fifth year, the eventual development of Mitchel Field was still a major challenge of the future.

The masses of urban workers drawn to the giant war plants and green subdivisions of Nassau County were exposed to a new experience in government. The suburban government of Nassau County was based on local home rule and provided a unique experience for these residents because of its attention and focus on the family and home. Political control, after the governmental reorganization in the late 1930s, had been firmly assumed by the Republican Party, which supported the home rule concept under the astute leadership of County Executive J. Russel Sprague.

Following a policy of letting taxpayers

Former Mitchel Field property indicating its vast resources to be planned and developed at the center of the county.

Nassau Veterans Memorial Coliseum.

Nassau GOP was early supporter of Dwight D. Eisenhower's presidential campaigns.

Nationally prominent leaders including ex-President Herbert Hoover and President Dwight D. Eisenhower gathered at Sagamore Hill for its dedication as a national historic site in 1953.

take part in local government to their heart's content, Sprague allowed them to run their school systems without any political interference. Volunteer fire departments were also excluded from regular governmental control and functioned independently. Sprague realized that to retain the GOP dominance, he must provide the new residents with an efficient, considerate government and, in his own words, "a humanized public service." Therefore, although he ran a highly disciplined and centralized party organization, Sprague ensured that all political appointees to local government positions could handle their patronage job and that they actually worked at it.

The Republican Party was organized around the elective officers of the town and county governments and quickly assimilated into the party structure the new businessmen, bankers and professionals who commuted to New York City. Although many of the new residents were urban Democrats, they shifted party allegiance and became suburban Republicans. Various influences created this political switch, including the overwhelmingly Republican environment into which the new residents moved and a tendency to vote as one's neighbors did. The rise in income that corresponded with many residents' movement to the suburbs also inclined them toward more conservative Republican politics. Some political analysts believed that even though these residents came from Democratic urban origins, many already had a predilection for Republican politics, and this was part of the influence toward their movement to the suburbs.

The Nassau Republican machine became one of the most efficient in the country and managed to roll up massive pluralities for its local and national candidates. In 1945 the Republican enrollment in Nassau County was 80,610 voters, compared to the Democratic total of 21,783. Throughout the growth of the fifties, the Republican Party continued to assimilate the newcomers and maintained an enrollment advantage of 332,594 registrants to 152,608 for the Demo-

cratic Party. During the late forties, most Republican candidates carried the county with over 70 per cent of the vote, and as late as 1960, John F. Kennedy could obtain only 45 per cent of the vote in the county.

Sprague, as both county executive and political party leader, exercised strong control over Republican campaigns both locally and nationally. On a local level, the GOP continually tried to connect the corrupt New York City Tammany machine and the Nassau Democratic Party. In local elections during 1951, a GOP radio commercial blared, "Would you surrender your village government for a system of Tammany wards?" Republican candidates asserted in campaigns throughout the fifties that they were fighting a tiger—a "Tammany tiger." Although the local Democrats denied such connections, they added to the conflict by maintaining relationships with New York City politicians such as Tammany Hall leader Carmine De-Sapio, who spoke to Nassau Democrats in 1960.

This reliance on the Tammany bogeyman extended into the next decade, when numerous campaign banners and folders were produced with the slogan "Keep Tammany out of Nassau, Vote Republican." The threat actually was not always a paper one, since in 1957, a proposal to call a new state constitutional convention included authorizing legislation to establish a procedure for the annexation of lands to cities. Sprague bitterly fought the proposed convention as "a most serious threat to our governmental and political existence and . . . designed to capture us in a Democratic ambush." Since many residents did not have a favorable view of city government due to their urban experiences, the Republican reliance on the issue was an effective campaign tactic during these years.

Even before the war, Sprague had become a major national Republican leader. Chairman of the New York State delegation to the Republican National Convention in 1936, he went on to manage Thomas E. Dewey's campaigns in 1940, 1944 and 1948, and participated as a member of the National Republican Committee. He was one of the first members of the committee to publish a plea to General Dwight D. Eisenhower to lead the GOP to victory in 1952, and was chairman of the executive committee that urged Eisenhower's nomination. In 1953 he nominated Leonard W. Hall as chairman of the National Republican Committee. The latter was a popular congressman and served as an effective national political planner during Eisenhower's presidency. Since Hall was from Nassau County, Sprague thereafter relinquished his national role in party politics.

The enormous changes within the county had begun to loosen Republican political control in the 1950s. It became evident that the assumption all new residents would vote the straight Republican ticket even though they had been Democrats in the big city was no longer valid. Although the Republican percentage of enrollment remained high, voting results were showing a different pattern. A. Holly Patterson, who replaced Sprague as county executive in 1952, was reelected in 1955 with 62 per cent of the vote. In his next reelection bid in 1958, he received 54 per cent, and the Republican candidate for the town supervisorship of Hempstead in 1959 squeaked through with only a narrow 50.8 per cent victory.

The swarms of new residents had become too much for the Republican Party to assimilate, and its committeemen were unable to continue the conversion process that had originally occurred. The large numbers of Democratic-oriented people who moved into

Shopping center rallies were a new campaign technique during the 1960s.

Republican leadership in Nassau County during early 1950s; left to right: William S. Hults, Genesta Strong, J. Russel Sprague, Thomas E. Dewey, John Bennett, Frank Becker, Leonard Hall and Joseph Carlino.

the unincorporated areas such as Levittown, East Meadow, Oceanside, Bethpage, Plainview and Hicksville had little contact with party officials and were outside of the older villages where traditional GOP strength existed. In these new communities, the major focus of politics was school district elections, which remained traditionally non-partisan. This influenced greater individual initiative and independence in voting patterns rather than party allegiance.

The GOP was also under increasing pressure from young and invigorated leadership elements within the Democratic Party. John F. English had taken over as Democratic county leader in 1958 and immediately began to whip up a storm of activity in the party. In his early thirties, English was a vigorous, experienced political leader and revitalized the local Democratic Party. The pressure of these changes and Democratic

criticism of his investments in local raceway stock caused J. Russel Sprague to turn over interim leadership of the Republican Party to A. Holly Patterson in 1959. Republican leaders were concerned over the decline in their voting percentage and a complete reorganization led to the elevation of young assemblyman Joseph F. Carlino to Republican leader, in preparation for the important county executive election of 1961.

The Republican leadership had been pleased with Nixon's plurality over Kennedy in the county the previous year and underestimated the Democratic strength in the county. After three terms as county executive, Patterson declined to run again and the party leadership had to find a new candidate. Although J. Russel Sprague was in retirement, he still was a major adviser to Joseph Carlino and other party leaders. Carlino was an active, astute assemblyman, who con-

Party leadership of GOP was passed from A. Holly Patterson, center, to Joseph Carlino, on left, to Edward Speno, on right, in turbulent 1960s.

sistently ran well even in Democratic Long Beach. He vigorously exercised party leadership and established a headquarters with its own four-color printing facility.

However, at a long evening meeting in May of 1961 in Sprague's office, the leadership clique decided to nominate Robert Dill, a political unknown, as the Republican candidate to succeed Patterson. Dill, a committeeman in his home community of Garden City, had served as United States customs collector for the Port of New York during Dwight Eisenhower's presidency. The Democratic Party nominated Eugene H. Nickerson, a lawyer from Roslyn Harbor. Nickerson proved a polished and intelligent candidate who was able to relate well to the professional and leadership elements in the county.

Democratic chairman English waged a vigorous campaign against the Republican machine, concentrating on the bossism issue, and labeled Dill as "Boss Sprague's candidate." Sprague responded to the Democrats' criticism of him and his intrusion in the election was a negative influence on the Repub-

lican campaign. The Democratic Party also accused Dill of a conflict of interest during his period as customs collector and waged an extensive campaign to ensure that their committeemen worked effectively on election day, including a countywide committeeman telephone marathon.

The GOP campaign, although well organized by Carlino, was led by a very inexperienced candidate. Dill defended the principles of home rule but was castigated in the press for refusing to debate with Nickerson. His inexperience caused several major verbal *faux pas* in speeches which were reported in detail by the daily press, particularly his slip terming the Democrats as "greasy, slimy pigs," which rebounded severely and stimulated the Democratic Party into even stronger campaign efforts. Dill's lack of acquaintance with members of the party organization diminished enthusiasm for his candidacy and his consistently bad press undermined party morale. Despite the poor campaign and *Newsday*'s support of Nickerson's candidacy, most political writers predicted, on the eve of elections, that the

Candidates for county executive in 1967 gather at public debate: (right to left) Werner Pleus, Conservative; Eugene Nickerson, Democrat incumbent; and Republican challenger Sol Wachtler. Courtesy of Newsday.

Republicans would again carry all the posts.

However, as the vote trickled in on election night, it became apparent that Eugene H. Nickerson was running far in front of the other Democratic candidates. He carried over half of the county's election districts, winning the Town of Oyster Bay by some six thousand votes, and defeated Robert Dill by 216,150 to 209,581. An era in Nassau politics had come to an end. Nickerson ran well in the strong Republican portions of the Town of Hempstead and scored sizable pluralities in East Meadow and Levittown. Despite his victory, all the other Democratic county candidates lost by some thirty to forty thousand votes.

The Democratic Party was wild with joy after Nickerson's election, and John English began immediately to plan for the future. The Republicans were able to retain slim leads in the town elections except for the election of Michael N. Pettito as Democratic supervisor from Oyster Bay in 1963. The next year Nickerson campaigned for reelection as county executive against John Burns, a popular official from Sea Cliff. To the local

GOP's dismay, the election fell at the same time as the national Goldwater-Johnson presidential contest, which dominated the campaign. Goldwater's conservatism did not appeal to the large number of independent voters in the county and Lyndon Johnson won a crushing Democratic victory. Johnson's county plurality of over 129,000 swept all the major county offices into the Democratic line, with Nickerson winning reelection and the Democratic candidates for sheriff, clerk and comptroller also winning. The GOP loss was so great that even Joseph F. Carlino, who was then serving as the powerful speaker of the New York State assembly and had been in Albany for some twenty years, lost reelection in the overwhelming Democratic landslide.

Shaken by this stunning defeat and the resignation of the Town of Hempstead's presiding supervisor Palmer D. Farrington in 1965, the Republican Party reorganized under State Senator Edward J. Speno of East Meadow. For the next several years, Speno had to deal with considerable dissatisfaction within the party as unhappy younger

GOP leaders J. Russel Sprague, A. Holly Patterson and Edward Speno join to support new chairman, Joseph Margiotta.

leaders attempted to take over. In 1967 Nickerson was again challenged by an able young Republican, Sol Wachtler of Great Neck, but was able to eke out a victory due to 13,626 votes which he received on the Liberal line. A growing Conservative Party in the county polled over 56,000 votes for its candidate, pulling many former Republican votes away from the GOP candidate.

Immediately after this election, the dissatisfaction in the Republican Party led to a major shake-up and the election of Joseph M. Margiotta as county leader. A forty-five-year-old lawyer, Margiotta had attended Hofstra University and was a popular, well-known assemblyman from the Uniondale area. An aggressive, hard-working leader, Margiotta immediately began to vitalize the Republican Party. He transformed the GOP executive committee into a group dominated by younger and more vigorous men, indicating: "You get the younger fellows with the energy to put in the long hours."

A strong central Republican staff organization was established, with an emphasis on fund raising. Earlier goals of raising $250 in each election district in the 1960s were replaced now by a requirement to raise $400 from each of the 971 election districts. Margiotta also initiated a series of other major fund-raising events to provide a central party fund of over $1 million a year for campaign activities.

The Republican Party's return to grassroots power was one of the amazing feats of American politics in a period when strongly disciplined parties were dissolving all over the country. The conversion of a disoriented party into one of the best financed and organized in the country was accomplished by Margiotta's strong leadership. The New York *Times* commented that "the modern-day version of the old-fashioned political boss is flourishing in Nassau County," while professionals of both parties credited Margiotta with directing the most efficient political machine in the nation by the early 1970s.

The rejuvenation of the Republican Party was tested in the 1970 election for county

Chairman Joseph Margiotta addresses young Republican training session.

executive. Warming up to the contest in the town elections of 1969, the Republicans won victory over the Democrats, who had proposed that the Town of Hempstead government be abolished. The presiding supervisor of the Town of Hempstead, Ralph G. Caso, was chosen as the Republican candidate. An experienced public official and tireless campaigner, Caso received strong backing from his party. Margiotta's well-organized campaign regained Republican election supremacy and Republicans swept the election, with Caso receiving 277,360 votes to Democrat Andrew J. DiPaola's 235,314. Margiotta had resisted any agreements with the Conservative Party, which ran a candidate that drew fewer than forty thousand votes. The Republicans followed up this victory with continued triumphs. In 1973, Ralph G. Caso was reelected as county executive with an enormous ninety-thousand-vote plurality over Democratic, Conservative, Liberal and Independent candidates. He maintained traditional GOP support and also attracted independent voters due to the

progressive record of his administration.

The recovery and retention of control over the county government restored the dimmed luster of the county Republican organization. The new election strength, developed by Joseph Margiotta as party leader, reestablished the major role of the local GOP in New York State politics in the early 1970s. Long Island power in the state legislature was based not only on the increased numbers of local representatives due to legislative reapportionment, but also on the high caliber of individual legislators such as Senator John R. Dunne and assembly whip John Kingston. Nassau-Suffolk legislators represented 20 per cent of the Republican vote in the legislature. Through seniority and political muscle, they had taken over many powerful committee chairmanships. This influence provided more state assistance and aid for local school finances and other municipal programs.

In a period of less than twenty years, the once dominant Republican Party in Nassau County was severely shaken, reorganized and

Democratic Party Chairman John English meets the press with assemblyman Eli Wager and Arthur Kremer in 1966. Courtesy of Newsday.

restored as a strong and vibrant party. The tradition of strong party organization initiated by J. Russel Sprague, although weakened by the tremendous postwar population changes, was renewed under the leadership of Joseph Margiotta. Republican Party leadership gave continual attention to strengthening its internal machinery, and committeemen were active in every election district, providing an annual house-by-house voter canvass. In contrast the Democratic organization, despite the infusion of new leadership, still lacked a strong base of party workers. The Democratic Party was also continually racked by internal disagreements, causing many lower-echelon leadership changes and constant debilitating party primaries for election nominations. The GOP always settled its problems internally and seldom had weakening primary battles.

Although the Republican Party was able to achieve consistent election victories, Democratic enrollment by 1970 had increased to 32 per cent of the total registered voters. The electorate was also changing in other significant ways. Women now made up over 50 per cent of the eligible voters and were a major electoral factor. The new importance of women was based not just on their outnumbering men but also on their important role in party activities. Suburban political parties required large numbers of volunteers and women were filling much of this need. Democratic chairman John English commented: "I think women ask less and give more. In politics, men talk more and do less; women talk less and do more."

Nassau's electorate was also dramatically changed by the increasing independent tendency of voters. Its new populace, with a high-income level and above-average educational attainment, had less need for the traditional assistance and favors of a political party. National trends toward independent political action were especially evident in suburbia. The most visible example of this influence in Nassau was during the statewide elections of 1962 when Governor Nelson Rockefeller won the county for the Republicans with over a 125,000-vote margin, while Democrat Arthur Levitt also carried the county for comptroller by 27,000 votes. This tendency was also aggravated by the build-up of a small but dedicated Conservative and Liberal vote. These minority parties could provide the swing vote in close elections and attempted to influence the choice of candidates by major parties. The increased Democratic strength, new influence of women and rising non-partisanship were creating a new era of independent voting for popular candidates.

The Democratic Party had experienced a tremendous revival under the leadership of John English during the years Eugene Nickerson served as county executive. After Nickerson's reelection in 1964, English began to push him as a candidate for statewide Democratic office. Nickerson attempted to obtain the nomination for the governorship but was never able to obtain sufficient financing to make a successful bid. English moved on to state and national Democratic Party politics and the local Democratic Party lost much of

Democratic candidates such as north shore congressman Lester Wolff had close ties with Robert Kennedy. Courtesy of Newsday.

Governor Nelson Rockefeller on the stump in Nassau with County Executive A. Holly Patterson.

its organization strength after Nickerson un-successfully sought the gubernatorial nomination and did not stand for reelection as county executive in 1970. It was evident that the Republican leadership had been able to regain the confidence of many voters, but the greatly increased Democratic strength in the county would hereafter provide a strong two-party system in local government elections.

Reapportionment of Supervisors

The ascension of the Democratic Party into control of the county government in 1962, after years of Republican supremacy, created a complete upheaval in county politics. Democratic Party officials began to press vigorously for ways to enhance their victory and attempted to push their proposals for the reorganization of the county's local governmental structure to obtain more representation on the Board of Supervisors. They felt citizen confusion between the responsibilities of the town government and the many special districts was unnecessary and urged a modernization of the county's government.

A petition drive was launched to force the Board of Supervisors into a referendum on charter review, and in August of 1961, County Executive A. Holly Patterson appointed the initial members of a Nassau County Charter Revision Commission. James N. Gehrig was appointed chairman of the commission, consisting of George L. Hubbell of Garden City, Walter E. Van de Waag of East Williston, Raymond French of Locust Valley, R. Gordon Hoxie of Oyster Bay Cove, Howard G. Wilson of Lynbrook, William J. Sullivan of Rockville Centre, William H. Walters of Manhasset, Rocco Campanaro of Valley Stream, Arthur Roth of Rockville Centre and J. Charles Zimmerman of Long Beach.

When Eugene H. Nickerson became county executive the next year, he added W. Harry Lister of Rockville Centre, M. Halstead Christ of Oyster Bay, Mrs. Edward Coffin of Brookville, Paul Godofsky of Hempstead, Norman Gross of Sands Point, Bertram Harnett of Great Neck, Henry Rigali of Seaford and George Soll of Roslyn. The seventeen members began extensive deliberations over the direction of the county government, and although Gehrig was chairman, the Democratic members of the commission asserted a leadership role. After the United States Supreme Court ruling in 1964, requiring that each resident of a state must have an equal vote in selecting state representatives, the major point of contention became the weighted voting basis of the county Board of Supervisors.

Under the revised county charter of 1938, each supervisor had one vote for every ten thousand persons in his township, with no town having more than half of the Board's entire votes. In 1960 the Board was using an apportionment of 62 votes for the two Hempstead supervisors, 28 for Oyster Bay, 21 for North Hempstead and 2 each for the cities of Long Beach and Glen Cove. Although these votes add up to a total of 115, the Board actually set 125 votes as its entire vote. This was done to meet the charter requirement that no town could have more than half the votes on the Board, and Hempstead with 62 was below half the theoretical total of 125.

In June of 1965, the commission released preliminary majority and minority reports. The majority report proposed that the existing Board of Supervisors be replaced by a new fifteen-member board elected from districts of equal population throughout the county, with each member having one vote. It also recommended that the county sheriff be appointive rather than elective, and that the sheriff's staff be composed of civil service personnel. Four members of the commission, led by Chairman Gehrig, opposed the majority proposal, contending that other alternatives should be reviewed, such as a board with weighted vote positions including the supervisors and other representatives from districts. The Democratic political leadership pressured for the consideration of the fifteen-member proposal, since such a change would materially improve their possibilities for increased representation.

Although there was some confusion whether this was a final recommendation, the Republican majority on the Board of Supervisors decided to submit the proposals to the electorate in the fall of 1965. Proposition Number One, providing for the change in the sheriff's office, was strongly supported and won approval with a plurality of over 200,000 votes. However, the creation of a fifteen-district Board of Supervisors was strongly opposed by the Republican Party. The proposition was defeated in the Town of Hempstead by a three-to-two margin. Since it would have meant the loss of their supervisorship, even the Democratic-controlled city of Long Beach voted against it by three to one. The total vote was 158,427, to 145,770 against the plan. County Executive Eugene H. Nickerson indicated disappointment in the defeat of the proposal, which he had supported, and contended, "It is hard to get a program of this kind through because its opponents are better able to focus attention on it than its supporters."

The commission continued its deliberations and at the end of 1966 submitted final proposals to the Board of Supervisors for the revision of government in Nassau County. It again concentrated primarily on the reapportionment of the Board, proposing a twelve-man body with equal votes from equal districts. In addition, it proposed that the county executive could introduce legislation to the Board of Supervisors, and in the event of his death or resignation, he would be succeeded by his appointed deputy.

The commission proposals also eliminated the town receivers of taxes, with their functions to be taken over by a new county Department of Finance. Mandatory reassessment of all property in the county was proposed to be done every fifteen years. The commission also suggested a series of changes in the county charter providing a Health Services Department, Parks Department and Office of Administrative Services, and changing the county budget year from a calendar year to a fiscal year beginning June 1.

Although there was agreement on most of the minor suggestions, the major recommendation concerning the Board's membership received a split approval by the commission, eleven votes to six. The commission's proposal to the Board of Supervisors was not mandatory and the Board began deliberations. Its Republican leadership opposed the reapportionment of the Board and Supervisor Ralph G. Caso indicated, "If weighted voting is legal then why change it? It has provided flexible and efficient government." Throughout 1967, the Board continued deliberation, including consideration of a board consisting of the existing supervisors and seven new county legislators.

In July, when it appeared that the Republicans would go ahead with their own plan, there was a sudden bipartisan agreement on a new compromise proposal. The Republican leadership and County Executive Eugene H. Nickerson agreed on an eighteen-member Board of Supervisors with one representative from each assembly district in the county. The county executive's power to introduce legislation was not included, but the abolition of the Office of Receivers of taxes was contained in the new proposition. There also was a provision for an ombudsman to provide countywide investigatory services.

The Board of Supervisors held several hearings on the proposition in the fall and widespread opposition was expressed to various aspects of the proposals. Both the Liberal and Conservative parties opposed the measure, indicating it would not assist minority parties in obtaining a voice on the Board. The Police Benevolent Association contended that the ombudsman would become a "one-man civilian review board" and persuaded Democratic supervisor Michael N. Pettito from the Town of Oyster Bay to urge that police review be excluded. In addition, there was a great deal of opposition to a provision which gave the county the right to challenge local zoning decisions in the courts. After additional negotiations, the Republicans obtained Nickerson's reluctant support for these deletions and the main proposals were placed on the 1967 election ballot.

Nickerson strongly supported the propositions but opposition developed within the Republican Party. Ralph J. Marino, Oyster Bay candidate for supervisor, strongly opposed the measure, and Edward Speno, Republican leader, also expressed the same sentiment. Citizen groups were organized on both sides of the issue. The need for an extensive coordinated campaign to obtain a charter change was again evident in this election, and the lack of such strong leadership led to defeat of the Board's reorganization by a vote of 282,311 to 163,963. The ombudsman proposal also failed, and a proposition for the election of councilmen by districts rather than on a townwide basis was also defeated in each of the three towns.

With this final defeat, the Democratic leadership realized that reapportionment of the Board to enable an increase in Democratic representation probably could not be achieved through referendum. Therefore, in 1968, five Democrats brought legal suit to force reapportionment in line with the new Supreme Court decisions applying the one man–one vote rule to local government. The Board of Supervisors, under its Republican leadership, appointed George C. Pratt as a special attorney to represent them in the suits and opposed the action. By February 1970, the action had moved through the lower courts, and the State Court of Appeals upheld their rulings that the Board was not properly apportioned and must reorganize itself by mid-1971, after the new population census was published.

The Democratic court triumph was soured by Republican Ralph G. Caso's victory as county executive in the 1970 election. After the court decision was studied, County Executive Ralph G. Caso supported reapportionment of the Board and its election by

equal districts. The new Republican town supervisors opposed the measure, however, and proposed another plan on a weighted vote basis including the principle that no town could cast the votes required for a majority. Under this plan, there would be 130 votes on the Board, with 35 for each supervisor from the Town of Hempstead, 32 for the supervisor from the Town of Oyster Bay, 23 for the supervisor from North Hempstead, 2 for the supervisor of the city of Glen Cove and 3 for the supervisor of the city of Long Beach. Passage of majority legislation was set at 71 votes, and a two-thirds measure would need 92 votes.

This proposal received the support of the Democratic supervisors from the two cities and was passed by the entire Board. Caso vetoed the measure but it was passed over his veto and presented to the court. Initially it was declared unconstitutional, but upon appeal to the State Court of Appeals in May 1973, the system was upheld. The Democratic leadership continued to fight the issue and attempted to bring the question before the United States Supreme Court, which finally settled the matter in February 1974 by refusing to review the matter. The long decade of controversy over the reapportionment of the Board and revision of county government had failed to achieve any significant change. Serious political partisanship, combined with the lack of widespread public understanding and support, mitigated several attempts to revise the essential structure of the Board of Supervisors.

The postwar years reflected the effect of the county's great population influx on all levels of government. Local government, particularly in special districts and at the county level, had to provide extensive new and costly physical facilities. The state government provided major resources for transportation improvements and the enlarged population created many new governmental service demands. The pressure of these demands, the changing base of the county's population and the increasing independence

County Executive Ralph G. Caso campaigning with youthful supporters.

of American voters caused a major political upheaval. The long-dominant Republican Party lost its executive control of the county government for a decade but through renewed and skillful leadership reassumed political superiority.

Although there were calls for reform of local government, citizens evidenced little interest and there were only minor modifications made after the reorganization of the late 1930s. As Nassau County entered the last quarter of its first century as a separate governmental entity, the major physical facilities required for its population had been completed. The extension of special services for the more complex problems of a larger population was creating increasing financial burdens that posed a challenge for future governmental leadership.

Conclusion

In 1869, *Harper's Weekly* acclaimed A. T. Stewart's purchase of Hempstead Plains and his plan to erect homes there for the working classes of Brooklyn and New York since "It will be the most beautiful suburb in the vicinity of New York. God speed the undertaking." During the next century, Stewart's vision was accomplished, and over a million people established Nassau County as one of the great suburbs of America. The growth of suburbia was part of a new direction in American life which, as a New York *Times* editorial concluded, "has reshaped the face of America since World War II and profoundly affected the country's life and institutions."

Nassau County was created in 1899 as a separate governmental entity due to its essentially rural character and incompatibility with the increasing urbanization of western Queens County. For the first decade of the 1900s, it remained essentially a rural area of small farms and villages, "a landscape of unself-conscious miniature beauty." The majority of residents derived their livelihood from the sea or agriculture, and had deep roots in the area.

However, a rapid succession of changes in the county's life not only propelled it into the space age but also toward full development as one of America's principal suburban areas. The Long Island Rail Road initially played a principal role when through rail service to Manhattan made commutation feasible for the industrial workers of the city. By the 1920s, the widespread use of the automobile was reflected in a major road network linking the county to the city. The availability of rail and auto transportation allowing any section of Nassau to be reached within one hour's travel time from Manhattan established the county as an ideal residential area for urban workers. Realtors quickly seized upon the opportunities and, aided by railroad promotion efforts, built major housing subdivisions in small villages during the boom years of the 1920s when Nassau's population doubled.

The county was a suburb with unique environmental and recreational attributes. The natural waterfront on its shores was a major attraction for many new residents. Its lush north shore woods were chosen by the very wealthy as the sites for New York country homes and a Gold Coast covered a great portion of the county's northern area. The extensive estates and manorial mansions cast a shine of high society over the county and retained a considerable area in an undeveloped, natural state.

There was also unusual glamour and excitement connected with early aviation, and many significant national aviation developments occurred at the various airfields located on the flat central plains land. This activity eventually created a great wartime industry in World War II, and provided a strong economic basis for the county's growth.

Although the initial suburban growth between World Wars I and II had expanded the small communities along the railroad lines, the county still retained much of its rural atmosphere. This rapidly disappeared, however, in the enormous doubling of the population in the 1950s, to a total of over 1,300,000 residents by 1970. This pervasive development affected every area of the county and created block upon block of residential housing as far as the eye could see.

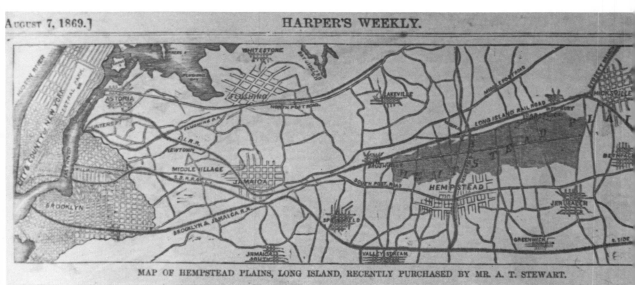

MAP OF HEMPSTEAD PLAINS, LONG ISLAND, RECENTLY PURCHASED BY MR. A. T. STEWART.

Despite the encroachment of suburbia, the maritime charm of the Freeport
Creek still remained in the early 1970s.

Nassau's past, present and future gathered in 1973 at the opening of Falaise, Harry Guggenheim's estate, as a historic house. Charles Lindbergh on right, who wrote We *at Falaise; Robert Moses, master planner of the postwar years; and County Executive Ralph G. Caso.*

The automobile became the master of suburban life as an absolute transportation necessity for most residents. The intensive suburban development of the county overcame its rural institutions and major realignments had to be accomplished to handle the rapid growth since, as a New York *Times* editorial indicated, "from behavior to politics, ecology to economics, there is virtually nothing this outward migration has not changed."

Local government was faced with a continual demand to provide increased services for the new residential population and business community. Consequently, the county was a pioneer in attempting to adapt the old framework of rural government to a suburban mission. Village governments were highly developed to provide local services while increasingly the county government assumed greater responsibilities to provide both physical facilities and special public services.

Due to the predominantly youthful nature of the county's population, its educational system of independent school districts provided a central role in community life. Enormous financial burdens, due to the extensive construction of facilities and rising operational costs, caused rapidly rising tax rates. Although there was great resistance to these costs, active citizen leadership and support enabled the districts to provide exceptionally superior educational services. The archaic geographical boundaries of school districts were not adapted to this new growth, and great financial inequities existed between areas with high and low tax bases. Demands for state assistance in education were responsible for greatly increased state aid to local school districts. The independence and development of local control in village and school district operations created a strong desire within the county's citizenry for "home rule" government.

Initially, the majority of the county's residents earned their living outside the county, but by the late 1960s, over half were employed within the county. The development of light industry after World War II, an enormous expansion of retail business, special service concerns and other economic resources created a new base of local employment. The development of massive regional shopping centers and small industrial parks not only reshaped the economic life of the county but significantly altered its environment in many areas.

From the development of small villages around main road intersections or harbors in the late 1800s, life on Long Island revolved around the local community. Growth of a commuter life-style confirmed this local interest, although many residents had strong commercial ties with New York City. Throughout the early 1900s, the people in Nassau County gave their primary allegiance and major attention to the social affairs of their local community. This caused an absence of any sense of county civic or social life.

After the extensive suburban development in the 1940s and the increasing political-economic interrelationships of the entire metropolitan New York area, more citizens recognized the need to be concerned with the area outside their own community. It was still difficult, however, for most residents to muster sufficient understanding or interest in the increasingly complex state of affairs outside local villages.

County Executive Eugene H. Nickerson observed in 1969 that residents of the county "have no sense of living in the town. They will tell you they live in East Meadow or Levittown or Rockville Centre but not in the Town of Hempstead." Residents not only had difficulty in sensing a town relationship, but a county consciousness was equally distant. However, the increasing scope of countywide activities, including the widening role of county government, provided a new county awareness. The impossibility of telling where one community ended and the next one began in the burgeoning suburban expansion directed newer residents toward a county location identification.

In the early 1970s, County Executive Ralph G. Caso particularly expressed the need to develop this attitude in residents to ensure adequate attention to the county's future growth. In addition, he also led a drive for greater recognition of the suburbs on the state and national level. Caso felt that "It is important now to bring America's perception of its suburbs up to date," and that the image of problem-free suburbia, unwilling to assist in solving the cities' problems, was not realistic. The future would require more understanding and discussion about the "interrelationships of the cities and the suburbs."

The problem of establishing such broader awareness was a major factor complicating the attempts to solve the problems of suburban growth. A Regional Plan Association report in 1969 indicated: "Overall Nassau County cannot be sensed as a place because until recently no one thought of it as a place." Thus even those residents comprehending the significance of countywide developments could not easily articulate or define Nassau County due to the enormous complexities and diversity existing within its boundaries.

The new financial, environmental and governmental problems of suburban Nassau County not only transcended village and community boundaries but even county lines. Transportation systems including the railroad and a bridge to Connecticut, future energy needs requiring atomic energy plants outside the county and the specter of eventual need to obtain water supplies from outside the county were concerns that required metropolitan area solution and cooperation. However, residents' identification was still essentially related to their familiar and closely associated local village, but the interactions required by a much more complicated life-style in the last quarter of the twentieth century were thrusting Nassau County into a new era. In this great county, the full impact of suburbia as a new American life-style can be traced—its initiation, growth, maturation and challenge for the future.

Nassau County Executive Ralph G. Caso and Suffolk County Executive John Klein discuss the future of oil drilling off the Atlantic coastline and the necessity to preserve Long Island's unique environment.

BIBLIOGRAPHY

The following books are those readily available works necessary for a study of Nassau County from 1900 to 1975. In addition, *The Nassau County Historic Society Journal*, published from 1937 to 1974, has many valuable articles, and a great many newspapers, including *Newsday* and the *Long Island Daily Press* and its predecessors, and major weeklies are available on microfilm.

Bailey, Paul, editor, *Long Island—A History of Two Great Counties, Nassau and Suffolk.* 3 vols. New York: Lewis Historical Pub. Co., 1949.

Bassett, Preston R., *Long Island, Cradle of Aviation.* Amityville: Long Island Forum, 1950.

Bassett, Preston R., and Arthur L. Hodges, *The History of Rockville Centre.* Uniondale: The Authors, 1969.

Bellot, Alfred H., *History of the Rockaways.* Far Rockaway: Bellot's Histories Inc., 1917.

Carpenter, James W., *The Mineola Fair.* Uniondale: Agricultural Society of Queens, Nassau and Suffolk Counties, 1965.

Chambers, Whittaker, *Witness.* New York: Random House, Inc., 1952.

Cox, John, Jr., *Oyster Bay Town Records.* 8 vols. New York: Town of Oyster Bay, 1916–1940.

Darlington, Oscar, *A History of the Hempstead Volunteer Fire Department.* Hempstead: 1953.

Dobriner, William M., *Class in Suburbia.* New York: Prentice-Hall, Inc., 1963.

Fitzgerald, F. Scott, *The Great Gatsby.* New York: Charles Scribner's Sons, 1925.

Franklin National Bank, *Statistical Abstract of Nassau and Suffolk Counties.* Garden City: Franklin National Bank, 1962.

Fullerton, Edith Loring, *History of Long Island Agriculture.* Jamaica: Long Island Rail Road Co., 1929.

Gabriel, Ralph H., *The Evolution of Long Island.* New Haven: Yale University Press, 1921.

Hagedorn, Herman, *The Roosevelt Family of Sagamore Hill.* New York: The Macmillan Co., 1954.

Hazelton, Henry Isham, *The Boroughs of Brooklyn and Queens, Counties of Nassau and Suffolk, Long Island, New York, 1609–1924.* 3 vols. New York: Lewis Historical Pub. Co., 1925.

Hicks, Benjamin D., editor, *Records of the Towns of North and South Hempstead.* 8 vols. Jamaica: Town of North Hempstead, 1896–1904.

Hodges, Arthur L., *Nassau County, the Netherland of the New World.* Rockville Centre: 1940.

Hodges, Arthur L., editor, *Know Long Island, America's Most Complete Community.* Hempstead: Community Yearbooks, 1960.

Jackson, Birdsall, *How They Lived.* Rockville Centre: Paumanok Press, 1941.

Kaiser, William K., and Charles E. Stonier, editors, *The Development of the Aerospace Industry on Long Island.* 3 vols. Hempstead: Hofstra University, 1968.

Long Island Rail Road, *Long Island, the Sunrise Homeland.* New York: Long Island Rail Road, 1924.

Merritt, Jesse F., *The Historical Importance of Nassau County, Long Island, New York.* Farmingdale: 1940.

Moger, Roy W., *Roslyn, Then and Now.* Roslyn: Roslyn Board of Education, 1964.

Nassau County, *Proceedings of the Board of Supervisors, Nassau County.* 1899–1973. Mineola: Nassau County, 1900–1974.

Nassau County Historical Museum, *A Catalog of Long Island Newspapers on Microfilm.* Mineola: County of Nassau, 1970.

New York Bureau of Municipal Research, *Government of Nassau County.* Albany: Comm. on the Government of Nassau County, 1915.

Overton, Jacqueline, *Long Island's Story.* Garden City: Doubleday, Doran & Company, 1932.

Prince, Nathaniel S., *A History of Long Island.* New York: Robert Carter, 1845.

Ransom, Charles E., *Gaslight and Gingerbread, A Photographic Recollection of Old Sea Cliff.* Sea Cliff: 1971.

Regional Plan Association, *The Future of Nassau County*. New York: Regional Plan Association, 1969.

Ross, Peter, A *History of Long Island, from Its Earliest Settlement to the Present Time*. 3 vols. New York: Lewis Publishing Co., 1903.

Seyfried, Vincent F., *New York and North Shore Traction Company*. Hollis: 1955.

Seyfried, Vincent F., *The Long Island Rail Road, A Comprehensive History*. 5 vols. Garden City: 1961–1971.

Smith, Mildred H., *History of Garden City*. Manhasset: Channel Press, 1963.

Smits, Edward J., *The Creation of Nassau County*. Mineola: County of Nassau, 1962.

Thomas, Samuel F., *Nassau County Its Governments and Their Expenditure and Revenue Patterns*. New York: City College Press, 1960.

Thompson, Benjamin F., *History of Long Island from Its Discovery and Settlement to the Present Time*. 3 vols. New York: Robert H. Dodd, 1918.

Tredwell, Daniel M., *Personal Reminiscences of Men and Things on Long Island*. 2 vols. Brooklyn: Charles Ditmas, 1912.

Uhlan, Edward, *Dynamo Jim Stiles: Pioneer of Progress*. New York: Exposition Press, 1959.

W. W. Munsell & Co., *History of Queens County, New York*. New York: 1882.

INDEX

A

Abilities, Inc., 229
Abraham & Straus, 26, 253
Acosta, Bert, 96
Adams, Franklin P., 124
Adams, John C., 219
Adelphi University, 172, 218–19
Adult education, 215–16
Aeronautical Society of New York City, 79, 80
Agricultural Society of Queens, Nassau and
    Suffolk Counties, 13, 75, 176
Agriculture, 13–16, 37, 73, 174–75, 260; dairy,
    14; market gardening, 14–16, 174; potato, 16,
    174
Airmail, 83, 99
Aldrich, T. B., 30
Allen, James, 217
America, 96
American Aeronautical Corp., 109–10
American Legion, 143
Amityville, 36
Amphitrite, 126
Apartment housing, 185, 204
Arnold, Lieutenant H. H., 84
Association for the Help of Retarded Children,
    229
Atlantic Beach Bridge, 241
Automobile, 47, 152, 226, 238
Aviation, 75, 89, 193; airfields, 102–8; between
    wars, 94–102; early 1900s, 79–86; industry,
    109–19; World War I, 89–91; World War II,
    113–14
Aviation Field No. 2, 89

B

Babylon, 39, 41
Bacon, Robert Low, 69
Badger, G. W., Company, 179
Baldwin, 19, 20, 25, 33, 36, 84, 104, 167, 177,
    184
Baldwin, Fred, 84
Baldwin, William, 3
Baldwin Naval Ordnance Plant, 193
Baldwin Savings and Loan Association, 181
Banking, 25, 180–81, 186, 254, 256

Bank of Rockville Centre, 25, 181
Baptist church, 34, 164, 201
Barbuti, Ray, 134
Barnum, P. C., 13
Barnum Island, 43
Baseball, 36, 132
Bassett, Preston R., 101
Bayman, 19
Becker, Frank, 273
Bedell, Theodore, Jr., 73
Bee Line, 158
Bellanca, Giuseppe M., 84
Bellerose, 168
Bellmore, 36, 184, 199
Bellmore Land Improvement Company, 12
Belmont, August, Jr., 129, 156
Belmont, Mrs. Oliver H. P., 62
Belmont Park, 80, 129, 237
Benét, William Rose, 125
Bennett, Earl J., 70, 71
Bennett, John, 273
Bennington Park, 146
Bernays, Edward L., 145
Bethpage, 28, 196, 251, 273
Bethpage State Park, 136
Bettis, Lieutenant Cyrus, 103
Bi-County Regional Planning Board, 266
Bicycling, 4, 36
Black, Governor Frank S., 42
Blacks, 145, 146, 162, 164, 200; school desegre-
    gation, 217
Blodgett, Frank D., 172
Boating, 237–38
BOCES, 213, 214
Bogert, Joseph H., 40
Bolling, Major Raynal, 86
Bostwick, G. H., 128
Bowling, 237
Boxing, 134
Boy Scouts, 143, 228
Brickmaking, 28
Brierly, Arthur, 67
Brooklyn Water Company, 23
Brookville, 17
Brower, Girdell V., 59
Brown, Charles F., 43
Brown, Paul, 127

Browning, Edward West, 184
Bryant, William Cullen, 8–9, 33
Buck, Frank, 234
Buck, Gene, 126
Burden, Arthur S., 123
Burden, James A., 121
Burket, Lawrence A., 72
Burnett, Francis H., 125
Burns, John, 249, 275
Bus service, 158, 244
Byrd, Commander Richard, 96, 98

C

C. W. Post College, 219
Calderone, Dr. F., 230
Calkins, Truesdale P., 169, 173
Campanaro, Rocco, 280
Camp Black, 37
Camp Mills, 88–90, 157, 163
Carle Place, 218
Carlino, Joseph F., 273, 274
Carll, John H., 39
Caso, Ralph G., 262, 263, 268, 277, 281, 282, 283
Cathedral of the Incarnation, 33, 35
Cedarhurst, 9, 36, 43, 204
Cedarmere, 9
Centre Island, 28, 55
Chamberlin, Clarence, 96, 98
Chambers, Whittaker, 161, 170
Charitable organizations, 145, 228–29
Cheshire, A. Burnside, 67
Childs, John Lewis, 16, 18, 42, 60
Chinese, 200
Christ, M. Halstead, 280
Christ, Marcus, 69
Christ, Philip J., 60, 62, 66, 67, 68
Christian Hook, 20
Christie, Robert L., 136, 146
Chrysler, Walter P., 221
Citizens National Bank, 181
Civic League of Nassau, 72
Civic organizations, 59, 138–39, 209, 227
Clamming, 21
Clapham, Thomas, 25
Clark, F. Ambrose, 9, 123
Coast Guard, 20, 137–38
Cochran, W. Bourke, 60
Cock, W. W., 39
Cocks, James H., 60, 66
Cocks, William, 60, 67, 130
Coe, William K., 17, 123

Coffin, Mrs. Edward, 280
Cohan, George M., 125
Coli, François, 96
Collins, Henry J. A., 70
Columbia Aviation Corporation, 117
Columbian Brass Foundry, 179, 193
Columbia Ribbon and Carbon Company, 179
Conservative Party, 276, 281
Cooley, James S., 30, 169
Corbin, Austin, 3
Cornelius Carman, 48
County Federal Savings & Loan Association, 254
Courthouse: temporary, 45; old, 47–48, 51, 270; new, 75, 77
Cove Neck, 55
Covert, William S., 169
Covey, F. Howard, 143
Cox, Smith, 42, 46, 59
Cox-Klemmin Aircraft Corporation, 110
Craft, Morris F., 59
Crocker, Frank L., 66
Cromwell, Edward, 42
Cuff, Thomas J., 68
Cuff-McNamara Charter, 69
Curtis, Elwood A., 70
Curtiss, Glenn, 78, 79, 102, 108–9, 119
Curtiss Aeroplane and Motor Company, 75, 91, 94, 179
Curtiss Field, 99, 104, 117

D

Dade, George, 86, 99
Daily News, 183, 256
Daily Review, 166, 282
Dana, Charles, 8
Davis, John W., 62–63, 69
Davison, F. Trubee, 67, 69, 87, 106
Davison, Henry Pomeroy, 92, 123
Davison, Sanford, 50
Davison's Mill, 17
Deasey, Edward J., 67
Deepdale, 130
Delafield, Lewis L., 75
Delancey Floyd-Jones Library, 33
Democratic Party, 51, 71, 272, 274–75, 278, 280, 282
Denton, Augustus, 42, 44, 46
Depression, 73–75, 185
De Seversky, Alexander, 106, 110
Dewey, Governor Thomas E., 271, 273
Dill, Robert, 274

Dime Savings Bank of Brooklyn, 196
DiPaola, Andrew J., 277
Doane, Jeanne Marion, 68
Dodd, John W., 169
Doolittle, James, 100, 106
Doubleday, Page & Company, 176, 178
Doughty, G. Wilbur, 43, 57, 62, 63–64, 68
Downing, Benjamin W., 67
Dowsey, James L., 60, 64
Dunne, John R., 277
Du Pont, Alicia, 123
Durant, Will, 125
Duryea country store, 2
Duryea Starch Company, 27, 28

E

Earhart, Amelia, 106
Eastman, Henry N. W., 42
East Meadow, 13, 196, 217, 222, 273, 275
East Norwich, 130, 199
East Rockaway, 1, 17, 19, 20, 24, 49, 55, 143, 155, 177, 210, 245
East Williston, 55
East Williston Road Cart Company, 28, 29
Education, 132–33, 134, 165, 214–18; parochial, 165–66, 213–14; public schools, 29–33, 166–70, 210–13; universities, 172–73, 219–22
Edwards, Elvin N., 60, 106, 138
Eisenhower, President Dwight D., 226, 270, 272
Elections, county, 1898: 42; 1910: 59; 1912: 60; 1917: 62; 1935: 69; 1936: 72; 1950s: 272; 1961: 274–75; 1963: 275; 1967: 276; 1970s: 277
Elmont, 2, 43, 168, 197, 212
Emory, George S., 66, 68
Endo Chemical Laboratory, 257
English, John F., 273, 274, 275, 278
Episcopal church, 33, 164, 201
Ethnic groups, 146–47, 162–63, 199–201

F

Fair, county, 13–14, 175
Fairchild Airplane Manufacturing Company, 110
Fairchild Camera and Instrument Corporation, 115
Fairchild Hiller Corporation, 118
Falaise, 98, 231
Fantasy Theatre, 137

Farmingdale, 2, 29, 55, 110, 179, 196, 204, 217, 258
Farrington, Palmer D., 275
Far Rockaway, 23
Finlay, Charles E., 162
First National Bank of Hempstead, 26
First National Bank of Rockville Centre, 186
Firth, E. Harper, 46
Fishing, 17, 23, 176
Fitzgerald, F. Scott, 125
Floral Park, 16, 18, 32, 49, 51, 55, 163, 168, 197, 204, 212, 249
Floyd-Jones, Elbert, 40
Fonck, Captain René, 96
Football, 133
Foster's Meadow, 43
Foulis, Lt. B. D., 84
Fox, William, 184
Franklin Shops, 179
Franklin Square, 2, 168, 174, 197, 212
Franklin Square National Bank, 254
Freeport, 1, 6, 19, 20, 23, 25, 26, 27, 36, 49, 50, 51, 87, 104, 136, 142, 146, 152, 155, 156, 158, 159, 164, 172, 179, 184, 186, 193, 197, 199, 204, 205; government, 55, 56, 234; schools, 31, 33, 132, 133, 165–67, 169, 170, 210, 212, 217, 238
Freeport Bank, 181
Freeport Creek, 3, 24
Freeport High School, 31
Freeport Land Company, 12
Freeport Lodge of Elks, 144
French, Raymond, 280
Friends Academy, 33
Fry, Ambrose J., 167

G

Gale, Cyrus B., 42
Garbage disposal, 248
Garden City, 2, 4, 12, 28, 33, 36, 43, 49, 83, 89, 92, 140, 151, 159, 162, 178, 185, 204, 210, 260
Garden City Aviation Field, 80
Garden City Company, 12, 43, 162
Garden City Golf Club, 36, 129
Garden City Hotel, xii, 1, 96
Gary, Elbert A., 123
Gatty, Harold, 101
Gehrig, James N., 71, 280
Germans, 28, 162, 199
Gibbons, Eugene, 265
Gibbs, Alonzo, 153

Nassau County Bankers Association, 181
Nassau County Bar Association, 144
Nassau County Clearing House, 186
Nassau County Firemen's Association, 140
Nassau County, government: A. Holly Patterson
   Home, 251; Board of Assessors, 73; Board of
   Supervisors, 64, 66, first, 42, reorganization of,
   280–82; Bridge Authority, 241; budgets, 47, 48,
   52, 264; Cantiague Park, 234; charter reform,
   1915: 65–66; 1922: 67–68; 1935: 69–72; Commission on Human Rights, 265; Community
   College, 219–20, 263, 264; County Executive,
   71; courts, 73, 264; creation of, 39–43; debts,
   193–264; Department of Public Transportation, 244; Department of Public Works, 245,
   247; Fire Commission, 140; Firemen's Training Center, 228; Meadowbrook Hospital,
   250, 251, 264; Mitchel Field Planning Commission, 268; Mosquito Extermination Commission, 53; Museum, 230; Nassau County
   Park, 225–26; Planning Commission, 266,
   268; police, 53, 54, 264; reorganization, 65–73,
   280–82; tuberculosis hospital, 52; Veterans
   Memorial Coliseum, 235; Vocational, Educa-
   tion and Extension Board, 214
Nassau County Medical Society, 145
Nassau County Review, 3
Nassau County Trust Company, 181
Nassau County Tuberculosis & Public Health
   Association, 145
Nassau County Village Officials Association, 55
Nassau Daily Review, 181–82
Nassau Daily Review Star, 72, 256
Nassau Hospital, 145, 251
Nassau Library System, 223
Nassau Light and Power Company, 50
Nassau-Suffolk School Board Association, 212
National Air Races, 113
National Bank of North America, 254
National Guard, 87, 190
National Municipal League, 69
NC 4, 94, 95, 108
Neutra, Richard, 218
New Cassel, 200, 258
New Hyde Park, 55, 168, 197, 212
Newsday, 189, 255–56, 274
New York Bureau of Municipal Research, 66
New York City, 41, 169, 176, 194
New York Institute of Technology, 222
New York and North Shore Traction Company,
   156
New York State School of Agriculture at Farm-
   ingdale, 172
New York Telephone Company, 49, 180, 249

New York Yacht Club, 128
Nickerson, Eugene H., 264, 265, 268, 274–75,
   281
Niemann, James, P., 42
Non-Partisan Civic Association of Oyster Bay,
   72
Norris, Kathleen, 125
North Bellmore, 164
Northeast Civic Association of Freeport, 72
Northern State Parkway, 153, 154, 238
North Hempstead, town government, 205
North Shore University Hospital, 251
North Woodmere, 234
Nungesser, Charles, 96
Nurseries, horticultural, 16, 175, 261

O

Ocean County, 40
Oceanside, 19, 140, 167, 199, 273
Office buildings, 259–60
Old Bethpage, 13, 199, 212, 228
Old Bethpage village restoration, 223–33, 263
Old Westbury, 17, 55, 123, 221
Old Westbury Gardens, 207
O'Leary, Martin P., 68
Olena, Alfred Douglas, 70
Onderdonk, Henry, 40
Orchard House, 145
Ordnance Engineering Company, 110
Orteig prize, 96
Ovington, Earl, 83
Owl, The, 61
Oyster Bay, hamlet, 2, 6, 23, 25, 28, 34, 36, 49,
   51, 87, 164, 172, 222, schools, 166, 167;
   town government, 52, 54, 237, 248, 266
Oystering, 19–23, 176–77, 261

P

Page, Walter Hines, 92
Painter, C. Chester, 64
Parent-teacher associations, 179, 212
Patterson, A. Holly, 64, 68, 133, 261, 264, 266,
   272, 273, 274, 276, 279, 280
Patterson, Alicia, 256
Patterson, Archibald, 67
Patterson, Thomas, 42, 44, 46
Pearsall, General James, 39, 40
Pearsall's Corner, 1, 20
Pendill, Dr. Willoughby C., 72
Peters, George H., 225

Telephone service, 48–49
Temple of Nassau Hebrew Congregation, 163
Temple Sinai, 201
Thayer, Dr. J. P., 50
Thorne's Lumber Yard, 25
Thorp, John S., 72
Thunderbolt, 112–13
Thunderjet, 115
Tiffany, Louis C., 123, 125
Titus, E. V., 174
Townsend, Edward N., 39
Trolleys, 156–57
Truex, Ernest, 125
Tubby, William, 46
Turner, William B., 88

U

Uniondale, 196, 200, 213, 251
United Cerebral Palsy Association, 229
United Fund of Long Island, 228
United Nations, 259
United States Merchant Marine Academy, 221
Urban renewal, 205
Uterhart, Henry A., 67
Utilities, 50–51, 249

V

Valley Stream, 1, 12, 55, 104, 105, 110, 162, 168, 174, 185, 197, 204
Vanderbilt, Virginia, 123
Vanderbilt, William K., II, 130, 153
Vanderbilt Cup Race, 130–31
Vanderwater, Lott, 40
Van de Waag, Walter E., 280
Vandewater, Edwin, 70
Vandewater, Colonel R. L., 190
Varipapa, Andrew, 236
Varney, William F., 138
Velsor market wagon, 15
Viscardi, Henry, 229
Volunteer firemen, 139–43, 227, 271

W

WGBB, 257
WPA, 75
Waag, Alfred H., 161

Wachtler, Sol, 275, 276
Wallace, Archer B., 39, 41
Wallace, Edwin W., 64, 67
Wallace, George, 30, 41, 43, 86, 181
Walters, William H., 280
Wantagh, 28, 91, 104, 184, 212, 234
Waterbury, Larry, 127
Waterbury, Monty, 127
Water sports, 36, 128–29
Water supply, 247–48
Watriss, Frederick N., 66
Wayside Home for Girls, 145
We, 98
Webb, J. Watson, 127
Webb Institute, 221
Webb & Knapp, 108
Weed, Leroy J., 66
Weeks, Charles R., 137
Weller, Augustus B., 193, 254
Westbury, 9, 14, 16, 79, 164, 166, 167, 214
Westbury Music Fair, 230
Westchester County, 67
West Hempstead, 197, 254
Wheatley Hills, 122, 168
White, Stanford, 122
White Bird, 96
Whitney, Cornelius V., 123
Whitney, Harry Payne, 123, 127, 128
Whitney, Jock, 127
Whitney, William C., 9, 50, 129
Wholesale business, 259
Whyte, William H., 208
Wildcat, 113
Willard, Charles F., 80
Williston cart, 28, 29
Williston Park, 55
Wilson, Francis E., 30
Wilson, Howard G., 70, 280
Wilson Taxidermy, 29
Winnie Mae, 101
Winthrop, Bronson, 66, 123
Winthrop, Dudley, 50
Wodehouse, P. G., 125
Wolff, Lester, 279
Women's suffrage, 62, 63
Wood, Jeremiah, 64
Wood, William, 42, 44, 46
Woodbury, 199, 258
Woodmere, 132, 167
Woodruff, Timothy, 83
World War I, 86–94
World War II, 110, 133, 190–94
Wright brothers, 82

Wurman, Andrew, 205
Wysong, A. C., 68
Wysong, Charles N., 66

Youngs, John, 260
Youngs, William J., 42

Y

YMCA, 89, 92, 145, 228
Yachting, 128

Z

Zimmerman, J. Charles, 280

DESIGN BY JOSEPH P. ASCHERL
BODY TEXT, 10 PT. BASKERVILLE
JACKET PHOTOGRAPH BY ROBERT TURNER
PHOTOGRAPHS FROM NASSAU COUNTY MUSEUM COLLECTIONS